THE MAKING OF A FEMINIST

THE
MAKING OF A
FEMINIST

Early Journals and
Letters of M. Carey Thomas

Edited by
Marjorie Housepian Dobkin

with a Foreword
by Millicent Carey McIntosh

THE KENT STATE UNIVERSITY PRESS

Library of Congress Cataloging in Publication Data

Thomas, Martha Carey, 1857-1935.
   The making of a feminist.

   1. Thomas, Martha Carey, 1897-1935. 2. Feminists —United States—
Correspondence. 3. Educators— United States—Correspondence. I. Dobkin,
Marjorie Housepian, 1923-   II. Title.
HQ1413.T48A37   301.41'2'0924 [B]   79-88605
ISBN 0-87338-232-3
ISBN 0-87338-237-4 pbk.

Library of Congress Catalog Card Number 79-88605
ISBN 0-87338-232-3 cloth
ISBN 0-87338-237-4 paper

Manufactured in the United States of America

Design by Harold M. Stevens

CONTENTS

ILLUSTRATIONS

FOREWORD

by
Millicent Carey
McIntosh

M. Carey Thomas was my mother's oldest sister, and the oldest in a family of four boys and four girls. My first memories of her were of meetings of the Bryn Mawr School Board of Managers, in the parlor of our Baltimore home. Miss Thomas, with her friend Miss Mary Garrett, had founded this school in the city of their birth to give girls a first-rate education. She, along with Miss Edith Hamilton, its headmistress, sat every month in consultation with the other three members of the board, which included my mother.

As a child I could hear Aunt Carey's voice coming up the stairs, the same beautiful clear commanding voice which later echoed through the chapel in Taylor Hall, or made itself heard in the farthest corners of the Bryn Mawr College gymnasium where we held Commencement. "One of the greatest handicaps women have in public life is that they cannot be heard," she used to say to us in chapel. How often I have thought of this throughout my own life, as I have listened to women mumbling in committees or rising in meetings to mutter an embarrassed comment which no one could hear. Even as a child I could understand what she was saying in our parlor: "Don't allow these soft Baltimore mothers to weaken their daughters by insisting that they drop Latin!"

For eleven years I was a student at her Bryn Mawr School, which was founded at just about the same time as the College, the idea being to give to girls an education equal to that given their brothers, and preferably better! I reaped the benefits of the uneasy collaboration between two extraordinary women: Miss Thomas and Miss Edith Hamilton. I can remember weeping over the fate of Leonidas at Thermopylae when I was only seven, and sighing over the death of Roland at Roncevalles two years later. In Class V we learned two of Keats's odes by heart, although we had no understanding of what was meant by "Thou still unravished bride of quietness." When I am driving alone, I still recite to myself the poems learned willy-nilly by me and all those tender products of Baltimore society.

When we graduated from the Bryn Mawr School, Miss Thomas—splendid in a flowing white lace dress, her hair even then snowy-white—sat on the platform with Miss Hamilton. Each of us rose in her turn, and grasping a bunch of buggy daisies, went up the steps to shake hands with her. We never forgot the few words she said to us, welcoming us to the company of young scholars.

My career at college spanned three of Aunt Carey's last five years at Bryn Mawr. She was on sabbatical leave during my senior year, and she retired two years later, in 1922. It was clear to me from the beginning that I was marked as her niece, and that it was a tough assignment. My freshman year (1916) happened to be the year after Miss Thomas had had her worst fight with the faculty and had been called a "tyrant" and sometimes even a "deceiving tyrant" in the *Public Ledger* and other papers in Philadelphia. I was a little puzzled as to why some of the faculty people regarded me with a certain amount of suspicion. If I had been a little more sophisticated, I would probably have revolted and left Bryn Mawr for another college. But such a thought never occurred to me, and I solved my problem by immersing myself completely in the life of the college at that time. No sport was left untried, including water polo, which we played at night in the winter term. No meeting was held without Milly Carey sitting in the front row. Class and college politics were fair game, and I had little time to think about my family problem. I suppose I must have done some work, because I got good marks; but I remember very little about my courses.

However, I couldn't escape from Aunt Carey in chapel. There I felt the burden of my relationship to her, and responsibility for what she said. And she said plenty to us in the three times a week when we thronged into the chapel to hear her. On Mondays she talked of her travels; on Wednesdays about books; and on Fridays, politics. Some of the outrageous sayings attributed to her are apocryphal, but most of them are authentic. My friends used to sit behind me so that they could enjoy seeing the blushes spread down my neck. One of her main objectives was to wake us up and to get us to cast aside the upper middle class chains of conventionality and respectability. She told us that the happiest moment of her life was when she no longer believed in Hell Fire. She cited the discovery of agnostic Swinburne as her great intellectual awakening—this to a generation brought up on Wordsworth's "Daffodils" and Shelley's "To a Skylark." She tried to break our feminine bonds to our parents, to the idea of marriage, to domesticity. "Give your parents a *month* of your time each year. The rest should be for your own independent life." Incidentally, when later I decided to study for my Ph.D. at Johns Hopkins and to live at home, she insisted that it would be impossible and tried to bribe me to go to Columbia. She made me so angry that just to prove her wrong, I got my degree in record time, a flat three years.

Her remarks about marriage are well known: "If you *must* marry, you can plan to have your children in August," presumably to continue your teaching career. Later when I was married, and my first children were twins, she wrote my cousin, "It's bad enough for Millicent to be handicapped by having twins; but that they are boys is the worst blow of all."

Less well known is her very modern attitude toward marriage. As early as 1901, she published an article on higher education for women and men. As the climax to a plea for equal education, she wrote: "This women's college education should be the same as men's . . . because men and women are to live and work together as comrades and dear friends and lovers."[1] I think she might have approved of coeducational dormitories.

Her accounts of her travels filled us with delight. Her picturesque, vivid speech came into its own here. At one time she persuaded the captain of a freight boat to take her from Constantinople to Troy. "I slept on the deck in great discomfort but it was worth it, when I stood on those ruined walls and looked out over the plains of windy Troy." She made her way into the Vale of Kashmir in much the same fashion. Women were not allowed in the Taj Mahal, but again she persuaded (or bribed) a guide to take her in the night. "There by the light of the full moon I saw the white monkeys walking hand in hand." Edith Finch has given an amusing account in *Carey Thomas of Bryn Mawr* of the style in which she traveled, taking linen sheets and handwoven shawls with her, and a rubber bathtub.[2] She once told in chapel of an expedition she took in the African desert, with Arab retainers led by a sheik. Every night the sheik brought hot water to her tent where she took a bath. Once, she said, the tent was pitched on a slope, and she found herself sliding out of the door in her tub, down the hill. The sheik covered his face with his full sleeve, bowed low, and escorted her back to the tent in dignity.

She told us that we must be prepared to read, always; that her greatest joy in life had been to read and that whenever she was free and had nothing else to do, she would read. She said to us in chapel, "I have never passed a day in my life without reading an hour or more in bed no matter how late it was." She always carried candles for reading in bed, in case during a voyage no other light should be available. Once my mother and another aunt

1. Quoted by Barbara Cross, *The Educated Woman in America,* Classics in Education, No. 25 (New York: Teachers College Press, 1965), p. 154.

2. *Carey Thomas of Bryn Mawr* (New York: Harper & Brothers, 1947).

x

went with her on a camping trip in the Adirondacks. Each had a separate tent, and one guide carried as his single burden a huge load of candles.

She was always excited by any new idea, especially one that would open fresh possibilities to women. At a time when girls were considered delicate flowers, the Bryn Mawr School included in its new building a swimming pool, a running track around the top of the gym, and rowing machines. She appointed a disciple of John Dewey as director of the Phoebe Anna Thorne Model School at the college, and approved the latest theories of education for its curriculum. She established at Bryn Mawr the first graduate department of "Social Economy and Social Research," which has recently become a full-fledged Graduate School of Social Work.

The crowning point of her career, I think, was the founding of the Bryn Mawr Summer School for Women Workers in Industry. When she was on a sabbatical leave she wrote to us in a family letter, "I sat in the desert and looked at the bright stars and felt the sorrows of all the women workers in the world." And this feeling of empathy for their sorrows, and the need for Bryn Mawr to do something about it, were responsible for the founding of this extraordinary institution.

She had a passionate interest in education and in buildings. One summer in the late twenties I consulted with her about the plans for the new Bryn Mawr School, which had been forced by encroaching industry to move to the suburbs of Baltimore. "We must have colonial buildings, campus style. Yes, they must be red brick, connected by a colonnade like the University of Virginia." This idea caught her imagination, and she went over the plans in detail with the architect. Alas, the school could afford only two of her beautiful buildings, but the colonnade was continued between all parts of the school.

She also never lost her interest in politics. She had been a great advocate of women's suffrage and she left the National American Woman Suffrage Association, which later became the League of Women Voters, because she felt it was not aggressive enough in getting the rights of women. She joined the National Woman's Party, which was working on the Equal Rights Amendment. In the late twenties she invited me to go with her to a meeting of the national American Association of University Women where she proposed to persuade them to endorse this amendment. The president was bitterly opposed to it, but Aunt Carey managed through her superior knowledge of Roberts Rules of Order to maneuver the meeting into passing her resolution of endorsement. I wonder what she would have felt about the women's movement at the present time. It is somewhat ironic that we are still—some of us—working for the passage of the Equal Rights Amendment.

My personal relationship with Aunt Carey was warm but faintly distant. I think that when I was in college she realized something of the situation I was in, and tried not to interfere with me. At the same time, it was hard for her to restrain the ambition she had for me. She often asked me to Sunday lunch (where I always burned my tongue on the boiling soup), a somewhat scary occasion, especially in freshman year. We usually went for a drive afterwards, in her Franklin, with her chauffeur sitting in the back seat. My friends would gather in Pembroke Arch to watch as we drove round the corner on two wheels, scattering students as we went. One time during the war, President Taft visited Bryn Mawr. She asked student officers to meet him in cap and gown, and on the way home we watched with horror as she drove Mr. Taft into the ditch near Pen-y-groes. One strange thing about my undergraduate contacts with Aunt Carey is that I cannot remember what we talked about. I know that she urged me to work immediately for a Ph.D., whereas I had decided on the Y.W.C.A.—a bitter blow to her. She tried again the spring after my graduation, offering to finance a year of study abroad. By this time I realized that one couldn't save the world through women's clubs, and I accepted gratefully. The only present she gave me before I set sail was a folding rubber bathtub (which I never used).

I had the exciting experience of joining her in Paris that summer for three days. We stayed in luxury at the Plaza

Athenée, where everyone knew her and looked after her. Each day we rose early and went to several art galleries; after lunch we went to a matinee, and in the evening to the opera. By 11 p.m. I was a wreck and she was gay as a lark.

After I had my doctorate and came back to Bryn Mawr to teach in the English Department, I saw her from time to time, when she returned to Bryn Mawr and at Haverford Court. She was much quieter in those days, but she still took in every good play and opera in both Philadelphia and New York, sitting on the aisle in the front row, with her lame leg supported by a folding footstool that she would take out of her petticoat pocket.

During the last years of Aunt Carey's life, she had various medical problems and, as always, she was fair game for any new remedy. She adopted Beemax (Vitamin B) as a preventative of all ills shortly after I was married. My husband and I went to visit her and found ourselves putting Beemax on all our food. She was equally enthusiastic about smoking, which she had avoided while she was president, and she did not seem to be disturbed by smoking the wrong end of her filter cigarettes.

Two and a half years before she died, she wrote me a long and very personal letter in answer to mine telling her of my engagement. It was marked "Confidential" and was filled with advice, with the notation: "I shall not refer to this letter again." She had pinned her hopes on my following in her footsteps at Bryn Mawr, and had been disappointed in me for leaving my position on the faculty to become headmistress of the Brearley School in New York. I know that she was fond of me, and suspect that she felt it urgent to "set me straight" at this important time in my life. Her letter is one of the most moving I have had from her, and one of the few I have in my possession and which I had not, until now, thought of sharing. It seems to me, however, that it serves to explain a good deal about Aunt Carey's attitudes toward men, women, and marriage, and I am therefore setting down the crucial passages:

Rome, May 22, 1932

Dearest Millicent,

Your letter of April 24 is before me as I write. I am pleased to hear that Rustin[3] is not a practising physician but a teacher and a research worker. It makes a great difference in the point of view. One disability remains only then—he is not as mobile as a college professor or a college executive. . . . On the pro side of the question we have the possibility that you and he will be able to make a "genuine contribution" as the social workers say, to the all important burning question of whether a married woman can hold down a job as successfully as an unmarried woman. This must be proved over and over again before the woman question can get much further and I have set my heart on your making a success of it and so bringing great help to the *"Cause."*

I am now going to tell you some of the observations I have made and as this letter is difficult to write, it will be still more difficult to answer. So it needs no answer—only a postcard to tell me that it has been received. Nothing more.

First of all comes to my thinking the question of children. It seems to me to be of great importance in creating the strong bond of friendship and congeniality on which all happy marriages must be based for two people who come together as you and Rustin have, without long years of friendship and association behind you, to have time— at least two years for the kind of intimate companionship that friends of the same sex have, and that cannot be realized if one of the two friends has the disabilities of pregnancy and care of babies. This requires careful planning. . . . I am ordering Brentano to send you Mrs. Margaret Sanger's last book on "Contraception" which has been endorsed by so many eminent men and women. I want you to read it. I hope also very much that you will go to her New York clinic so as to understand the proper

3. Dr. Rustin McIntosh until his retirement in 1960 was Carpentier Professor of Pediatrics at the College of Physicians and Surgeons in Columbia University, and director of the Babies Hospital. He is now Professor Emeritus.

procedure. It is for a woman, not for blind chance to decide when she wants a child. . . .

And now a few words on the subject of men as the result of my observation and experience. In thinking it over I have really known and worked with many more men than women. I have had several (eight I think) in love with me and with one I was wildly in love, so wildly that I fled and never saw him for many years. When I met him again he had become everything I most disliked although eminent and in a way famous but I should, I think, have committed suicide if I had had to live with him. But my choice was made easy by the fact that in my generation marriage and an academic career was impossible. I knew myself well enough to realize that I could not give up my life's work, but I thought of him for three years night and day and then suddenly I was free. It was completely over. It was an amazing experience.

Men seem to me the unreasonable sex and far more romantic than women. They are more like children than women are. I am comparing of course educated men and educated women. . . . If I were starting out as you are to make the greatest possible success of a husband and a job I should take every legitimate means to preserve his illusion about me. I should never occupy one room with him. . . . Make it a fixed rule on the steamer, in all hotels, that you are firm. You get what you want for the same price. Do not stay with people who will not or cannot give you two rooms. Stay in an hotel and eat your meals with them. Mary Garrett and I made this a fixed rule. Never in travelling have I shared a room with Lucy or Alys or Georgiana King or with Edith. It costs no more and preserves the reserve and romance of friendship with women and how much more with a man. . . .

I said this was the last piece of advice—but there is one more and that is do not attempt the impossible. . . . No woman and no man can keep the vitality and alertness of attention requisite to success in his other work who tries to do a double job. Men know this by a long traditional experience of the failure of mere routine work, but women almost always make the fatal mistake of trying to unite domestic work such as housekeeping, nursing anyone who is ill, managing servants, buying food or at least ordering it, and having babies, under old conditions with a full man's job. You will have to have all this done for you. . . .

How I wish you could keep your own name like Miss Perkins.[4] "Millicent Carey" is *you*. . . . At least I hope you will be Mrs. Millicent Carey—and not filch Rustin's name which has an entirely different significance. If you had been born twenty years later you would have kept your own name as a matter of course. . . . It is one sign of enslavement that is bound to go, with the wedding ring and all other warnings to keep off the premises of an owned human being such as the difference between "Miss" and "Mrs.," while all men are "Mr."

Goodbye dearest Millicent. Remember, no reply—only think over what I have said and use your own very good judgment as of course you will. I have told you everything that I wanted to say. I shall now feel satisfied. As you know I wish you all happiness and all success.

With love,
Aunt Carey

---

4. Frances Perkins, secretary of labor under Franklin D. Roosevelt.

INTRODUCTION

Difficult as it may be for an older generation of Bryn Mawr College alumnae to understand, there is a world of educated women who have not yet heard of M. Carey Thomas, the first dean and second president of their college. I have to confess that until five years ago I had thought of her primarily as the aunt of Millicent Carey McIntosh, President Emeritus of my own college, Barnard; although, having heard quoted a number of Carey Thomas's pithier comments exhorting women to live up to their brains, I sensed that she must at one time have been a formidable presence on the Bryn Mawr campus.

The extent to which her spirit still looms over that campus became clear to me soon after I settled into the college archives during a year's leave from Barnard in 1974-75 and began reading and sorting her voluminous personal papers. It took me somewhat longer to note that her influence on women's higher education, by sheer force of her personality as well as more tangible achievements, is more profound than has generally been acknowledged. Judging by what has been published to date about her colleagues, Carey Thomas was certainly the most compelling and dramatic figure among pioneer leaders in higher education for women. Having come to know her through the various images she projects in her letters, speeches, and journals, and having heard, as well, of the spell she cast on her audiences, I think of her as something of an actress manqué. Although devoted to the theater, she would assuredly have scoffed at such a notion. Yet, whatever else is said of her, there is no question that she very deliberately made, and left, an impression.

In fact, I had not been reading her letters for very long when two of the campus guards on the night shift were reporting a ghost hovering around Canaday, the modern library building that houses the college archives. Canaday is located on the very site of the rambling Deanery Carey Thomas built, lived in and loved, where many of the letters I was reading were written. It was my habit to keep working until the building closed down at 11 P.M. when, thanks to the hospitality of Mary Patterson McPherson, then dean (now president) of the college, I would run through Pembroke Arch and across the road to the elegant old carriage house that now serves as Deanery. According to the guards, a figure in academic robes would materialize as soon as the library lights dimmed behind me. Roving restlessly from window to window it would peer into the darkened halls of Canaday. It looked, they said, "the image of the portrait" (a portrait of Carey Thomas by John Singer Sargent hangs in the M. Carey Thomas building), and when approached it would turn and vanish in the direction of the cloisters where Carey Thomas's ashes are buried—in an area of the magnificent old library building named after her.

It strikes me as thoroughly appropriate that Carey Thomas's spirit should be outraged by a stranger's riffling through her personal papers. She had set aside, in one trunk, the materials she had sorted out for an autobiography of the M. Carey Thomas she wanted the world to know. Her urge to plan ahead included instructions for the disposal of her papers, as well as virtually every other item that she owned. Her burial, too, is described in some detail in her published will running to 107 printed pages. She had not been one to brook interference with her intentions.

The M. Carey Thomas Library building exemplifies better than any on the Bryn Mawr campus her urge for

The M. Carey Thomas Library at Bryn Mawr College, architect's sketch

perfection, her taste for solid conventional elegance, and her refusal to be constricted by such relatively minor considerations as a limitation of funds. When completed, in 1906, the building cost a rousing $313,153, a high price for a college building at that time. Raising the money had taken stamina: John D. Rockefeller, Sr. had already paid for a new dormitory and heating plant on the understanding that the library would be funded by other donations. She cajoled his son, John D., Jr. into giving another $60,000 to complete the complex—chiefly the library; although she did not dwell on the point, it was here that costs outdistanced plans. But the stairs of the entryway, modelled after the chapel of Oriel College, Oxford, are of teakwood, in blatant disregard of the trustees' vote against such an extravagance. The cloisters, too, are laid out exactly as Carey Thomas decreed. The summer before, she had gone abroad with a flexible metal tape and measured her way through the finest cloisters in Europe.

A month before she died, at age 78, in 1935, Carey Thomas returned to Bryn Mawr to preside over the college's fiftieth anniversary celebrations. As dean when the doors opened for students in 1885, and president from 1894 to her retirement in 1922, she had more than any single person shaped Bryn Mawr's destiny for those fifty years, making certain that no college in the United States, or for that matter as far as she knew anywhere in the world, could claim higher academic standards, a more rigorous course of study, or a campus better designed to elevate the spirit in accordance with her conviction that beautiful surroundings nurture the intellect and enhance the work of the mind.[1]

She had almost literally built up the college stone by stone, for among her innumerable passions, as already noted, was one for the raising of buildings. Her supervision during their construction was so inexorable that according to legend one of the stonecutters, driven to distraction, had carved her face on a gargoyle. If so, he chose an unlikely model; Carey Thomas was a spirited, intelligent, handsome woman with a shapely figure, regular features, golden brown hair, and a flawless complexion: with every attribute, in short, to attract a nineteenth century man except for an iron will that would submit to no man or woman.

Her diary and journals show how early her strong will was in evidence. The stubborn, competitive, rebellious spirit they illustrate may be the rule today in preteens and young adolescents but it was less commonly observed in the 1860s and 1870s—and rarely in girls. The journals show her in full immaturity determined to have her way, a penchant she never relinquished and which, combined with certain opportunities that she seized upon energet-

---

1. She also felt that intellectual endeavor was incompatible with such menial tasks as making beds, setting tables, and washing dishes—not to mention cleaning house. Consequently, all through the war years Bryn Mawr College students, unlike their counterparts in other women's colleges, continued to have their housekeeping chores attended to.

ically, led to the making of a career. The feminism she had invoked as a child took on its direction at the same time. Because her feminist inclinations were so much a part of her character, and because both her character and the opportunities thrust her way are so clearly drawn from family influences, an introduction to her parentage is in order.

M. Carey Thomas, christened Martha Carey Thomas after her paternal grandmother, and called "Min" or "Minnie" throughout her childhood, was born in 1857, in Baltimore, into a family of Quakers on both sides. Her mother's parents, the Whitalls of Philadelphia, were descended from Quakers as far back as anyone could remember; at least to the 1680s when the first Whitall was said to have emigrated from England and settled in the area of Red Bank, New Jersey. Carey was brought up on the legend of Ann Cooper Whitall, her great-great-grandmother, whose stubborn adherence to principle in the midst of the battle of Red Bank during the American Revolution had made her a heroine in the family annals.[2]

Carey was drawn to this side of her family: a warm, extended family of aunts, uncles, cousins, and a pair of generous, prosperous grandparents who gathered the clan together on holidays and summers at the Cedars, their country place in New Jersey,[3] and at Storm Tide, their beach house in Atlantic City. These holiday reunions remained among Carey Thomas's happiest childhood memories, and to the end of her career she carried on the tradition in her own large family of brothers, sisters, nephews, and nieces by gathering them together at the Bryn Mawr Deanery every New Year's Eve and presiding over a three-day celebration encompassing her birthday, 2 January.

2. Evacuated from her home during the battle of Red Bank (New Jersey), Ann Cooper Whitall had returned and taken up her spinning (according to her principles, war was to be ignored) when a cannon ball destroyed the room overhead. She retired to the cellar and continued her work, emerging after the battle to take charge of the wounded.

3. Near Haddonfield, New Jersey, the area is now a bedroom community for Philadelphia commuters.

Her mother's branch tempered religion with liberal doses of humor, blinked at minor infractions of religious rules,[4] upheld individualism even more than the Quaker creed demanded, allowed girl children the same freedom as the boys, and indulged them all, believing, as Grandfather Whitall put it, that "every child is entitled to a happy childhood tucked under the belt." He had gone off to sea as a youth, worked his way to becoming captain of a sailing ship, and returned to settle down and raise a family, firm in his Quaker beliefs and with tales to tell his grandchildren.

The tradition of strong Whitall women was carried on in Carey's aunt, Hannah Whitall Smith. She appears to have been the first adult who would not let young "Minnie" have her way. Still, even Aunt Hannah had to give in and indulge her every whim after Carey, aged seven, came close to death, having scalded herself playing cook.

Carey had for the first years of her life been the adored only child of soft-hearted parents. With the arrival of successive babies after her second birthday (she was eventually the oldest of ten, eight of whom survived infancy), Carey, by age seven, must have become resigned to sharing a measure of attention. A serious burn, which covered the center portion of her small body and was most severe around the region of her thighs, and the long, painful period of recovery, put her once again at center stage, a position she appears to have been reluctant thereafter to yield. There is evidence, at any rate, that members of her

4. Although Carey's mother, Mary Whitall, and her sister, Sarah Nicholson, had periods of religious overzeal, they were, like their sister Hannah, willing to stretch a good many strictures beyond recognition. Indeed, Hannah, the family maverick, attended not only the theater after emigrating to England, but also the races at Ascot. Sarah has recorded that "I am not burdened with convictions myself...but I shall stick to certain rules for my children until they get older in order to give them a bias on the *safe* side .... We shall all scrabble through I reckon and get to the same place at last—some of us however will have had more fun in our scrabbling than others of us" (Sarah Whitall Nicholson, Letter to Hannah Whitall Smith, November, 1881). Carey Thomas's mother wrote to Hannah (8 April 1874), "... I will yield to no one in point of being a Quaker out and out, and yet I take the largest liberty in all non essentials . . . ."

family took her sufferings and recovery as a sign that "Heavenly Father" had singled out Carey Thomas to serve "a noble purpose." The message could not have failed to reach her.

Carey Thomas's Aunt Hannah did not mind "putting in an oar," as she herself has noted, behind the scenes in the educational circles in which her male relatives held influential positions on boards. These included the Johns Hopkins University and Bryn Mawr while still in embryo and called Taylor College after its founder and benefactor. In orthodox Quaker circles Hannah Whitall Smith was a celebrity, having gained fame as a writer of popular religious tracts. A biography of her oldest son who died at eighteen, titled *Frank, The Record of a Happy Life*, was a best seller for nearly fifty years, was translated into many foreign languages, and was still paying out royalties well after World War II.[5]

Hannah and her immediate family eventually expatriated to England where they became the center of a "radical chic" group,[6] and she an ardent feminist.[7] But that came after the years of influence that concern us here. More

5. Hannah Whitall Smith, *Frank, The Record of a Happy Life* (London: Morgan and Scott, 1873-74).

6. The group included, among others, Bertrand Russell and Lady Henry Somerset. Alys, Hannah's younger daughter, was Bertrand Russell's first wife. Hannah's older daughter, Mary, married Bernard Berenson after leaving her first husband and two daughters to go off and study with him in Italy. Hannah brought up her two granddaughters after their father's death, according to his wishes in the Roman Catholic faith. One of the granddaughters, Ray, married Oliver Strachey and the other, Karin, married Adrian Stephen, the brother of Virginia Woolf. Hannah's surviving son, Logan Pearsall Smith, in time became an author of distinction, having taken Carey Thomas's advice to become a writer. Ray Strachey's daughter, Barbara Strachey Halpern, is at this writing working on a biography of her great-grandmother Hannah Whitall Smith.

7. "I do not see how *women* can ever feel like anything but aliens in whatever country they may live, for they have no part or lot in any, except the part and lot of being taxed and legislated for by men." Hannah Whitall Smith "to her friends," from London, 6 June 1888, explaining why she cannot feel herself a citizen of any country. Quoted in *Philadelphia Quaker; The Letters of Hannah Whitall Smith*, ed. Logan Pearsall Smith, (New York: Harcourt, Brace, 1950), p. 102.

directly relevant was her aunt's insistence, when Carey was at an impressionable age, that no married woman could be happy.[8] She encouraged Carey to read her journals that made no secret of her regret at having married and her misery at being subjected to frequent pregnancies. Nor did she make any bones about the fact that she found her husband, Robert, a cross to be borne.[9] She had a good deal more to say about husbands and men, none flattering,[1] and she was consumed with indignation at having been denied a college education. In 1873 when Carey was fifteen, Hannah was writing: "Girls have a *right* to College education. They ought to be *made* to get it, even if at the point of a bayonet . . . . I regret my own loss in this respect every day of my life; and the world has cause to regret it too; for as I *will* be a rather public character and will *insist* on undertaking to teach, it is a monstrous pity that I have this great lack of want of education. You don't any of you know what I might have been if I had had it; I do! . . ."[2] Aunt Hannah became increasingly outspoken, even outrageous,[3] the older she got, and to the end of her long life Carey Thomas's correspondence maintains toward her a

---

8. "It is hard for me to believe that any husband and wife are really happy together . . . ." Smith, *Philadelphia Quaker,* p. 211.

9. Robert Pearsall Smith must at times have been a trial. His religious passions showed more than a hint of sexual undertones (a not uncommon condition), and his behavior on at least one occasion threatened to be so scandalous as to require a temporary exile. Hannah herself had a darker side, which showed when she admitted to beating her infant son, Logan, until he was "literally black and blue" because he would not stop crying.

1. "Men are by nature unreasonable and have to be cajoled." Letter to Mary Berenson, 14 December 1909, quoted in Smith, *Philadelphia Quaker,* p. 201. "It gives me solid satisfaction to see *men* obliged to walk around in this muddy Rome with long, flapping skirts." Ibid., p. 102.

2. Letter to Mrs. Anna Shipley, from The Cedars, 14 August 1873, quoted in Smith, *Philadelphia Quaker,* p. 19.

3. "Yes, we did rejoice in the assassination of the Grand Duke [Sergius, of Russia], and we only hope there will be some more! I have always said that Quaker or no Quaker, if I had lived in Russia, I should have been a Nihilist!" Letter to Mary Berenson, 22 February 1905, quoted in Smith, *Philadelphia Quaker,* p. 167.

tone of respectful admiration and genuine affection, tinged with awe.

Aunt Hannah's influence was offset by Carey's mother, who was soft-spoken, conventional, and a loving wife. Unlike her eccentric older sister Hannah, she cared very much both for her husband and for what people thought of her and those close to her—and in this last respect, at least, Carey grew to be more and more like her mother.[4] She was strong in spirit and character, but her strength was nonetheless feminine, and Mary Thomas was not altogether pleased at having her oldest daughter a tomboy. She wrote disdainfully of "woman suffrage *twaddle*" and advised her sister Hannah, when the latter entered into the battle in England, in 1882, that "the *principle* can be spread by thee with much greater acceptance and power if thee keeps free from the Platform." Still, she too had longed for higher education and been denied it. Carey's battle against the unfairness of the status quo was doubtless fought, consciously or not, on her beloved mother's and aunt's behalf as well as her own.

Mary Whitall Thomas was by all accounts a beautiful, gentle, tender-hearted woman who loved all her children, boys as well as girls (Hannah unabashedly favored daughters)[5] and was in turn adored by every one. She was active enough in religious affairs and "good works" to pass for a career woman.[6] Certainly Carey approvingly thought of her as one. In an autobiographical fragment titled "Mothers with a job," she has noted, "My experience has been these are the mothers whose opinions their daughters care for." Her earlier attitude appears ambivalent: she was proud of

4. According to those who knew her, confirmed through interviews.
5. "Daughters are wonderful luxuries; they are well worth a bad husband in my opinion: at least mine are." Letter to Mary Berenson, 28 September 1910, quoted in Smith, *Philadelphia Quaker*, p. 210.
6. Among her activities was her leadership of the Baltimore chapter of the Women's Christian Temperance Union. According to a family account, when in the course of her temperance work Mary Thomas went in and out of saloons exhorting the men to leave their drinks and return to their homes, she invariably ended, Pied-Piper fashion, leading a parade of men down the center of the street, totally oblivious of her own attractiveness and with the full conviction that the men were saved.

her mother's activities and at the same time intensely demanding of her attention and resentful when it was diverted.[7]

While it would be misleading to suggest that Dr. James Carey Thomas, Carey's father, was a man ruled over by women, his wife exerted a quiet influence on him, especially in his attempts to direct the course of Carey's education; she would never openly have questioned his authority, however. He was a reputable Baltimore physician,[8] successful both in his medical practice and his work as a Quaker preacher. He was, as well, a respected member of prominent Quaker and educational circles in Baltimore and Philadelphia: on the boards of Haverford College, the Johns Hopkins University and Medical Board, and, of course, Bryn Mawr. Dr. Thomas's attitude toward women's higher education was in fact a liberal one. There is on record a "quite confidential" letter from her mother written to Carey in 1874 when she was at Cornell, describing a meeting of the Johns Hopkins University Board which Carey's father had attended and during which coeducation had been discussed. He had spoken up in favor of it.[9] And when, after graduating from Cornell, Carey spent a year

7. "I have had a lovely time with her [mother]. I tell her my ideal of happiness would be to have her born a widow and be her only child and travel about . . . ." To a friend, Julia Rogers, 10 July 1879, shortly before Carey Thomas left for Germany and after she and her mother had spent a few days alone together at Atlantic City.

8. His father had an active medical practice in Baltimore, and was a professor in the medical school of the University of Maryland, which he had helped to found.

9. "They had the woman question up at the J.H.U. Board the other day and had a most interesting discussion. Johnson set his foot down flat on one side as being totally unwilling to let women in, in any way or shape—Frank White and Gwinn agreed with him—Father urged the other side, and Judge Dobbin spoke first rate, and Garrett and Francis King and Uncle Galloway, in fact the weight of the Board was on the woman side, and finally President Gilman when called out said he would be glad if they would leave the matter to his discretion, with liberty to make such arrangements for special cases as would seem best . . . . All this is quite confidential." Letter (undated) to M. Carey Thomas, who was studying at Cornell, from her mother.

enrolled at the Johns Hopkins in hopes of eventually obtaining a second degree, and found the conditions too limiting and humiliating to continue (she was allowed tutoring but refused permission to attend classes), her letter of resignation to the University president had her father's approval.[1]

Dr. Thomas's own father died early in Carey's childhood, leaving his third wife and a family of half-brothers and sisters: "the Grove people," she calls them, after the name of their family summer home near Baltimore. Religious zealots were rather more numerous on this side, although needless to say her father, fully abreast of the latest scientific thought, was nothing of the sort. As she drew away from her religion, Carey Thomas grew increasingly concerned about the various forms of "craziness" (her word, used often on extensive lists she drew up of deranged family members) brought on, she was convinced, by in-breeding among some of her Quaker ancestors.

Her antipathy to her given name, "Martha," is undoubt-edly related to her admitted antipathy to her father's mother—the Martha Carey Thomas after whom she was named, although no one ever called her Martha[2]—on ac-count of the latter's religious fanaticism. Later, in her autobiographical notes, she has characterized her Thomas grandmother as "certainly unbalanced" and "almost a religious monomaniac." Carey had never known her, but a testimonial booklet published after this grandmother's death indicates that this is exactly what she was. Carey

1. "Father agrees with me that unless they grant me full privileges I should resign." Letter to Mary Garrett, whose father was the aforemen-tioned Garrett on the Board, 27 August 1878. (See note 9, p. 10.)

2. According to remarks in the correspondence, "Minnie" decided that her name was too childish ("for a girl of eighteen summers," as her brother John wrote in an ode to his sister on her birthday) and wanted to be called "Miriam." Her father suggested she use the initial "M." and be called "Carey." To Anna Shipley she wrote, "Father is rampant [she may mean 'adamant'] but wants me to drop the 'Minnie' and keep the 'Carey'—old family name etc., and sign my name M. Carey Thomas. What does godmother think of it? 'Miriam' he repudiates." Letter to Anna Shipley, 11 August, probably 1875. Her brother Harry addressed his first letter of the new year 1876 to "Dear Carey, ex Minnie."

Thomas has recorded her terror, when a child, of someone's voicing a "concern"—that is, a signal from God—that she was destined to follow in the path of the religious grandmother whose name she bore. She had believed that from such a prophecy there would be no escape.

Carey Thomas's preoccupation with hereditary influences was undoubtedly fostered by the concern with eugenics, which became prominent in the United States after World War I. She believed in the Establishment view that took for granted the superiority of the northern European races. In her talk at Bryn Mawr's opening convocation in 1916, for example, she boasted that the student body was "overwhelmingly English, Scotch, Irish, Welsh and other admixtures of French, German, Dutch largely predominant. All other strains are negligible. . . ." Therefore, she said, "You, the students of Bryn Mawr have the best intellectual inheritance the world affords."

It is only fair to point out that in holding this view Carey Thomas was by no means alone in academic circles. In May, 1924, she was invited to join the Eugenics Committee of the United States of America (there is no indication that she did so) whose letterhead listed, among others, Charles Eliot, president of Harvard, William Allen Neilson, president of Smith, Dr. William Welch, a founder of the Johns Hopkins Medical School, such distinguished academics as Edward Thorndike, Robert Yerkes, C. H. Danforth, Harry Emerson Fosdick, Raymond Fosdick, Franklin Giddings and dozens more, including Dean Virginia Gildersleeve of Barnard College, where the Committee's executive offices were located. The Committee's aim, according to the invitation, was to protect America from "indiscriminate immigration," "racial degeneracy," and "the dumping on our shores of incapables now going on." The Committee's first step in safeguarding "damage to the American race," was to lobby—as it turned out, successfully—for a selective immigration law, which favored northern and western European immigration and kept to a bare trickle immigration from southern and eastern Europe and elsewhere.[3]

3. It is pertinent to address this issue because M. Carey Thomas's views on Nordic superiority have been singled out (see the entry on her in

For some time Carey Thomas had been intensely concerned with the birth control movement, which disturbed the more orthodox eugenicists because birth control was already being practiced by those well-to-do Americans of acceptable ancestry whose birth rate was declining, and who were the very people, it was felt, who should be practicing it least. Carey Thomas's distaste for large families of any ancestry would have given her mixed feelings about the eugenics approach, which in any event became discredited, along with its racist theories, by the late twenties.[4] (The Immigration Restriction Act nonetheless remained in force until the presidency of John F. Kennedy.)

Carey Thomas's Quaker background ran counter to such racist views. It also mitigated the excessive male chauvinism of the "gilded age" in which she grew up. Her Aunt Hannah has noted that as a Quaker she felt at an advantage because, she has written, "When I first waked up to the injustices of the position of women in the outside world, I was able to congratulate myself continually that it was so much better among 'Friends' and that not the most tyrannical 'man Friend' even if he wanted to, would ever dare to curtail the liberty of his womankind, if only they could say they 'felt a concern' for any course of action."[5]

Hannah Whitall Smith doubtless felt more free than many Quaker women to invoke such "concerns." It is true that Quakers believed in the equality of the sexes when it came to the spiritual life; women could rise to speak in

---

Notable American Women [Harvard University Press, 1971], p. 448) without reference to the context of the times, while her academic colleagues who actually joined the Eugenics Committee appear to have escaped unscathed. (See, for example, the entry on Charles W. Eliot in the *Encyclopedia Britannica*, 15th ed.)

4. Two excellent studies of the Eugenics movement are: Mark H. Haller, *Eugenics: Hereditarian Attitudes in American Thought* (New Brunswick: Rutgers University Press, 1963), and Kenneth M. Ludmerer, *Genetics and American Society* (Baltimore: Johns Hopkins University Press, 1972).

5. Hannah Whitall Smith in her tract, "The Unselfishness of God," as quoted by M. Carey Thomas in her autobiographical notes.

public Meeting and could become leaders in the church. The Quaker influence in Pennsylvania since colonial times had in fact made that state considerably advanced with regard to public education. As early as 1683 the state law required that girls as well as boys under twelve years of age be taught to read and write. And the Quaker tradition made it easier for women Friends, at various times in the nation's history, to agitate for reforms in the society at large.[6]

But Carey Thomas's parents were more in touch with the wider Baltimore Establishment than were earlier generations of Friends, or those less affluent in their own time. To a greater extent than Carey (and perhaps even they) acknowledged, in their secular lives they had adopted a good many of the attitudes of their era. To young Minnie Thomas they must have presented a contradictory picture, bringing to her childhood and adolescence the principle of equality between men and women, and the practice in religious matters, while maintaining the principle of male superiority and domination in the secular world and in the home. The paradox must have exacerbated her sense of injustice.

The situation in which Carey Thomas was raised, as the favored child within a leading family in a community she considered to be unbearably parochial, tended to strengthen her aspirations toward a position of leadership in the wider community—especially as she drew away from her religion.[7] The segregated world of her childhood (segregated not so much for Quaker men as for women) would scarcely have contained her considerable ambition even had she remained true to its principles; in this sense she was temperamentally like her Aunt Hannah, "a public

6. Ernest R. Groves, *The American Woman* (New York: Greenberg, 1937), pp. 48-49.

7. Although it was not until 1927 that Carey Thomas formally resigned from the Society of Friends, she had well before the turn of the century recorded her opposition to the dogma and her resentment that her beloved mother had been "fettered" by it. Her mother died in 1888 of breast cancer, having rejected medical treatment in favor of "prayer cures."

figure," and her ambition was constantly aimed toward the conquest of larger worlds.

Having made her mark in women's higher education—as a successful graduate of a coeducational college and recipient of a Ph.D. summa cum laude from a distinguished European university, next a dean, then president of a first-rate American college—she went on to work for women's suffrage, the first college president to do so. She promoted birth control as a liberating force for women long before the term could be safely voiced aloud, and after World War I she became a vocal and active supporter of the League of Nations. Her urge to conquer larger spheres reached new heights when, freshly retired from Bryn Mawr, she focused her attention on assuming a role of leadership on the world scene. She pinned her hopes on winning the American Peace Prize[8] for a proposal that would best ensure the maintenance of world peace. She seems to have convinced herself of certain success and been unpleasantly surprised and depressed when she did not win, even though her plan appeared in a volume containing "the twenty most representative" entries along with the winner's.[9]

She had, not long before, established the Summer School for Women Workers in Industry at Bryn Mawr, a breakthrough in the education of American women, who during the war had begun working in ever-increasing numbers at industrial jobs. Carey Thomas undertook to expose some from the ranks of labor to eight weeks on the Bryn Mawr campus. After the first year, the nature of the instruction offered them was determined by a committee on which the worker-students had equal representation with the faculty. The graduate department of Social Research which she

8. The prize, of one hundred thousand dollars, was bestowed by Edward Bok on the author of "the best practicable plan by which the United States may cooperate with other nations to achieve and preserve the peace of the world."

9. Esther Lappe Everett, ed., *Ways to Peace: Twenty plans selected from the most representative of those submitted to the American Peace Award for the best practicable plan by which the United States may cooperate with other nations to achieve and preserve the peace of the world* (New York and London: Scribner's, 1924).

15

had established in 1915 was the first to offer the Ph.D. degree. Yet Carey Thomas did not feel especially redeemed by these feats. In a letter to her friend, Mary Garrett, written on 2 January (her birthday) at the peak of her career, in 1898, is recorded her yearning "to amount to something more than the President of Bryn Mawr College."

Still, Bryn Mawr has been the living, lasting monument to Carey Thomas's feminism, which was primarily an act of proof that she, that women like her, given an equal chance are as capable as men of achieving intellectual excellence, of pursuing the most rigorous courses of study in the liberal arts, in graduate schools, and in training for the professions. In this sense she was unquestionably an elitist. She felt it her mission to inspire the few at the top of the pyramid so that they in turn might inspire others.

This aim never waivered. "I am convinced that we can do no more useful work than this," she wrote in 1908,[1] "to make it possible for the few women of creative and constructive genius born in any generation to join the few men of genius of their generation in the service of their common race."

As early as 1833, Oberlin College had opened its doors to women, the first full-fledged college in America to do so. But from that time until 1885 when Bryn Mawr opened, and until Carey Thomas proved it wrong, the argument prevailed in the foremost medical circles that subjecting women to the rigorous standards demanded at the ranking men's colleges (Harvard, Yale, Johns Hopkins and the like) would be detrimental to their health. Women in Carey Thomas's youth could choose from among a dozen coeducational institutions. They might also attend all women's colleges such as Vassar, Smith, Wellesley, and the Rutgers Female Seminary, which granted the B.A. (or the Mount Holyoke Seminary, which at that time did not). But in none of these places could the brightest of them obtain an education equal to that offered at the best of the men's colleges.

1. "Women's College and University Education," (reprint) from the *Educational Review,* January, 1908: p. 85.

Bryn Mawr was the first to be a little more than equal. Carey Thomas insisted that the entrance examinations exceed in difficulty those given at any men's college in the country. She refused to allow a chapter of Phi Beta Kappa on the ground that any woman receiving the B.A. at Bryn Mawr was at the very least of Phi Beta Kappa caliber elsewhere, hence an award restricted to a percentage of students was unacceptable.[2]

Carey Thomas succeeded, as no one else had, in quelling any further dispute about women's intellectual capacity. At the turn of the century she began attacking the argument that college educated women were prone to spinsterhood and with characteristic logic squelched it in short order. "One by one women have patiently and successfully met and silenced all the a priori objections to college education," she wrote in 1901,[3] "insufficient physical health, inferior scholarly endowment, indecorum of conduct in coeducational colleges—and now they are again face to face with this new argument of the most insidious kind. Even Mr. Howells, in the November *Harper's* in one of the wittiest and wisest of his "Easy Chair" talks, which has to do with the impossibility, undesirability and latent cruelty of the suggestion that college women should be educated to be wives and mothers, says that 'cold statistics represent that only about one out of three, or four, or five educated or coeducated women marry, and of these as few again become mothers, or, if they do, survive the cares and duties of maternity.' But cold statistics, begging Mr. Howells' pardon, seem to me to prove just the contrary."

Arguing that investigations showed that 50% of women of the social classes from which most college women came married *whether or not* they had been to college, she went on to say that "college presidents who enjoin upon us to teach women womanly virtues and educate them to become wives and mothers should begin by educating their own college men to become husbands. . . . Justice, righteousness, truth, love of knowledge, sympathy, reasonableness,

2. Bryn Mawr to this day has no chapter of Phi Beta Kappa.

3. "The College Women of the Present and Future," (reprint) McClure's Syndicate, 1901: p. 4.

are both womanly and manly virtues," she insisted, "and happy are our men's or women's colleges if they teach some tiny fraction of them." She confessed to not knowing how women could be educated to being wives and mothers, and to never having met a woman who did. She said the very idea was laughable and preposterous. "What requires the perfection of all our human powers can scarcely be taught to women in high schools or in colleges by rule of thumb."

The college woman of the future, Carey Thomas predicted in 1901, would be "able to stand shoulder to shoulder with the man she loves in the support of the family," and for these women there would be "one hundred per cent and no longer fifty per cent of marriages. She will indeed be the only woman the man of moderate income can afford to marry."[4]

In 1908 she was insisting that every college woman would have to be prepared to support herself, whether wealthy or not. Circumstances could change, and in any event the educated woman would not simply settle for marriage but would be prepared to devote time to "some form of public service," whether paid or unpaid.[5] She argued for identical courses for men and women, and for research chairs for outstanding women at all leading colleges and universities. The next battle to be won, she wrote in the same article, was to see to it that gifted women in future generations be given as favorable opportunities in their careers as their male counterparts.[6]

Years before her death in 1935, Carey Thomas had thus promoted the status of the educated woman to the point where it remained, with scarcely a change, until recently when a new breed of feminists emerged to prompt another leap forward. Having anticipated advance, she would have been surprised only that women waited so long. In 1901 she had described her attitude toward marriage as a partnership between equals, and in her speech at Bryn Mawr's half-century celebration, shortly before her death,

---

4. Ibid., p. 6.

5. "Women's College and University Education," (reprint) from the *Educational Review*, January, 1908: p. 80.

6. Ibid., p. 85.

she directed the force of her message once again to urge that the thousands of women scholars and professionals who had been trained in those fifty years be given the same opportunities and financial rewards as men.

At Bryn Mawr, in addition to setting a new level of excellence for women, Carey Thomas instituted many "firsts." There had to be a graduate school: from the beginning she insisted on this as a means of attracting and keeping the finest scholars and offering brilliant women a place to teach and work. Every member of her faculty devoted one third time to teaching a graduate seminar and conducting research in a specialty. (The college opened with five graduate fellowships; at her retirement, in 1922, it offered twenty, all to women.) Years before the exchange of scholars between countries had begun elsewhere, ten foreign scholars came to Bryn Mawr each year, beginning in 1909. The college was the first to employ unmarried men to teach women, prompting President Seelye of Smith College to prophesy that Bryn Mawr would fold within two years. Contrary to the prevailing practice, married women on the faculty at Bryn Mawr were encouraged to go on with their work even when their husbands were also on the faculty. From the outset Bryn Mawr students governed themselves, and for better or worse were allowed to smoke on campus. An innovative curriculum emphasized general education on the Johns Hopkins model. And Bryn Mawr was the first women's college whose dean had a Ph.D.

Carey Thomas's ideas on women's higher education are encapsulated in her letter to Dr. James Rhoads (on page 277), her antipathy for sectarian control appropriately toned down for the benefit of the good brethren to whom she was offering herself as Bryn Mawr's first president. With a small group of friends she set up the Bryn Mawr School in Baltimore the year the College opened. (The school continues to thrive.) Initially, at least, such a preparatory school was essential to serve as "feeder" such as the best men's colleges had, to fill the freshmen classes with qualified students.

In her day Carey Thomas raised as many hackles as any feminist before or since. Her goals were anathema to many; her methods alienated some who professed sympathy with her aims. All this, too, seems contemporary, so much so that it is hard to believe she was born before the Civil War—long enough before to have a memory of it. She lived to anticipate World War II; a life filled with achievements and involvements in addition to the building up of a first-rate college. With her close friend, Mary Garrett, using Garrett money and funds collected from women throughout the country as bait, she and Miss Garrett contrived to force the Johns Hopkins Medical School (it opened in 1893) to admit women on the same terms as men. They further insisted that the B.A. degree be a prerequisite for entrance. This made it the most demanding and prestigious in the country and the women reasoned, correctly, that if such a medical school admitted qualified women as students, others would follow suit.

It was undoubtedly the force of her character no less than the list of her achievements for The Cause, or Her Causes, that made Carey Thomas a legend long before she died. Strong willed and impulsive, she had little patience with protocol[7] and tended to follow the precept that if you wanted something done, life being short, you did it without delay. She had not the temperament to tolerate interference or opposition with equanimity, and her career is therefore studded with dramatic encounters that left her supporters exhilarated and her enemies limp. Her own energy was prodigious.

Her adversaries, including members of her faculty, found her tactics so high-handed, even ruthless, that on several occasions there was rebellion in the ranks. Yet she never admitted to losing a battle, and perhaps she never did. On those rare occasions when the opposition became sufficiently formidable, she had the wit to yield points with the grace of a full-blown winner. In the end no one could deny

7. Except when it suited her. She never forgave Woodrow Wilson, whom she had appointed to his first job on her history faculty, for going over her head to President Rhoads whenever he wanted to discuss his status on the faculty. Among Carey Thomas's autobiographical notes and scraps are a number about him: "Woodrow Wilson did not play cricket," is one, and another is a sarcastic statement designed to illustrate his attitude toward women: "Put your sweet hand in mine and trust in me!"

that in addition to her other qualities she was endowed with abundant common sense.

In 1922, after her retirement from the presidency of Bryn Mawr, Carey Thomas took a villa on the French Riviera and sat down, so she vowed, to write her autobiography. She had not the patience to write for long; her insatiable appetite for travel, for reading and discovering new ideas— she read every contemporary memoir she could get hold of, and took copious notes, presumably in preparation for writing her own—her passion for the theater and opera, her affection for friends and family, her inability fully to let go of her many causes, these she could not resist indulging to the end. Her attempts to record her life consists of fits and starts, cryptic fragments, dozens of lists (e.g., "My Character," "Lovers," "Famous People I Have Known"), illegible scraps, some whole sentences, a number of unfinished paragraphs and a few completed ones. There is enough material among these fragments to allow me to piece some of them together, in a gratuitous but I trust more or less logical order, to form an essay of her ancestry and family life. This appears on page 289 of the Appendix. Except for some connectives, which are indicated, I have used only Carey Thomas's own words. Placed at the end of this volume, they provide a view of her childhood feelings and attitudes with the added perspective of hindsight. A few additional paragraphs, also found among her autobiographical scraps, were used to conclude the essay.

The notes for her unwritten memoir, together with Carey Thomas's journals, speeches, articles, and voluminous personal and college correspondence, provide a total picture quite different from the dynamic, autocratic, single-minded public figure. The private Carey Thomas reveals many of the complexities of a woman torn by ambivalence, conflicting needs and drives, and who reflects the tugs and tides of extraordinary change that occurred in the course of her span of life: 1857-1935.

The memories that others had, and some still have, of M. Carey Thomas point to the fact that among her greatest achievements was her ability to inspire in others her own enthusiasms, to provide the spark that gives reality to daydreams. Most striking of all is the clarity with which there emerges from the dusty memorabilia Carey Thomas's consummate love of living. It is revealed in these early journals and letters, along with her determination, her energy, her exuberance and occasional depressions, her need to dominate, her farsightedness, and above all, it seems to me, her abiding curiosity.[8] At the root of her feminist indignation about the inequality of opportunities for women, there appears—in addition to a strong sense of justice and of her own worth—an inability to suffer the thought of missing out on one vast portion of human, but heretofore exclusively male, experience.

The papers from which the following journals and letters have been selected were for many years stored in four large steamer trunks in the old Deanery on the Bryn Mawr college campus. Some time before that Deanery was torn down to make way for the Canaday Library, the trunks were moved to the basement of Taylor Hall. A fire subsequently broke out in Taylor, and although damage to the building was not extensive, soon after the event, on a sunny, windless day, the contents of the trunks were spread out on the lawn to dispel any dampness that might have penetrated the trunks when the building was hosed down. The papers were replaced more or less at random, but not before the then president of Bryn Mawr, Katharine McBride, had been made aware of their importance.

A few years ago Millicent McIntosh, who was M. Carey Thomas's last living executor, formally released the papers to Bryn Mawr, and I was assigned the task of sorting them out. When I first opened these trunks, I found the papers in

8. Among the autobiographical scraps is the notation: "I was born with an eager desire to understand things, that I have never been able to satisfy. There is an intense pleasure, unlike any other that I have experienced, of coming to understand at least in some way satisfactory to me, things that have puzzled me, and the passing of this satisfaction into a rapture of delight, as sometimes happens to me in regard to questions such as women's intellectual abilities, or the command of their own lives given by birth control. Such matters I have cared supremely about and they seem to me to fall into their proper places in the scientific order of the universe."

chronological disorder and most of the letters still in their envelopes and likewise in a jumble. In the course of a year and a half these materials were roughly organized into 105 file boxes of letters and papers and another 10 cartons containing the larger items such as school notebooks, diaries and journals, theater scrapbooks and the like. Carey Thomas was a "saver" and seems to have been unable to part with even such items as shipping invoices, medical reports, and laundry lists. She was also an avid clipper of articles, especially when she agreed with their messages. The clippings date from the years of her retirement when, instead of writing, she appears to have spent most of her time reading.

The following selections from her youthful journals and letters constitute roughly two-thirds of their entirety. She was often negligent about keeping up the journals and there are therefore gaps of months and even years between some of the entries. (The journals are handwritten in four separate bound notebooks.) I omitted those entries or passages which seemed to me to become tedious—chiefly those with pages of rambling adolescent philosophy, rhapsodies on "life" and "art" and similar "noble thoughts," as young Carey would have called them.

Consistency was not prominent among Carey Thomas's virtues, hence, as readers will note, her attitudes on occasion reverse themselves from one sentence to the next. There are a number of startling examples in the following pages; one of my favorites occurs on page 48: "Went to the lectures. Lowell's lectures are worth all the other lectures put together. Bessie was there and we had so much to tell each other it was a great trial to listen to Lowell." The same sort of abrupt shift can be found in the autobiographical fragments she jotted down some sixty or seventy years later. She was also offhandedly inaccurate about names, dates, and figures, sometimes with hilarious results: "Thirty percent of our graduates marry and fifty percent have children," is one of her famous slips, articulated resoundingly from a platform in the course of denying rumors that most Bryn Mawr graduates did not marry. Mrs. Esther Cushman of Cambridge, Massachusetts, her last secretary, told me that she was constantly referring to the Athens Hostel, with which she was actively involved for many years after her retirement, as "the Naples table." And she once introduced Caroline Ruutz-Rees, the founder of Rosemary Hall, with the tag line to a glowing introduction: ". . . and moreover, her father was a *great Dane!*" (Mary Roche, who has been working on a biography of Caroline Ruutz-Rees, tells me that there was not a Dane among that lady's ancestors, "so," she writes, "in addition to the blooper, Miss Thomas must have got her nationalities crossed!")

From all accounts Carey Thomas was unquestionably a captivating speaker, and like all good story tellers she must have embellished a tale for effect. The well-known legends of her having attended lectures at the Johns Hopkins behind a curtain (so as not to distract the male students, presumably), of her mother and she weeping her way to college and graduate school by melting the resolve of an overbearing Victorian father, of her family being as ashamed of her studying abroad as they would have been had she "married the coachman," are not sustained in her letters and papers. They are probably examples of graphic exaggerations which she herself came to believe.

Carey Thomas's spelling, especially before the age of fifteen, is appalling, and her punctuation often nonexistent—which may give hope to parents of contemporary teenagers. She remained a weak speller to the end of her days but had fortunately overcome the worst of this defect by the time she entered the Howland School. Up to that time I have for the most part kept the misspellings (although I added or changed some of the punctuation), correcting only where spelling errors become annoying, as for example in the case of her faulty contractions: "did'nt," "have'nt," etc. To enhance readability I corrected misspellings (except where noted) in the journals and letters after 1872.

With one or two exceptions I have presented the dates at the beginnings of journal entries and letters in the conventional form, even though in writing to her family Carey sometimes used the Quaker form: "Fifth Day, Third Month, 1872," for example. When she resorted to the abbreviated form, "2/10/71," she appears sometimes to have lapsed into the European manner of placing the month first and the day second, so that in the absence of a dated envelope one can only try to surmise by the context whether "2/10" is the second of October or the tenth of February. Dates, when she gave them, are unaltered, even though in some cases the day of the month for a particular year does not check out accurately on the perpetual calendar.

Cousins of friends and friends of cousins were numerous in Carey Thomas's family, and visiting Friends (and friends of Friends) even more so. It seemed unnecessary to identify every childhood friend mentioned; virtually all, including Richard Cadbury with whom she corresponded from Europe, were members of leading Quaker families in Baltimore or Philadelphia and environs. In many instances it was impossible (and often inconsequential) to trace identities. Unfortunately, I have not been able to identify a few who do appear to have been important in her life, as in the cases of two gentlemen, one "Mr. Jones" and a "Thomas Guard," whose lectures provoked her violent outbursts against the ideas they expressed and reinforced her determination to see justice done. Absence of identification ought not, therefore, to be taken as an oversight.

The distinction between a "diary" and a "journal" is not clear; dictionaries tend to use the term interchangeably. "Journal" nonetheless connotes entries bearing somewhat more depth than those in a diary, which tend more toward the listing of events, as in a log. Thus a writer's journal often serves as a kit of ideas, reflections and observations to be used in works to come, and journal entries are usually longer than those in a diary. The keeping of a journal, or diary, was more prevalent in the nineteenth century than in these days of more frequent happenings and less time in which to record them. Carey Thomas's earliest diaries were probably written at her mother's instigation; the very earliest are in her mother's handwriting and were evidently dictated while she was recovering from her burn. Mary Whitall Thomas's own diary records the births of her children and their temperaments as infants (including some succinct observations about her oldest daughter almost from the day of Carey's birth), and a description of her daughter's near fatal accident soon after it occurred. Extracts from these seemed pertinent enough to place at the outset of this collection.

Another editor would doubtless have chosen differently, and perhaps more wisely. I am happy to say that the opportunity, for those interested, to study the entire collection of M. Carey Thomas's personal and college papers is not far off. A grant from the National Historical Publications and Records Commission has made it possible to microfilm the collection, which is now being prepared for the process and should be completed and available to libraries by the spring of 1980. The collection includes correspondence and documents that predate Carey Thomas's generation and should therefore provide riches for a variety of scholars, particularly social historians and students of Quaker history, as well as the history of higher education and of women in America.

I am in debt to a number of Carey Thomas's connections—a few, alas, whom I can no longer thank—who gave me their time and memories and on whose recollections I have drawn in comments preceding the following sections or in my notes. Her nephew, the late Harold Worthington; the late Lady Russell who as Edith Finch was Carey Thomas's authorized biographer; James Flexner, her youngest nephew; Esther Landman Cushman; Katie Doyle Gaffney; and Richard Gummere have provided angles of vision no one else could possibly duplicate, as has David Robertson of Barnard College in sharing with me his remembrances of Julia Rogers who was a close family friend. My Barnard colleague, Katharine Stimpson, writer, teacher, and editor of *Signs,* took the time to read through the manuscript and gave me the benefit of her astute and expert comments.

The joy of coming upon a lode of fresh materials has been enhanced by all those in the Canaday Library and at Bryn Mawr College who made my work so pleasant and shared my enthusiasm for my project, including former

President Harris Wofford and Mrs. Wofford and the reassuring members of the night watch who managed to safeguard me from Carey Thomas's ghost.

This work would not have reached fruition without the patient help of Gertrude Reed, Bryn Mawr archivist and reference librarian. And without Julie Shibata and Harriet Lightman, respectively undergraduate and graduate student assistants, I should never have seen the bottom of the trunks. More recently, Lucy Fisher West, in charge of arranging the Thomas collection for microfilming, has graciously, time and again, taken the trouble to help me make up for my lapses in the final stages of this manuscript. I thank her, as I do all those mentioned, and assure them and my readers that remaining lapses are all mine.

My warm gratitude to Mary Patterson McPherson, now president of Bryn Mawr and dean during my stay, for inviting me to share her beautiful home on campus and making my year easier and more enjoyable than I could possibly have imagined. In my seemingly interminable trips since then, I bless Elizabeth Graham Bailey—most patient and hospitable friend.

Lastly, although actually first, and always, go my deepest thanks to Millicent McIntosh, to whom I owe more than I can here express, and who has always made working with her the purest of pleasures.

Marjorie Housepian Dobkin
West Lebanon, New York
July, 1979

CHRONOLOGY

PART I (THIS VOLUME)

PART II

1904	Mamie Gwinn leaves the Deanery and Bryn Mawr to elope with Hodder
1904	Mary Garrett moves into the Deanery
1905-1906	Faculty crisis at Bryn Mawr
1906-1913	Begins association with women's suffrage movement
1915	Mary Garrett dies
1915-1916	Faculty crisis at Bryn Mawr
1921	Summer School for Women in Industry at Bryn Mawr opens
1922	Retires from Bryn Mawr
1935	Fiftieth Anniversary of Bryn Mawr College in November
1935	M. Carey Thomas dies on 2 December

I

CHILDHOOD AND SCHOOL

EXTRACTS FROM THE JOURNAL OF
MARY WHITALL THOMAS

1857—1st month

Our precious little daughter was born the 2nd of 1st mo. 1857 and on the 3rd we named her Martha Carey Thomas, hoping that she may not unworthily bear the name which is held in such dear rembrance [*sic*] by us both. . . .

24th day of 6th month the little baby was laid in her crib wide awake[1] which she protested against most vehemently and took it so much to heart that her mother was obliged to give it up after persevering for three weeks.

1858—4th month

In the 2nd month Minnie paid a visit to Philadelphia which she enjoyed highly. While there we had two daguerreotypes taken of her. She began to say "Papa" and "Mama" about this time and called her nurse "Adga". . . .

1859—1st month

Minnie is two years old today and a darling little treasure she is. She calls herself "Marsa Cay Toppin" and talks away quite like a big girl. She says her papa's name is "Gocker James Marsa Cay Toppin." . . .

1860—1st month

Minnie began to learn her letters the other day. She

---

1. Evidently a milestone in a baby's life at that time. Mary Whitall Thomas recorded the dates and reactions to being put down awake for the first time of all her children.

puts a piece of paper with large letters on it, on a pin cushion and "stabs" them with a long needle. . . .

Minnie seems to feel dear Grandpa Thomas's death a good deal. She says "Heavenly Father called him and he went." She says "I am not happy without him . . . when will Heavenly Father say 'come come ittle Minnie'?" Poor little Minnie, she has a hard time often—she is so anxious to have her own way, and that way is often very far from being the best way, and she is obliged to yield. She said today, "Mamma I do want to be good *so* bad, but then the naughty angels will come in. I don't let them come in, but they just come in themselves."

1862—6th month

Minnie goes to First Day school regularly now. . . . She reads very well, and has done so for six months. She sits down and amuses herself reading by the hour. . . . She is a dear daughter and I hope trying to exercise a little self control though she does love to have things her own way. Grandma gave her a silver sugar spoon today, and she was very much pleased and wants it marked Martha Carey Thomas instead of Minnie—as Grandma thought of—

1863—12th month

Minnie is growing a very companionable girl. She reads a great deal and plays very nicely with her brothers and sits up in the evening to have tea with her father and mother and beguiles them into allowing her to sit up much too late. She is a great pleasure and joy to us all. . . .

1864—1st month

On Minnie's 7th birthday her father wrote her a little piece of poetry which pleased her very much. He gave her a Bible also for her own. . . .

The year opened upon us very pleasantly enjoying our home and children, delighting in our Darling Daughter who seemed to grow dearer every day. I fear we thought too little of the rich blessings that were bestowed upon us, and settled down in the enjoyment of the gifts somewhat

Above: Mary Whitall Thomas
and Dr. James Carey Thomas

Right: Hannah Whitall Smith

forgetting the giver. And so our nest was stirred. On the [left blank] of this month Minnie came into the nursery and said "Mamma I'm going to be assistant cook," and then washed her face and hands and put on a clean white apron and came to the lounge to kiss me before going down stairs; as she went out of the room I thought what a darling, satisfactory daughter she was. The vision of her dear little figure had scarcely left my mind before I heard a scream which filled me with horror. I rushed to the door and met my darling child in flames—it was but the work of a few moments to envelope her in blankets and put out the fire. Then I cut her clothes off, and wrapped her in cotton soaked in lime water and oil and laid her in the lounge and tried to comfort her with assurances that she would soon be well. She seemed altogether calm and natural for some time after she was burned. She said she did not see why Heavenly Father was not with her then, that He was with Shadrach, Meshach, and Abednego in the fiery furnace and she thought He might have been with her. . . . Towards evening she began to grow feverish, and her mind to wander, and then began the struggle for life—for days and weeks she lay, and tossed on her bed of suffering, and we watched in agony beside her not knowing whether she would be left to us. The one only desire of her heart seemed to be to have her Mamma near her; night and day I remained beside her, took every meal at her bedside for four or five months, and never left her. . . . Sometimes she would wake up and say, "Oh, Mamma I want to go so bad, up to Heaven." And I could not wonder, darling child, and yet I could not give her up if it was the Lord's will to let her remain. The dressing of her burn was the most distressing time of all, it hurt her intensely and she was so terribly excited and nervous as to make it a most heartrending thing. I always did it, no one else could touch her. She always wanted father in the room, but no one must touch her but Mamma. . . .

The winter passed away but with little change—the parts which were slightly burned healed, but the large burn remained as it was very much. In the spring her papa had a basket work tray made which would fit in the

34

The infant M. Carey Thomas

carriage and it proved a great comfort—a crib mattress was put in it and she could lie on it very comfortably. In that little basket she went to Philadelphia twice, and to Atlantic City during the summer. Aunt Hannah[2] came in the spring . . . she amused Minnie with her stories and cheered us all up very much. We all went back with Aunt Hannah and paid a nice visit to the Cedars. Minnie used to ride every day and drove often herself lying in her basket. Darling Grandpa and Grandma did everything they could to make Minnie's stay there pleasant and her sufferings were certainly greatly alleviated by all the kind care bestowed upon her. Still no one could take her mother's place. Day and night I was still with her—she could not be happy if I was out of sight. Sometimes she would consent to let Aunt Hannah sing her to sleep, rubbing her foot the while, but "I want Mamma" was generally the cry in such a plaintive little voice that it could not be withstood.

After staying at the Cedars five or six weeks we returned to Baltimore and went out to the Cottage which Papa and the dear kind Aunts at the Grove had nicely fixed up for us. We spent two or three weeks there in which Minnie seemed to grow worse, and Baltimore was threatened by the Rebels, a raid being expected down our road and altogether Papa was very anxious that we should go into town which we did one afternoon, passing several fortifications on the way thrown up to keep the Raiders out.[3] Poor little Min was very sick the next day. . . . Dr. Smith said he had never seen anything like it and strongly advised her going to the seashore. So off we started . . . and there Minnie improved very much. . . . In the 9th month she got up and walked about a little though her sore was still very large and very painful when being dressed. The day they [presumably the Whitall grandparents] left to go home Minnie did not seem well, and in a few hours was *very ill* so that we gave her up almost. Our merciful Heavenly Father again gave us back our darling

2. Her mother's elder sister, Hannah Whitall Smith.
3. This is one of the very few references to the Civil War in the Thomas family correspondence.

from the very verge of the grave and we were able to bring our children all safe to our home in Baltimore again in the course of a week. . . .

On the 4th of 3rd month another darling boy was given to us—a noble beautiful baby we named James Whitall and desired that he might inherit some of his dear Uncle's virtues.

EXTRACTS FROM THE EARLY DIARY OF
M. CAREY THOMAS[4]

1865, January 2
Dressing, as usual.[5]

My birthday. I am 8 years old. For my birthday present Father and Mother gave me "The Children's Garland" and some paper.

Father prayed for us this morning in the Nursery.

We had a show this morning. The log cabin with a garden around it, soldiers frightening a poor old woman nearly out of her wits, and several other things. Father told me about the Heathen gods today.

January 4
Aunt Julia[6] at the dressing today. After breakfast Mother made me learn a spelling lesson which I very much dislike. Afterwards she wrote a little in my diary. She writes just what I tell her. . . .

January 17
How kind Heavenly Father is not to let my fall stop the healing of my sore. . . .

January 20 [child's handwriting]
England is my favorite country.

4. All but one entry in mother's handwriting.
5. The dressing of her burn.
6. Her father's aunt, Julia Thomas Cheston.

March 5

This morning I saw my sweet little baby brother for the first time. He was lying asleep and all covered up. I wish mother would let me name him—I should name him Arthur or Herbert. . . .

March 8

Baby is named James Whitall Thomas after Uncle Jim.[7]

September 6

Dear little Jamie died at the Grove cottage—the sweetest and dearest little baby that ever could be.

September 7

I could not bear to see my darling, beautiful little brother shut up in that dark coffin and put in the ground. I should have screamed out loud when they did it if it had not been for the thought that he was so happy, and that I should see him in Heaven.

"PRIVATE JOURNAL KEPT BY JO MARCH[8]—
COMMENCED JUNE 20, 1870"

June 20

Mother, Father and Polly[9] gone to Quartly meeting and I'm housekeeper. Don't find it very amusing taking care of babies and scolding boys. After breakfast went down to the Library— full of men and so I didn't venture. Bought a volume of Tennyson with my currencies then read *Tom Brown at Oxford* till dinner. While Eliza was at dinner I

7. Her mother's brother, James Whitall.

8. The tomboy heroine of Louisa May Alcott's *Little Women,* which was first published in two volumes, 1868-1869. Carey took the name for this journal, thereby showing a strong identification with the character. Legions of young readers, for over three generations, have identified with Jo March.

9. The housekeeper or a servant.

outraged her by letting Daisy eat her rice herself instead of feeding her.

School broke up last 6th. Got 4 prizes. I'm tremendously proud. Learnt The Cloud by Shelly. Goody. I wish "that the hours would go faster nor long day bide so late," because I want them all to come home. Boys are very poor company for a *young lady* like me. . . . About 9 o'clock Father and Mother came home. I was delighted to see them. They seemed to have had an elegant time.

June 21
. . . People seem to think that girls don't want any fun, and even if they do they want to row and climb they are shocked and say it isn't LADYLIKE but P[1] and I are going to resist to the last!! After dinner mother let us take a ride in the carriage. I tell you we astonished the natives. . . . After [riding around town] we got up on the stable roof and couldn't get down and as we had white dresses on every body stared. We got down with a determination not to get on a roof where we would be seen. It was very embarasing.

November 12
. . . Read Ruskin on arcutecture until K [Bessie King] arrived wanting something desperate to do. We looked out the back window and were going to let ourselves out of it by blankets but we forbore went up to my room and READ a little then took a walk way out by the fountain. I wanted to go farther but did not exactly like to as neither of us had a plain bonnet on. Came back looked longingly at Father's horse and carriage but Bessie's father has forbodden it so we didn't dare. We then went to a store and bought lots of *bad* candy came back laid on my bed and ate it from a *sense of duty* of course. Then went into the yard, swang on the trapeze and walked on stilts at the back gate and astonished passers' by. Then dinner bell rang and dinner being serenely over bright idea seizes us

1. Probably her friend and distant cousin Elisabeth King, who is usually referred to as "K" when not "Bessie," "Bess," or "Rex." Carey Thomas's papers show her tendency to scramble her letters.

and we quietly stole the parlor matches and rushed down in the cellar and brought up an armful of chips to the boys' room and made each a little bonfire and tried whose would keep in the longest. . . . Had a real nice day it is a consolation that seventh day comes once in a while. "All work and no play makes Jack a dull boy." Then learnt a terrible hard lesson in Greek and read till bed time.

November 16

Went to School and down to Greek. We none of us knew our lesson extra. I got in with a lot of girls and went down to Mercantile Library with them. Got out Green Mountain Girls—ain't worth reading—*perfect trash*. Bessie was *very* unreasonable today and abused me at a fine rate saying that the reason I wouldn't go with other girls was because I thought myself too good. Went to lecture and didn't larn my naturel history but I knew it.

November 17

Went to Meeting sat way up the aisle and I was right next to Miss Marble[2] I was so afraid I would laugh I had to repeat Isabella of Austria to keep myself solemn. I know it is wrong but I can't help it.

After Meeting we drew. I undertook to draw an innocent looking baby dressed as a sailor boy and when I had finished him he resembled a *vishion* leering, wicked, repulsive 50 year old looking sailor. So I have concluded after the manner of sour grapes that I would rather be an authoress than a paintress and so I will turn my attention that way.

November 18

Miss Marble read us about Our Lord turning out the money changers and then described the different courts of the temple and drew a picture of them on the blackboard and told us a good deal about them that I *wise as I am* didn't know before, and then said that "if we went to Meeting and did not behave as we ought to that even though we weren't making it a *house of thieves* we were

2. Rebecca Marble, her teacher from 1868 to the spring of 1872.

"Minnie" Thomas and her brothers; left to right, Harry, John, and Bond

making it a Play house." I thought it was a practicul illustration.

November 19
Out shopping today with mother to get gloves and stopped in at the library to take back *Green Mountain Girls* which by the way is the most trashy immoral miserable *Yankey* bad book I ever read. Saw Bess in the library, talked with her and didn't watch mother who got out *Josephus,* 4 great big volumes for me to read. The idea. But we compromised and got out *A Prince of the House of David.* Had quite an allarn this evening. The boys saw a man under the porch and rushed in the house and locked all the doors and windows even in the third story and when Father came home he took a lantern and looked high and low and above and below but minus man. . . .
So this is the end of a week and in reading over what I have written I am afraid my life hasn't been of much use to anybody . . . haven't read a single useful book just *trash trash trash.*

November 20
. . . Got a letter from Laurie[3] telling about the fuss at Haverford. The managers have made a new set of rules saying they mustn't whistle sing or in fact do anything that is fun. Bessie and I were congratulating ourselves we weren't there for we would have been suspended certain sure like poor Cap Haines. . . .

Thanksgiving Day
Slept till after breakfast 'cause I was so tired of getting up to go to school. About 10 o'clock put on my shandy dandy and went to Bessie's then we went to Dr. Bachus's church to hear Mr. Jones. We didn't know what to do when we got to Church but the Sexton bowed us in to a right good seat.

3. Frank Whitall Smith, her first cousin, Hannah Whitall Smith's oldest son. She called him "Laurie" after the character in *Little Women.*

After singing Mr. Jones commenced. He is the ugliest man, Daniel Havlin excepted, I ever have seen, and his gestures correspondingly so. He preached a splendid sermon but Bessie and I disagreed, for I thought he wasn't reverent enough and Bess thought he was. For instance he said things like this: He was saying that the minority in politics was always dissatisfied whereas they ought to be thankful that in this government where the whites, blacks, Chinese, and Indian were all together they didn't fight like the Kilkanny Cats till nothing was left but the nose of one and the tail of the other whereas they are living and thriving.

Then again he was saying that people were so good when anything was the matter with them why "when the Devil was sick the Devil a monk would be." Of course this set the people laughing and Bessie and I had to laugh, although we tried awful hard not to. When we got out Bess was off in raptures and thought him splendid but I thought his preaching was nice but not (amen) what real preaching ought to be. . . . I said we didn't come to church to be amused but converted or at least made better . . . so we fought like the kilkanny cats about it. Then after dinner Mother was sick and I took care of the little *boserations*[4] all the afternoon and didn't learn my lessons.

November 25

Have come across such a glorious book called 'Boys Play Book of Science' am going to read it through and see if whether ain't some experiments Bess and I can try. Won't it be jolly if we really can? But it takes money money money even for the priviledge of blowing ones self up. . . .

November 26

Set a mouse trap last night in case Bess and I might want to get his skeleton caught him but he wasn't dead.

---

4. Meaning "botherations," her name for her young brothers and sisters.

Neither Julie nor Netty[5] would kill him so I heroicly dropped the trap in a pail of water and rushed out of the room. Then took my slippers into Mother's room who is lots better and is sitting up and sewed sewed sewed. "Oh the monotony of worstered." Laurie ain't worth half this bother.

Pretty soon I heard someone calling "min" and knew it must be Bess 'cause no one else ever calls me "Min." Well first we roasted some chestnuts then proceeded to the more important duty of getting to skeleton of a mouse. The poor fellow being drowned by this time we took our victim out in yard, bared our glittering knives and commenced operations. But the horrid mouse's fur was so soft that we couldn't make a hole and besides it made us sick and our hands trembled so we couldn't do a thing. But concluding it was *feminine* nonsense we made a hole and squeezed his insides out. It was the most disgusting thing I ever did. We then took off his skin. It came off elegantly just like a glove, and then holding it by the tail we chased poor Julie all around. She was so afraid of it just as if it were even worse than a chicken and finally put it on the fire to boil to Julie's great disgust. When it had boiled we took it again and picked all the meat of it and saved its tongue and eyes to look through the microscope and then the mouse looked like a real skeleton. We then put it out the window to bleach and then as Bess had to go I walked with her.

Wasn't it funny she had been thinking about experiments too and so we planned together and are going to spend our money in instruments instead of candy and then we will invite our friends to see our experiments. I think I'd almost rather be a chemical fellow than a doctor.

When I got home I found that Netty had thrown away our tongue and eyes, and worst of all woe woe is me that our skeleton that had taken us 3 mortal hours to get, had fallen out of the window and smashed. Oh Science! Why will thou not protect thy votaries!

In the afternoon lolled around learnt Greek and sewed everlasting slippers. Bess said when she told her father

5. Julie may be a servant. Netty is the cook.

about our getting the mouse he looked grave and said, Bessie Bessie thee is loosing all thy *feminine* traits. I'm afraid I haven't got any to loose for I greatly prefer cutting up mice to sewing worsted.

December 6

Oh my I made my oration today at Marble hall before an audience of 36 persons. It really was awful. I had no idea I'd feel so embarassed—the way of it was this: Miss Marble had us to say pieces on fifth day while the girls are sewing and so she appointed me and said as I was a woman's righter I could deliver an oration and so I had a great time writing and today I spoke it.

"MY POETICAL EFFUSIONS"[6]

O cruel and stony hearted teachers
To you I would address my song
To you who have the care of children
To you who can redress the wrong.

Have you no pity for the children
Who're intrusted to your care
That you load them down with lessons
Almost more than they can bear

When you see their cheerless faces
Growing every day less gay
Think oh think! Upon the hours
You have kept them from their play

Hear the mourning of the children
Heed their broken hearted wail
For a time is slowly coming
Which will make e'en your hearts fail

For soon will the seats be vacant
Which today the scholars fill
Soon green graves of little children
Will increase upon the hill

6. From a notebook so titled, and marked "Autobiog. MCT poems 12 years old" in her adult hand.

45

Behold arising to reproach you
Thirty little tomb stones white
Each one bearing this inscription
Died from studying day & night

Then cruel and stony hearted teachers
You'd best take warning by my rhyme
And shorten our unending lessons
While there yet remains the time.

"JOURNAL KEPT BY JO MARCH, COMMENCED JAN. 1
WITH THE FIXED DETERMINATION NOT TO LET IT
DROP BUT CONTINUE IT UNTIL JAN. 1872.
AIM TO BE A WORTHY MEMBER OF THE S.S.S.
MOTTO: "PRIMUS LUDUS, SUPREMUS LUDUS,
SEMPER LUDUS"[7]

January 1, 1871

Well!! I am determined to keep up *this* Journal even though my last attempt was *not* successful and in order to begin right I have commenced on the first day of the new year.

Now my resolutions. Everybody makes resolutions and of course I do too. I put them down here so I can see how far I carry them out. I ain't going to be afraid of saying what I think as my journal ain't going to "peach" and I am going to do my best to seclude it from the public gaze.

Here goes for the resolutions. I am going to study my lessons a great deal harder, especially Latin and Greek. I am going to bend my energies to get a good knowledge of Chemistry even though I *do* have to study it by myself. I am going to try not to read many novels as I really think it a waste of time and I *do* want to be a *real* Christian and not a half a one and really let my light *'shine'*. . . .

Meeting over ate dinner and went with Grandfather [Whitall, in Philadelphia] to his colored school. Had a

7. "Ludus" is the Latin for "school," "game," or, rather loosely, "fun," in which case this could mean "Fun first, last, and always."

class of 10 old colored women and got along right well. Would like to be their teacher right well. Then went to Annie Groths bible class. Was very much interested. Oh my if she wouldn't have those horrible little curls down her neck I really think her preaching would do *me* more good. I know it took her an hour or two to fix them this morning and she preached about *simplicity*.

January 2

I'm 14 years old today just think. I am afraid I don't know half enough for 14 but bygones are bygones and even if I don't it can't be helped now. So I leave moralizing and come to facts. . . .

Today Grandma and Grandpa had their grand New Years dinner. They had to buy a new table for the occasion and at 3:30 all their sons and daughters and all their sons and daughters-in-law and all their grandchildren except Frank sat down making 26 in all.

Oh the dinner we had: 4 turkey, 2 geese, beef a la mode and all the vegetables you could imagine almost. For dessert 2 sharlet ruskes, water ice, ice cream bisque, all sorts of fruits, almonds, raisons, pound and white mountain cake, jelly, in fact everything good.

Rich[8] came in this afternoon and we had a splendid time. I tried to persuade him to study harder but no go. Duke came this evening and talked the greatest pack of nonsense. Aunty Hal[9] and mother had told Bess and I to go to bed at 8 o'clock and Duke came and stayed till 10:30—so much for our obedience.

Just as Bessie and I were going to get into bed Bess hit me with a towel and I siezed it and was just about to give her a smasher when with my usual good luck I knocked off one of Grandma's elegant vases. I was terribly sorry but went and told Grandma and she never scolded a bit. I think she is a "brick" as Whit[1] would say. . . .

8. Probably Richard Cadbury, a Quaker friend. Later referred to as "Dick" or "Richard" and even (in letters from Europe) "Mr. Cadbury."

9. Sarah Whitall Nicholson, her mother's sister.

1. Her first cousin, James Whitall Nicholson.

January 3

Came home today and the holidays are over. Went to the lectures. Lowell's lectures[2] are worth all the other lectures put together. Bessie was there and we had so much to tell each other it was a great trial to listen to Lowell.

Bess's Uncle Elias has given her a ring. I told her I didn't approve of it and neither I do. I reckon she will have earrings next. . . .

January 6

Went off to school to-day same as usual and spent the afternoon getting together our chemicals about 5 Bessie came up and we did our Greek fable. After supper we went to Anna Dickonson's[3] lecture. She was dressed very simply and her subject was "Joan of Arc" and she gave some splendid descriptions of the way she led the french in the thickest of the fight she got right in to the spirit of the thing and got carried away by her own eloquence and on the whole I liked it very much. She said one very true thing she said "that if a boy had genious and tallent and splendid abilities, and when he had grown to man-hood should come to his parents and tell them he felt it his duty to go out into the world and do his part elevating the human race, they would dry their tears and send him forth with their blessing resting upon him; but if a girl grown up in the same way with the same talent same genious same splendid abilities should in the same way express her desire, they would put her in her chamber lock the door and put the key in their pocket and think they had done their duty." Oh my how terrible how *fearfully* unjust. A girl certainly [should] do what she chooses

2. James Russell Lowell, according to his biographers, was doing a good deal of lecturing between 1869-72 due to harrassment in money matters.

3. Anna Dickinson, noted Civil War orator, known as the "Joan of Arc" of the Unionist cause. Became a post-Civil War star on the Lyceum circuit, her most popular lecture being an apotheosis of Joan of Arc. She demanded women's emancipation and attacked the double standard in morals.

as well as a boy. When I grow up—we'll see what will happen.

Dr. Morris[4] walked home with us and talked all the while about the "sacred shrine of womanhood" and that no matter what splendid talents a woman might have she couldn't use them better than by being a wife and mother and then went off in some high faluting stuff about the strength of women's devotion completely forgetting that all women ain't wives and mothers and they I suppose are to fold their hands and be idle waiting for an *ellgable* offer. Bah! Stuff and nonsenses! Well when we got undressed we skedaddled around went over in the laboratory, ate candy and talked until I happened to look at my watch and found it was half past one. My we went to bed in a *jiffy*.

February 9

Went to school and said the "Diver" by Schiller. It's quite an imposing thing to get up and say a piece before a school of about 35. Well any way its a good preparation for *lecturing*. Frank, Aunt Hannah and *all* her children came today. Frank is tremendously tall and oh let me breathe it to my journal alone—a very very little Philadelphialised. May he out grow it.

February 14

. . . We had a company of about 20 here. Had a real nice time. Aunt Hannah played like a trooper. She is my idea of a jolly woman. She is splendid.

February 16

Frank went home, real sorry, had elegant time.

February 26

I have at length come to the conclusion that it will be more interesting to me when as an old dried up woman with aid of spectacles I decipher these scrawls to read what I thought than what I did and accordingly I am

4. A friend of her father.

going to commit my reflections to paper trusting to kind fortune to keep them from careless eyes.

An English man Joseph Beck was here to dinner the other day and he don't believe in the Education of Women. Neither does Cousin Frank King and my such a disgusson as they had. Mother of course was for. They said that they didn't see any good of a womans learning Latin or Greek it didn't make them any more entertaining to their *husbands*. A woman had plenty of other things to do sewing, cooking taking care of children dressing and flirting. "What noble elevating things for a whole life time to be occupied with." In fact they talked as if the whole end and aim of a woman's life was to get *married* and when she attained that *greatest state of earthly bliss* it was her duty to amuse her husband and to learn nothing; never to exercise the powers of her mind so that he might have the *exquisite* pleasure of knowing more than his wife. Of course they talked the usual cant of woman being too *high* too *exalted* to do anything but sit up in perfect ignorance with folded hands and let men worship at her shrine, meaning in other words like all the rest of such high faluting stuff that woman ought to be *mere dolls* for men to be amused with, to kiss, fondle, pet and love maybe, but as for associating with them on terms of equality they wouldn't think of such a thing. Now I don't mean to say these two men believed this but these were the principles they upheld.[5] I got perfectly enraged. How *unjust*—how narrow-minded—how *utterly uncomprehensible* to deny that women ought to be educated and worse than all to deny that they have equal powers of mind. If I ever live and grow up my one aim and consentrated purpose *shall* be and is to show that a woman *can learn can reason can compete* with men in the grand fields of literature and science and conjecture that opens before the 19 century; that a woman can be a woman and a *true* one, with out having all her time engrossed by dress and

5. It is interesting to compare this statement to one she jotted in late age: "I have never known a man who is really a feminist. They think they are but deep under the skin they are not."

society—that the woman who has fought all the battles of olden time over again whilest reading the spirited pages of Homer, Vergil, Heroditus, who has sympathised in the longings after something beyond mere daily exhistance found in the works of Socrates, Plato and Eschelus, who has reasoned out all the great laws which govern the universce with Newton, Cirago, Galleleo,[6] who has mourned with Dante, reasoned and speculated with Shiller, Goethe and Jean Paul,[7] been carried away by Carlyle and "mildly enchanted by Emerson" who has idealised with Milton and emerged with strengthened intellect from the intricate labyrinth of Geometry, Trigonometry and Calculous is not any less like what God really intended a woman to be than the trifling ballroom butterfly the ignorant doll baby which *they* admire. My firm fixed purpose (for Puncheon,[8] I heard him lecture on Eliga yesterday says that unless you have one you will never *do* or *be* anything) is to have a thorougher knowledge of French, Latin Greek and German and then to read and study carefully all the principle authors especially the old german metaphyseans and to go high in mathametics for even if they ain't any "practical" use they strength[en] the mind. I think I would like to take some science for my espesiality and then my greatest hope and ambition is to be an author, an essayist, an historian, to write hearty earnest true books that may do their part towards elevating the human race towards inducing some, at least, to let their money bags on which they are wasting such a wealth of hope and desire and intellect drop from their hands and aim at something higher than merely providing for our miserable earthly exhistance, to look higher than the miserable disappointments of every day life and not to live on in utter forgetfulness of God, but their duty to their fellow men. In the words of Longfellow

6. Newton, Arago (French astronomer 1786-1853), Galileo.

7. Jean-Paul Friedrich Richter, German novelist 1763-1825.

8. Probably Thomas Ruggles Pynchon, Episcopal clergyman, professor of science and moral philosophy, and president of Trinity College, 1874-83.

"When departing leave behind me
Footprints on the sands of time
Footprints that perhaps another sailing
    on lifes dreary main
A forlorn a shiprecked brother
    Seeing may take heart again."[9]

It seems to me that is a purpose worth striving after. Oh may it not be *only* a purpose.

"I wait for *the future* the birds cannot sing it.
Not one as he sits on the tree
The bells cannot ring it. But long years
On bring it. Such as I wish it [to be?] it."[1]

March 12

I really have such lots to do that my poor journal gets crowded out and a great many other things too. I'm afraid just think I only read TWO books in February ain't that dreadful? Oh by the way it came up at dinner today about Development and I had thought all along that it was perfect nonsense and that Adam and Eve were created all at once but to my *intense* astonishment I found out that Mifs M. [Marble] and Uncle Allen[2] don't believe it [the biblical account of creation] and that even Father won't positively say that they were created all at once but says that even if they were created in a lower state and gradually were develloped into men that there is nothing in the Bible to contradict it. It says that God created man but it doesn't say He created him all at once or by a serries of developments. Oh my I must find out about it I don't see how people can be content to live without studying all about it and finding out. My purpose is a little changed. I'd like to be a great geologist and scientist for my own satisfaction if nothing else. How glorious it would be to spend your life in studying it out. Oh my I *must* go to Vassar. Mifs Marble says that she thinks I might possibly

9. From Henry Wadsworth Longfellow's "A Psalm of Life."

1. This has the ring of her own unexceptional verse.

2. Allen C. Thomas, her father's half brother.

be prepared to enter the Freshman class by next summer if I study real hard till then; and then Bess and I could go and she enter the Sophomore and I the Freshman, and then with a splendid groundwork we could go on and experiment and all. And I really think Mother might possibly let me go. But I must study hard and I really ain't and it's a crying shame. I must finish my Caesar this year and I can't do it unless I average a paragraph a day and that will be hard, but still "If a thing is worth the having." And there are such heaps I want to find out that I must read like fun, and not any more trash but real solid essays and such. I have made a good beginning for this month and read *Fireside Travels* and *Hero Worship*[3] which last has interested me more than any book I ever read almost.

Yesterday Bess and I tried to make some wax fruit and made a lemon. Next seventh day we shall go on and who knows but we may become celebrated in that line.

April 27

Well here I am just the same as ever and this stupid old journal of mine would never have guessed what has happened since I last wrote if I didn't tell it as I am going to. 1st place Easter Holidays have come and passed. Mifs Marble went home and the 1st day of the holidays I was taken with a very high fever and sore throat and was sick four or five days, in bed about three. Then Bessie and I went on to Philadelphia and had gay fun. We went on fifth day and were at a party at Nina Trevilles on 7th day evening, had a very nice time. Oh my there are such a nice lot of girls and boys [starts out to write "boys and girls" but crosses out the first "boys"] there; you can't go out of the house with out meeting 4 or 5. But dear journel I have notised one thing about theese Philadelphians and especially the SHIPLEYS[4] that are *tremendous* kissers (I don't mean the boys) if you met 'em 9 times a day they'd kiss each time coming and going away; it was inexpress-

3. Thomas Carlyle, *On Heroes, Hero-Worship and the Heroic in History* (1841).
4. The Shipleys were a leading family of Philadelphia Quakers.

ibly funny to Bessie K and myself and they mix up prayer-meeting and flirting in a remarkable way but really they do have real nice meeting and they are all such *real earnest consecrated* Christians and are really doing such an amount of good that it makes me think I ain't one at all. Maby if I lived in Philadelphia it would be different for the very atmosphere is goodness consentrated. I do hope that I ain't luke warm but I afraid I am. Annie Murray is so lovely and sweet and a real Christian too. I fell "heels over head" in love with her. I wish I knew her better. She and Bessie Nie[5] are the kind of Christians I like, but as for being sober when you're a Christian I don't believe in it now, "frinstance" there's Frank he has just consecrated him self and I may be wrong but he is a great deal more sober than he was before, and *I* don't think it's a mark of a Christian to be so awful sober. And Mame Wader who used to be so full of fun is as solemn as an owl now *she* has become a Christian. I can't tell why we are placed in such a beautiful bright earth if we are to go wading through all its beauties drenched in tears. . . .

May 28

The C A T A S T R O P H E has come and they have been and gone and done it. When we, MM and I came home from Meeting, Uncle Allen walked up and when Mother met Miss Marble I noticed that she kissed her *very* affectionately. They went upstairs and I stayed down in the parlor with Uncle Allen. He seemed rather embarassed. When Miss M. came down she had a *furrous* color and mother asked U.A. to stay to dinner which settled it in my mind. . . . Uncle Allen didn't stay and so as soon as he went Mother said, "Has Uncle Allen been confessing his sins to thee?" I said "No, but I know what they are," and so I gave my approval and ain't it fun. I knew it, I knew it. I'm delighted to think it's splendid. I'd rather have MM for an aunt than anybody else and I like a little romance, it's a little exciting.

After dinner Miss M came up in my room and I had great fun reading B. Browning's love sonnets to her and

5. Bessie Nie, probably spelled "Nye."

making her blush but she wouldn't let me read the one about "the first kiss." Well, U.A. came in about a half an hour, and Miss M tried to pursuade me to come see him. Catch me, I ain't going to be in the way when very likely they're melting from overcharged softness and can't get rid of it while I'm in the way. There really must be something in love after all, for they seem real happy and yet it is funny that two people only having seen each other such a short time should profess to love one another better than anybody else in the world. I wonder if it is happier in the end to fall in love or not to be married or an old maid. However that may be, it's fun to be a spectator. O romance, romance, enlivens this prosaic world of ours a heap. . . .

June 20

I went to Meeting to see Mary Ellicott married. She had no bridesmaids and it was very quiet. She looked very pretty and sweet and all that but still I think people ought to have bridesmaids, and if *I'm* ever married I shall have 4 at least. It's due to your friends, due to the public and due to yourself. . . .

At school we all had to read our compositions. Mine was on Twilight . . . I romanced and climbed into the clouds over it and all to what effect—it was nothing more than an ordinary school girl's composition. Well I got up to read it and my voice trembled so I could hardly read. It is *so* foolish it really makes me mad, and I can't help it. I just as leave read it as not. Then school broke up and Miss Marble bid us all goodbye and told me I might tell about her engagement . . . I really hardly like to bid Miss Marble goodbye because I do love her and think she is so splendid and I really don't see how she can like me because I have given lots of trouble and I believe school wouldn't have had half the fusses if one Thomas had been missing.

. . . My, I intend to study my Classics and Mathematics next year, because I do so want to finish at Vassar and then come to Philadelphia and study for a doctor. I can't stand being dependent on anybody, even mother and father, and I want to do something besides eating, reading and dressing. . . .

June 22
We arrived at the Cedars safely today. . . .

July 3
We are having elegant fun. Frank hasn't come from Haverford yet so there are only three of us.[6] The program for a day is early in the morning to go to Haddenfield to do errands and buy some candy if you have any money and mine hasn't run out yet, then we come home and go in bathing. . . . Dinner at 12. . . . After dinner we read in some old willow trees by the road which are just as nice a shade as possible. . . . Then we hunt bugs . . . it is terrible hard to classify them. All the books I have got hold on have such long names that I can't make head or tail of 'um. But I'm determined to proceed for there are such lots of interesting things about insects and after a while maybe I may be a natureelst.

July 10
Charley Haines, one of Whit's friends about 16 has come to stay a week at Linden. He is about the best looking boy I ever saw. Dark eyes, dark hair, dark complexion, but rather feminine. We have a great deal of fun playing cricket. It is an elegant game only I tear all my clothes and Mother threatens to make me a suit of red flannel jacket and pants.

July 13
. . . I do despise Sam Hillis, he is a real *baby* boy. Well, after dinner we were going to ride on their little pony and I got on and Sam Hillis was just going to hand me a stick, when all at once the pony began to cut up and jump and rear. Still Sam came on holding up the switch until at last the horse reared and tumbled backwards on me and there we lay rolling together. Sue Howland and I just before had been talking about Women's Rights, and so I determined to let her see they didn't scream, so I didn't say a word and at last crawled out all right much to their

6. On hand were probably her cousins Whit and Bessie Nicholson who lived at Haddonfield very near "The Cedars."

astonishment for they were ever so frightened. I then got on again and rode nicely. In the evening we went to William Hillis' to tea and afterwards rowing. It was a long way down to the warf and the moment we got out of the door William Hillis took my hand and talked to me all the way. We had an elegant row Allen and I rowing most of the way. Then the next morning after a ride on that delightful pony we went home. I think Sue Howland is splendid, decidedly the nicest of the lot.

September 29

Oh my my my here I've missed lots and lots of months and now there is nothing for it but to tell what has happened since in as short a way as possible. . . . And oh such lots has happened. I have a baby sister, Hellen and Whit has gone to Providence, and school has commenced, and I have begun Virgil and Frank has entered Princeton and Rich has gone back to Haverford, and how I'm just as mad as I can be for Miss Marble told me we didn't have spelling today and so I didn't learn it and then she kept me in for it but I determined she should lose her dinner and so I wouldn't learn it. . . . Now I don't care one solitary penny and intend to take my ease and not learn one single thing more—

October 1

Of course I had to ask Miss Marble to excuse me for I know I did wrong, though I still think she was terribly unjust. She just takes me and makes an example of me which to say the least is real unkind. . . . School is getting along right nicely only I can't behave to save my life, and I'm really afraid Miss Marble thinks I purposely trouble her, but I like her . . . but I'm all out of sorts and nothing goes right and I'm tired of studying and there's no fun and "nothing new under the sun" and I despise everybody and Bettie Arnes ain't so nice as she was and girls never can have any fun . . . and I nearly 15 and each year I have less fun and am more grown up and everybody seems satisfied to go on living without any variety but I *ain't* and never will be and never want to be. . . . I ain't good and I ain't bad. I ain't a tomboy but I ain't *ladylike* and I'm everything that's disagreeable and I do want a little excitement and I do want to go to Vassar. . . . I *do so want* to, and I am *perfectly determined* to get a good education. Oh I think its cruel when a girl wants to go to college and learn and she can't and is laughed at and absolutely kept from it while *a boy* is made to go whether he wants to or not. I don't see why the world is made so unjust and I don't see why all unjustness should be turned against girls in general and me in particular.

More and more every day I'm making up my mind to be a doctor for when I grow up I can't be dependent on father and mother and I ain't going to get married and I don't want to teach school, so what can I do? I can't imagine anything worse than living a regular young ladies life. And I have a taste for doctoring and could study at Philadelphia and mother and father could *have* to let me if I was *determined.* I don't *care* if everybody would cut me. I *despise* society and I *detest* girls. . . . It makes me mad to see everybody so contented. . . .

Our life is so horrid and petty and little and proper. I wish I lived long ago in the old chivalrus days when there would at least of been the satisfaction of dying in the Crusades and living to some purpose, but now there isn't a bit of romance in the world. The only thing that has the slightest remains is love, and there's precious little in that anyway. Even fighting has lost its nobleness, for men just stand up and shoot each other down a hundred at a shot and all the kings are the most practical money making rascals in the lot, and you'd about as soon catch one of them risking his life and charging at the head of his troops as you'd catch a young lady saying anything sensible.

I'm just mad mad mad and I do wish I was either awful bad or awful good, cause if I was bad I'd have lots of fun. I mean real *bad.* And if I was good I'd go to about 12 prayer meetings a day like the Shipleys and enjoy 'em which I don't do now. But as it is I can't do anything that is real bad cause it ain't right and I can't do anything real good cause I don't want to, so I appeal to anybody to know if I'm not to be pitied.

Now I'm going upstairs to read though it is first day, cause there's nothing else to do and Maude Kennedy's with Mother. I don't see why being a Friend should level all distinctions of society. If that woman wasn't a Friend she would eat with Eliza, but as it is Mother actually treats her like an equal just because she's a Friend.

October 27

Yearly Meeting is over and we've had a real nice one. . . . I feel a great deal worse than I act but I do hope I'm a Christian in spite of all. . . . And now my journal I must tell you of quite an adventure. Franklin McCay and David Whey, both young men or boys, stayed here this yearly Meeting and I thought just for fun I'd make myself agreeable to them. Well, Franklin was right devoted and I went to Meeting several times with him and all that. Well the last evening he was here we walked home from Meeting and walked very fast and got home before anyone. Well as soon as we got in, he said, "Minnie I want thee to give me something that I'd rather have than anything else in the world," and he went in the office and opened a drawer and there to my *utter* amazement and surprise I saw a little porcelain picture of myself. I told him I didn't give my picture to young men and so on but he was real serious and I do believe thought I would give it to him— the goose. Then the rest came and we hadn't any more conversation.

Jim Grenshaw was here to tea and dinner and I walked home from Meeting and saw a little of him. He seemed real nice and was at Earlham[7] and I believe was sent away for behavior and I'm afraid I like him all the better for it. . . . Miss Marble's friend Mary Harris is come today. She was at Vassar a year and thinks it's elegant. Oh I do so want to go. . . .

November 10

Oh my there's so little fun in this world and I'm real lonely and there isn't a girl in Baltimore I care a cent for except Bessie King and Bettie Arnes but I never see her

---

7. A Quaker coeducational college in Richmond, Indiana.

out of school. . . . The other day Lizzy, Bess and I went to the physiology lectures which we're attending, by Dr. Miles,[8] and which are very interesting as I'm watching them with a critical eye to see if I'd like to be a doctor for I haven't quite made up my mind yet. I didn't like the way Bess behaved exactly—sort of patronising, and if I'm nothing else I'm proud. Oh maybe it's fancy but I won't be a drag on her and if she wants our friendship to drop why I shan't do the slightest thing to prevent—but however there's nothing to do. There ain't a thing that's *real* nice in this world and the fact is I don't care much for anything except dreaming about being grand and noble and famous but that I can never be. . . . I wish the air were pure oxygen and then as it says in chemistry our life would sweep through its fevered burning course in a few hours we would live in a perfect delirium of excitement and would die vibrating with passion. . . .

November 19

Of course I made up with Bessie again and she came up and stayed all night 6th day. . . . In the morning we bought 2 calfs hearts and cut them up (as Dr. Miles did in the lecture) and found the oricles and wentricles and it was real interesting only they smelt bad—ain't the name for it. Then we moved our chemicles back to our laboratory after great difficulty distilled water, and then Bessie went home and I talked to MM until dinner time.

After dinner I took an elegant ride on Lady Die behind Father's carriage of three or four miles, and Father says I ride real well and Lady goes so splendidly, she canters all the time.

There is the effect of perseverance. This summer with great trouble I persuaded Grandma [Whitall] to let me have the saddle brought home, and then I hadn't any bridle or riding dress and father utterly refused to let me ride. But from that time to this I have been working, and now I have riding dress, bridle, and the liveliest little

8. Probably Dr. Manly Miles (1826-98), physician, naturalist, author, and teacher.

whip grandma Grove[9] gave me, and Oh what splendid duds I have!

December 1

Weren't we good? We read *Aunt Jane's Here* through in the afternoon and I went down to Bessie's for tea and from thence to the lecture.

Just now Bess and I have a great deal of fun over "catalacis" which name we give to every disease we don't know the name of, and in *Aunt Jane's Here* she dies with a very mysterious one and we call it "catalacis" and on sixth day evening when mother was telling about someone who died, Bess and I commenced to shout "because of catalacis."

On last 4th day evening we had a dreadful time . . . as we were returning home (it was pitch) with our arms full of biscuits Bessie tumbled *flat* right down in the gutter but she didn't let go her bundles but held them on high and when I looked around all I saw was two arms full of bundles emmerging from the gutter. When at last supper was ready and we hoped to have a little peace we were assailed by about 20 old maids all screaming in our ears at once:[1]

"I want some hot water."
"I don't want sugar."
"I want coffee."
"I haven't gotten tea."
"Where's the warm water."
"I don't want any milk."

Still we were driven wild, but at last after Horace had gone for some hot water, (we had forgotten it) and after each old maid that wanted coffee had poured tea in their cup, and every one that wished tea had got coffee, and after all these mistakes had been rectified, and we were eating quietly, Rachel Brooks and "Jemima Somebody" entered and commenced by looking into the tea pot.

9. Father's stepmother, third wife of grandfather Thomas, so-called after the Grove cottage, her summer home near Baltimore.

1. Evidently a gathering of Friends at her home, which was a frequent occurrence.

"Why Jemima, look at that tea!" Jemima looked, and Bess and I saw four hands raised in holy horror. "Why its enough to have done 20 sewing meetings," said Rachel, "and it tastes just like persimion."

"Yes," said Jemima with a reproachful look at Bess and myself, "I had a very bad headache and I took tea hoping to make it better but now my throat's raw from top to bottom and its green tea too." And with that they both fixed eyes of such melancholy sorrow on Bess and myself that SSS's couldn't stand it any longer. We caught each others eyes and with one last vain effort at self composure we laid our heads on the table and *shook*. The fact was we had put in a cup and a half of tea when a tablespoon full would have been enough. The last word we heard was Alice Gothergil's remarking to a friend, "I shall have to take opium to put myself to sleep tonight." And we agreed with her.

Last sixth day night Bess and I went into father's office and there we found this vaccine matter and lancet all ready so we determined to vaccinate ourselves so we beared our arms and I took the lancet to cut, and cut and cut Bessie's arm but made no blood, but we remembered that Dr. Miles had said the arteries were on the insides of the arm so I made a ferocious dig and Bessie's bled like fun then we scientifically put the crush on it, and she commenced on mine. She lacerated mine like a good fellow and stuck about half a crash on it and all night it hurt like fun and today it is festered and I do believe it'll take.

December 30

Oh, my now it is the end of the year and I have to close this dear old journal. . . . I am devoting my energies to skating, for be a good skater I *must* and will if possible. And now I must write Finis only saying that in the whole of this year I have only read *8* useful books and 55 novels. What am I coming to, just think of it.

"JOURNAL KEPT BY MINNIE THOMAS. COMMENCED JAN. 1ST, 1872, FINISHED JAN. 20TH, 1878"

January 1, 1872

This is the first day of the new year and last night Frank and I sat up and watched the old year out. Aunt Hannah had gone to Watch Meeting and Bessie had gone to bed, so we had the house to ourselves. We turned down the light and sat in the dark with the window open to listen while we got "talked up" and Frank told me his love secrets.

He is very much in love with Anna Shipley who by the way is perfectly splendid. I put this down about Frank so as to see if anything comes of it by the end of this year. After all it is nice to fall in love though I don't intend to commit the unpardonable crime myself, yet it's fun to see Frank and Anna do it. Miss Marble and Uncle Allen ditto. . . .

What I want almost more than anything else in the world is to go to Vassar. When I go to bed I think about it, and when I get up I think about it. Mama has almost promised to let me go when I'm 17, so that this time two years I would be there. My plan is to try for the sophomore class if possible because if I didn't, the four years there and three years in Philadelphia [at medical school] will make seven years away from home. But the trouble is I'm afraid I can't enter the Sophomore for I have to be examined in Algebra and Geometry besides lots of Greek. The truth is I don't study hard enough . . . I *will* and *must* . . . I do want a good education so much and I've got as good sense as most people and *can* learn if I get a chance and therefore what's to prevent it? Only my laziness—*Bah.*

And then I do so want to be a doctor, for what is a woman to do if she don't marry I'd like to know? Be dependent all her life, I suppose. If I can't be a doctor I'll have to be a school teacher or live at home on Father and do just as he says. I can't. . . .

January 2 MY BIRTHDAY

15 years old. Just think! How "Tempis Fugit." It seems as if yesterday when I wrote 14 in my journal last year but

still somehow I feel a great deal older it seems as if I knew much more, yet I'm sure I can't tell how. I ain't any better Christian if as good. I maybe know a little more about lessons but even there *precious* little to be sure. I have more experience in one way certainly (having sent both a story and a poem to *Harper* to which the only answer I got was "Respectfully returned") but *n'importe*. I shan't try again.

Well 9 o'clock we started and after a long ride in the horse cars found ourselves there [in the outskirts of Philadelphia]. Oh I do wish we had a river like the Wissahickon,[2] it is perfectly beautiful, just exactly the sort of stream Indians ought to have paddled their canoes in. Well we climbed up the most dangerous precipices when to have slipped would have been a headlong plunge into the river and maybe something worse. We did everything we could think of, especially Frank and myself, for I'm a better climber than the rest, one of which was there was a decayed branch of a tree and I dared Frank to walk out on it. It was real high and there was a perfect sea of brambles underneath it. He walked out to a certain point and then stopped, but I called him a coward and he went to the extreme point—of course I had to do it though I was oh so afraid. And just as I reached the extreme point behold I slipped and tumbled head foremost into the brambles. There was a shriek of dismay from the spectators but after a great deal of difficulty I succeeded in extricating myself. . . .

In the evening we went to Shipley's to tea. They started an elegant plan. Vincent, a boy from Yale was there, and the plan was that next summer we should explore the Brandywine[3] to its source, staying about a week or two and having one or two haycarts and a boat in case we get tired. Now wouldn't that be splendid—just think. Oh but I'm afraid it'll never come off.

January 3

Today I went home. Frank went down to the cars with me and we had quite an affectionate parting. He promised

2. Now a creek within the Philadelphia city limits.
3. River near West Chester, Pennsylvania, home of the Shipleys.

M. Carey Thomas at fifteen

to write and tell me all his secrets etc. . . . But now I must tell what I think of Anna Shipley. She is just too nice for anything and I'm perfectly in love with her, the way she speaks and all. Oh she is too splendid. I like her better than any girl, of course excepting Bessie. . . .

January 20

I have just come from a lecture on "Soul and Body" by Thomas Guard, and though it is 10:30 and I have a composition to write this evening I must tell something about it.

It was splendid. I liked it better than almost any lecture I have ever heard. It was about culture and etc. and oh so noble. It seems when you hear a man speak like that as if everything was better and real and sure as if life was something grand, something noble and not such a horrid prosaic thing as it is.

And if there really was some hope of doing something splendid after all. Oh my I do wish I could be famous for above all things I should like to write *well*. No, not well but *splendidly*. In the course of his lecture he said that men's brains in comparison with their size weighed more than any other animal. That the whale's with his immense size only weighed 80 oz. and man's almost 50, but he said one very insulking thing, that *ladies' brains weighed a few ozs less than men's.* He said, "But let them ask *us* for counsel, here are our brains! Let them ask *us* for love, here are our hearts! Let them ask us for worshipers, here are our knees!" And the stupid audience applauded him. However, he's an Irishman and not a judge, as St. Paul, being a bachelor, wrote so many horrid things against women. But if our brains did weigh less, what does it show? Why that for hundreds and thousands of years women haven't had the same education as men, that they have not had the same chances for developing, that with all their force and power men have been keeping them down and forcing them to remain in the narrow sphere of *household* duties and anything beyond that was in the highest degree "undecorous, unrefined, coarse, UNladylike." What a burning shame! And then they sit down and laugh and say

"Don't talk any more to *us* of *your* equal powers of intellect, *your* very brains weigh less. The thing is ridiculous!" IDIOTS! Why if woman's brains *did* weigh as much with the infinitely inferior education they receive, what would they weigh when cultivated to the extent men's are? Well! One thing I am determined on, and that is that by the time I die *my* brain shall weigh as much as any *man's* if study and learning can make it so. Then I'll leave it in the hands of some physiologist to be weighed so as after that no miserable man can stand up on a miserable platform and tell [that it is] a "FEW (that is eight ounces)" less than any other man's.

Just wait till equal education takes place and see if that remark can be made!!!!!!!!!!

January 23

Today Bessie and I had real fun . . . we started for the pond, arrived there the men told us they were very sorry but we couldn't skate, they said there is no way of ladies getting on. We laughed in our sleeves and immediately put on our skates. The pond crackled like all creation and one of the fellers about 19 skated all around to show that it was safe, and just as he was quieting an anxious lady with the words, "I assure you it is as firm as can be" slam bang, in he went up to his neck. After that catastrophe the lady took her son off and we had the pond to ourselves for 2 or 3 hours. My! but it was dangerious. The ice just waved up and down and heaved on great billows while we passed over it. It was perfectly elegant fun.

On the shore were 7 or 8 little coloured boys and at every heave they'd shout, "Now she's in this time," and their look of disappointment was pitiful to see as we triumphfully skated on. If ever two mortals deserved skating Bess and I are those two for no matter if the thermomenter says 212 we take our skates and hot out there on the barest supposition. Respectability is nothing. All the roudy ponds in the city of Baltimore are frequented by us. All the skating roughs in the city know us by sight, but the upshot of it all is that where other "ladylike" girls (if such there be that skate) have one skate, we have twenty, and so roudy-

67

ism pays in this instance as it *always* does. For my journal the result of cogitations of my 15 "summer suns" resolves itself into this advice:

Go ahead! Have fun! Stop short of nothing but what is wrong (and not always that). Never mind if people call you "wild" "tomboyish" "unladylike" "masculine." They like you all the better for it in the end. Be a child while you can. For twenty years of your life you may as well be wild, for at least 50 anni you'll *have* to be tame! Imagine Grandma pitching around climbing trees, skating, sledding. . . .

February 4

I must write to Frank. By the by I've come to the conclusion that Frank is ever so nice whenever he and I are *alone* we have such nice times. And then the general run of boys are so horrid for the other day I was thinking, suppose I should want to fall in love, though of course such a thing never *would* and never *shall* enter into my doctorial brains, who on earth would there be to fall in love with? What a *nice* selection there is in our Meeting. . . . Ugh—Nobody I have ever seen, man, woman or child comes up to my ideal.

I was reading a book the other day called *Hannah*[4] it was about a man falling in love with his sister-in-law (in England they can't marry) and oh it was so nice! They loved each other so wildly and passionately; Hannah had such a strong, noble, tender nature and Bernard was so fierce, firey and intense and they couldn't hardly see each other and Oh they suffered so. It seems to me that if I ever fell in love it must be like that and with such a splendid passionate man as Bernard and not in the miserable commonplace way everybody else does. "Frinstance" like MM and U.A. They are in love everybody knows it; they know it themselves. MM is sure Uncle Allen loves her. U.A. is sure MM loves him. There is not the slightest uncertainty about it. Why you might as well be married and be done with it. Whereas in *Hannah* they were to be sure unhappy, but when they did see each other they were 1000 times happier than the aforementioned pair. I don't think

4. *Hannah,* a best-selling novel of its day by Dinah Maria Craik (Harper, [187—]).

there's a speck of romance in life nowadays (Bessie thinks it's hidden) but I don't think there is *any* to hide. I don't mean particularly about love, but about everything.

February 23

I have missed lots but really I'm halting between two opinions—whether to give up this journal at once or keep it along for I really have not time to keep it up properly and so I've almost determined either to give it to the winds or only to write just when I feel like it and not even attempt to keep a connected account. And now for what I've been reading which is all absorbing at present seeing as it's *Jane Eyre.* At last I persuaded mother to let me read it and when I once began it I never stopped till I finished it. It is perfectly burning and full of concentrated passion and oh so powerfully written! My throat was parched while I was reading it, cheeks fairly scorched. Oh, though I dare say it isn't a good book, yet it seems to me as if it were something worth while to be able to write something that should have power to excite and intensely interest to such a degree. The part of it where it tells about the mad woman has a perfect fascination for me. What a vivid imagination and power Charlotte Bronté must have had. . . .

March 14

Besse and I have changed our names. I call her Rex and she calls me Rush and I suppose we'll call each other by them all our lives.

Yesterday was the Sewing Meeting. The last one I guess, and we had a real nice time. None of those horrid boys were there and so after the supper we went up in the Meeting house by ourselves.

It was so still, such a sort of solemn gloom hanging over it, and the windows let in just enough light to cause dim uncertain shadows on the long rows of empty benches. Our voices only disturbed the intense silence. It was so lonely, so deserted in the midst of the busy whirling city around that it possessed a perfect fascination under every bench in the recess of every shadow there seemed to lurk strange fantastic figures and forms that had taken refuge from the glare and bustle in this perfect stillness. It was just the very time to build air castles and we walked up and down the aisle and talked of what we wanted to be and do and formed plans.

How after we had come home from Vassar having taken bright honors we would do everything, we would devote our selves to study, live together, have a library with all the splendid books, with a bright wood fire always burning, dark crimson curtains and furniture, great big easy chairs where we could sit lost in books for days together. A great large table covered with papers for we would be authors. Adjoining this should be a laboratory where far into the night we would pour over Crucibles, mixing our mystic engredients and perhaps making discoveries which should affect the whole world and there we would live loving each other and urging each other on to every high and noble deed or action and all who passed should say "their example arouses me, their books ennoble me, their ideas inspire me and behold they are women!" Of course these were only our widest fancies but oh if only some of them might come true. Why can't two girls love each other in life's struggle just as well as a man and a woman! But I suppose one of us'll have to go and fall in love or something or other horrid. The more I see of lovers the more thoroughly I despise the whole lot so I don't think it will be me at any rate.

April 1

Today is April Fool's Day but I don't feel in a very April fool's state of mind, for last evening after meeting I said that I thought S[t]. Paul was very unjust to women and that I disbelieved him as far as I possibly could any thing in the Bible. Then father said no, that he was right that the man *was* the head of the woman as Christ is the head of the church—that God made it so—that a woman was weaker than a man—the woman was made for the man not man for the woman. Take a woman and man of the same abilities and the man would be the stronger in every way— that *sweetness, gentleness, gracefulness, beauty, love* belonged to a woman, that power, strength, force, intellect to a man—that a wife must reverence her husband that the

70

man always took the lead and was made by God to do so and all such things. It made me so mad almost beside my self that men can sit up and say to the smartest woman that ever lived "I am the head, I am made by God with more power. My will is the strongest. You are out of your sphere."

Oh, I think it's dreadful to be told that *Tom Carey* and *Charles Thomas* have more power than *we* have. Of course they have more *brute* strength but so has a prize fighter more than a gentleman. Oh I can't stand it. It's *too* unjust, *too* horrible that things should be so, of course I don't believe it. I believe that I have as much sense as any boy I know. Tom Carey, Net Coate, Charley Whitall, Frank, Jimmy, Carey, and more too and if I live we'll see who'll be worth the most. It seems to me I'd die if I could do *anything* to show that a woman is equal to a man, it is such a burning shame that a woman should have it always poked in their faces. If I have to give up my freedom in the slightest degree, *I'll never marry*—and I don't expect to any how, for if Heavenly Father spares me my senses I'll never be dependent on any one man or woman. . . . Oh, how I wish I had the intellect to do something only to show that all my talk ain't gabble. I am throughly and heartly woman's Right and never expect to change my opinion. I'll *despise,* and *hate* and *abhore* myself if I do. And now if I'm ever going to do anything I must study. . . .

April 27
Now my journal prepare yourself—Mother, father, Grace, Daisy and Helen[5] went to Ohio yearly meeting and so I was left to keep house. Rex [Bessie King] was sick and I was all by myself and real lonely but 4th afternoon, that is two days before Father and Mother came home, Anna Shipley, Sue Howland, Frank and Bessie came down and I tell you we had real fun. . . . Now I must give my thoughts on things—1st Anna—I like her ever so much. She is just too nice for anything. She is real smart, and interested in everything. Next to Rex she is the jolliest girl I know. She

5. Her three younger sisters.

and I have made a compact, that is, that I will go to Vassar and study with all my might and she will read and at the end of 4 years (we are almost even now) we'll see who'll know the most. Oh she is too elegant. Frank also is ever so much improved. He is much more wide awake, full of theories and everything and altogether is by far the nicest fellow I've seen. And now a secret—I only put it down because I want to see how it all turns out—Frank and Anna have [nine handwritten lines crossed out too heavily to decipher]. I do believe I'm a perfect goose! I think I must feel towards Anna for instance like a boy would, for I admire her so. Not any particular thing but just an undefined sense of admiration and then I like to touch her and the other morning I woke up and she was asleep and I admired her hair so much that I kissed it. I never felt so much with anybody else.

August 8

Today at 4 o'clock Frank died.[6] I am really writing this on Sept. 7th for it seemed as if I couldn't bear to write before.

He had been sick 10 days but I had *no idea* of his dying till today as I was asleep on the sofa; they waked me up and said "Get up, Frank is dying." I went in his room and from 1½ to 4 we watched him. He lay perfectly still not even able to swallow. We all sat around and Aunt Hannah bent over him, stroking his hair and laying her hand on his forehead. He breathed fainter and fainter and at last stopped. We all sat still for a few minutes, then Aunt Hannah and Uncle Robert closed his eyes and we all went out. And that is all—I never knew what death *was* before. I hardly knew there was such a thing but now, Oh it seems too dreadful, I can hardly believe it. Frank and my lives have so intermingled ever since we were children and we planned all our future together and everything. To think that I'll have to go on all alone.

This summer especially we have been together the whole long day, we'd lay in the hammock and on the grass and

6. He died of typhoid fever.

read and talk and dream. We were reading *Phantasies,* Oh all through the long twilights we sat under the trees and read and read and read like we ourselves seemed lost in the story and when it was too dark to see we talked of ourselves, our past, our futures, and how we were going to help each other on and stick by each other. Oh we were such regular friends and I loved him so so much and now I'll never see him anymore. Oh if we had only known! How much we might have said that we didn't. It wouldn't have been so bad if I could only once have told him how nice I thought he was, and how much I loved him for I don't believe he half knew.

Oh everything seems so lonely. The Cedars ain't the Cedars any more. Every book I take up is so associated with Frank that I can't bear it. We were right in the midst of the *Inferno* and through the long first day afternoon we used to read *Paradise Lost.* We were just at the 5 book when he died.

Poor little Maye's "Never coming back any more never coming back any more" seems to ring in my ears, Oh Frank, Frank—

This was the last piece we learned together Frank and I:

"I go mine thou goest thine,
Many ways we wend;
Many days and many ways
Ending in *one end.*

Many a wrong and its curing song,
Many a road and many an inn.
Room to roam, but only one home,
For the whole world to win."

[Extracts of last letters to Cousin Frank Whitall Smith]

[No date, but probably September 1871]

Dear Frank,

Hurrah for thee! I'm ever so glad thee passed. I think it was splendid of thee and so now thee is a Princetonian for certain. Do write and tell me all about the examination and what sort of rooms thee has and what the fellows are like and everything about it. Oh my I wish I was a boy and we had both entered Princeton together. I hope thee recognizes thy advantages and Oh Frank *do* graduate first, just think how splendid it would be! . . . I hope thee sympathises with thy poor cousin who has to struggle against the bigotted predjude of her paternal and maternal ancestors and very likely will be conquered in the end, whereas thee just walks into Princeton without any opposition. . . .

[No date, but notation on letter says "Answered 2/16/72"]

Dear Frank,

. . . Thee knows that talk we had in the cars about thy being a lawyer etc. Well Frank, if I was thee I certainly would be one. I have been thinking about it since, and it seems to me thee has such a splendid opening and not being *extraordinarily* stupid I see no reason why thee might not stand at the head of the profession and one day acquit a "Mrs. Wharton"[7] or empeach a president[8] etc. And then thee knows thee'll be a lawyer and I a doctor and we can try who'll get topmost. And thee'll invite me to thy court rooms and I'll invite thee to my desecting rooms and so we'll keep up quite an exchange of hospitalities and our "Alma Mater" the SSS Society shall be known throughout

7. A famous trial in Annapolis, Maryland, from December 1871 to January 1872. A Mrs. Elizabeth G. Wharton was accused of poisoning General W. S. Ketchum, and was acquitted. See *The Trial of Mrs. Elizabeth G. Wharton on the Charge of Poisoning General W. S. Ketchum,* published in 1872 by *The Baltimore Gazette.*

8. Obviously a reference to the impeachment of President Andrew Jackson in 1868.

the world for having produced the greatest lawyer and doctor ever seen from the times of Esculys (I haven't an idea how to spell his name as I suppose thee perceives) and Demosthenes. But seriously Frank do think about being a lawyer for I've almost determined to be a Dr. and think how I'd look down on thee as a humdrum old merchant in whose mouth butter wouldn't melt. Ugh.

Nov. 5th, 1872

Dear Frank,

. . . Oh is it true that you've had a row at Princeton? Bess and I read in the papers that the whole Sophomore class refused to recite, because they wouldn't let 'em rush the Freshmen, is it so? Oh my I hope thee was rushed like all creation, nothing would delight me more cause I don't think thee gets half thy share of abuse. . . .

Emmerson (if thee don't know who he is find out I had to) is going to lecture here about Christmas so if thee comes thee'll have a chance of hearing him, though I don't suppose that will be much inducement to a boy who won't lead his class, Pshaw! I am awful sorry thee's my cousin. Wait till I get to Vassar and then see how I'll distinguish myself. Oh by the way, mother has positively promised me that I shall go when I am 19, ain't that *elegant?*

Au revoir, thine truly
Dr. Minnie Thomas that is to be.

[No date, but notation reads:
"Ans'd May 4, 1872"]

Dear Frank,

. . . It does seem to me a poor state of affairs when a boy can't admire a girl or a girl a boy without people saying they're *in love* so don't be afraid that I'll ever do thee that injustice.

And now Frank if I was thee I don't think I would write to Amy Tatum. In the first place if she is a *lady* I don't think she'll answer but if she does thee knows you'll never write common sense letters. Amy, as I understand it, is a regular flirt and if you don't write nonsense she'll know it, as for her being cousin, that's no reason—she's a most distant one anyway, besides I wouldn't really like any girl who would write to a boy and don't believe thee would either. . . . And finally are they in the same station of society as we are? Thee knows what her mother was—not that that would make the *slightest* difference only I don't think the girls are refined or—hardly—well, perfect ladies, does thee? . . .

I had a real serious talk with father about being a doctor the other day. He said that if I was a boy he would disuade me just as much and also he talked about lawyers which conversation if I had time I would repeat. . . .

[Journal]
August 12
Frank was buried today on his eighteenth birthday.

Funerals are dreadful. I can never forget the dull heavy thud of the earth as it fell upon the coffin. All is over now and life goes whirling on again, but it will never be the same to me as it was before. I do hope Frank's life and example will make me a realer truer Christian. I do want to be and I suppose his death was all right but it's so hard and I miss him so so much.

August 25
Anna has been here for a few days and then I was up at West Chester. She knew Frank and so we could sympathize for we both love and miss him so. She and I know each other better than ever before and I think we can be real earnest friends. She is ever so nice and I love her dearly next to Rex. Oh I do miss Rex, she has been in Europe ever since May and I have been very lonely—O she is all I have left now—

BOARDING SCHOOL AND COLLEGE

When Carey Thomas took up her journal after the usual summer hiatus—more marked, in the summer of 1872, by the sorrowful note on which it had ended—she was writing from the Howland Institute at Canandaigua, New York, a Quaker boarding school for girls, near Ithaca. With her was her first cousin Bessie Nicholson, as well as Bessie King, her longtime friend and more distant cousin.

It was at Howland that Carey first came to the attention of Miss Jennie Slocum, a teacher who encouraged her resolve to prove the case for women's intellectual equality, and who influenced her decision to dismiss thoughts of Vassar in favor of a coeducational college where the challenge would be heightened and the degree more generally esteemed. The University of Michigan and Cornell are the two mentioned. Sage College, Cornell's first women's dormitory, was completed in the fall of 1875, and after graduating from Howland and spending a year at home studying for her examinations, Carey entered Cornell in 1875 with the first class to include women as boarders. She received her B.A. in two years.

At Howland, as at Cornell, Carey's strong emotional and romantic attachments (known then as "smashes"[1]) to various classmates provided a respite from her studies. "Smashing" was a common phenomenon among young American women in the nineteenth century, and especially among those thrown together in boarding schools and colleges. (In young adolescents in the same circumstances,

---

1. Her friend Anna Shipley, in a letter to Carey at Cornell, writes, "I have been reading that book of Mahaffy's as we are at Greek architecture now, and I was especially struck with the origin of the SMASH! Does thee remember? How is Miss Hicks. Sweet lamb I should like to annihilate her with a strong British stare—I am madly jealous." J. P. Mahaffy was a prolific writer of works on ancient Greece, and I may well have missed "that book." The only one of his works I was able to find that bears considerable reference to the subject (though not the term) is *Social Life in Greece from Homer to Menander* 2nd ed. (London:

"crushes" on older classmates have been common in this century, especially before coeducation swept through the preparatory schools.)[2] A letter in the 1873 *Yale Courant* described it thus:

> When a Vassar girl takes a shine to another, she straight-way enters upon a regular course of bouquet sendings, inter-spersed with tinted notes . . . locks of hair perhaps, and many tender tokens, until at last the object of her attention is captured, the two become inseparable and the aggressor is considered . . . smashed. The mortality, so to speak, resulting from these smash-ups is frightful to contemplate. One young lady . . . rejoices in more than thirty. She keeps a list. . . . How, "In the name of the hogshead of batter/Devoured at each breakfast at Vassar," such a custom should have come into vogue passes masculine comprehension. But the solemn fact remains, and Vassar numbers her smashes by the score.[3]

An excellent essay on the network of intense friend-ships between nineteenth-century women is Carroll Smith-Rosenberg's article "The Female World of Love and Rit-ual," which studies these relationships within the context of the existing cultural norms and moral strictures.[4]

Macmillan, 1875), pp. 329-30. Mahaffy quotes another authority as follows: "Still more remarkable is the fact that the elevation of senti-ment, which is regarded by Plato as the first step in the upward progress of the philosopher, is aroused not by female beauty but by the beauty of youth, which alone seems to have been capable of inspiring the modern feeling of romance in the Greek mind. The passion which was unsatis-fied by the love of women, took the spurious form of an enthusiasm for the ideal of beauty. . . . "

2. The chief difference between twentieth-century "crushes" and nineteenth-century "smashes" is the degree of demonstrated affection, which is in fact totally absent in the former. Indeed, the object of the "crush" has often been unaware that she is so intensely admired, and in most cases would undoubtedly feel uncomfrotable if she knew.

3. Quoted in "Changing Patterns of Sexuality and Female Interaction in late 19th Century America" by Nancy Sahli, p. 8. Paper read at the Berkshire Conference on the History of Women at Bryn Mawr College, 11 June 1976. Copy in Schlesinger Library, Harvard University.

4. Carroll Smith-Rosenberg, "The Female World of Love and Ritual: Relations between Women in Nineteenth-Century America," *Signs,* 1 (Autumn 1975): 1-29.

Nancy Sahli convincingly contends that these cultural norms and acceptable patterns of behavior changed radically between 1870 and 1880, causing a dramatic shift in attitude toward "homoemotional" relationships and, correspondingly, a sharp reduction in the open display of affection among women who had earlier shown no such reserve. She cites one of the factors causing the change to be the proliferation, in this country, of scientific inquiry on the subject of sexuality, and paraphrases Havelock Ellis's definition of lesbianism as encompassing "an emotional phenomenon that did not necessarily include either physical involvement or sexual activity."[5]

The term "lesbianism" is today used to imply both emotional and physical involvement, and Carey Thomas has been assumed, in and out of print, to have been a lesbian in terms of her sexual preference and practice. I find it necessary here to clarify the nature of Carey Thomas's relationships with and attitudes toward her close friends. Such clarification is pertinent to an understanding of her character and motivations, which in essential aspects did not change in the course of her life. No one can know for certain about personal and private behavior, and I find it hard to understand why anyone should very much care except as it throws light on public behavior and achievements. I would not feel it necessary to dwell on what is to me a relatively inconsequential matter were it not that at least one reputable historian has recently gone so far as to attribute Carey Thomas's motivation and considerable achievement to her "sexual preference."[6]

5. Sahli, p. 15.

6. ". . . for those young women who would not accept the male/female division of professions Bryn Mawr was something of a shrine. At Bryn Mawr, M. Carey Thomas encouraged young women to become scholars and college professors. It may have been at Bryn Mawr, on the edge of the unknown, that faculty and students ignored their sex and for the first time in an institution of higher education in the United States allowed human beings to be human first, men or women second. M. Carey Thomas was a lesbian and surely not the first person to head an American college or university whose sexual life was an influence on

The tendency persists to perceive relationships of another era in terms of contemporary attitudes, whereby nineteenth century "smashes" take on a uniform coloration in favor of lesbianism, in spite of studies avowing the contrary. For example, a recent book by Anthony Wallace[7] describes the "sisterhood" among women of the managerial class in a manufacturing district of Pennsylvania. Carey Thomas's idealized friendships with women fit the pattern Wallace describes of intense emotional and romantic attachments that were free of sexuality, although not of physical as well as spiritual intimacy. While latent homosexuality was undoubtedly nurtured under such circumstances, for a number of reasons it is my conviction that Carey Thomas did not harbor this tendency and that such unfounded statements as Frederick Rudolph's fall wide of the mark.

Carey Thomas's tendency to enjoy, and in fact often to prefer, the company of men to that of most women, which is obvious to anyone who reads through the letters and autobiographical notations, does not in itself make a case for her heterosexual preference. There is, however, the indisputable fact that her rebellion was not against men as a class and was not psychosexually oriented; indeed, as her early journals attest, it precedes her awareness of what sexuality was all about. Her rebellion was against the social role assigned to women and the limitations imposed on their lives. Her indignation was fired by the rationalization which most people accepted: that women had not the same intellectual capabilities as men. She was determined to see to it that she, and others like her, should one day be allowed the same intellectual opportunities and rewards as their male counterparts, but she at no time indicated her desire to have been born a man; on the

---

the college course of study." Frederick Rudolph, *Curriculum: A History of the American Undergraduate Course of Study Since 1636* (San Francisco: Jossey-Bass, 1977), p. 170.

7. Anthony F.C. Wallace, *Rockdale, the Growth of An American Village in the Early Industrial Revolution* (New York: Knopf, 1978), pp. 104-13.

contrary, she has written that despite everything she preferred to be a woman (see p. 121).

When Carey Thomas learned the "facts of life" in detail (through her father's medical books and rather late, considering the many pregnancies she had witnessed), her revulsion was a common one in young women brought up in an age that considered the noble ideal to be the nineteenth century concept of a classical platonic relationship. In her case the aversion was doubtless aggravated by the trauma of her burn, which had caused her such excruciating pain in an area extending from her waist to her thighs.

In spite of her initial revulsion against "the bestial nature" of the male sex,[8] Carey was attracted enough to Francis Gummere to have been tempted to marry him. Her failure to do so appears due to a number of circumstances, including his failure to propose. After she received her Ph.D. and was appointed dean at Bryn Mawr, marriage was less of an option; it was certainly ruinous to her career ambitions even if the ideal candidate had appeared. Like many strong women, Carey Thomas would in any event have had a hard time finding a satisfactory husband. Ambitious, aggressive women never have been likely to attract the strong, ambitious, successful men they most respect.

Carey Thomas's aversion to sex would have applied to homosexuality even more, since that behavior was not even socially sanctioned. Those who knew her well have been unanimous in attesting to her conventionality, even though she was in many ways ahead of her time—certainly with regard to education and the position of women in society. She was also capable of changing her attitudes to conform with socially acceptable behavior as society's attitudes changed. For example, in the 1920s she proudly mailed to a number of friends, including her last secretary

8. An interpretation of the evolution and consequences of this attitude is brilliantly argued in an article by Nancy F. Cott, "Passionlessness: An Interpretation of Victorian Sexual Ideology 1790-1850," *Signs*, 4 (Winter 1978): 219-36.

who supplied me with a copy, a poem written by a nephew titled "Perfect Abandon," which would certainly have shocked her earlier in her life:

As fresh as hill-top wind
In tall green pines
So clear
And yet the sparkle of a thousand precious stones
Set in a ruler's crown
What bliss
To strip
And dive off from the rocky bank
Of staid old-world conventions
With this clean graceful girl
Into the deep dark pool
Of naturalness.

Speculation about her lesbianism has involved her relationship with two friends and has evolved from gossip, in Bryn Mawr circles, around the turn of the century. Carey's friendship with Mamie Gwinn, who eloped with a former Bryn Mawr English professor in 1904, and who will be more prominent in later sections of this volume, became the subject of a minor novel by Gertrude Stein (*Fernhurst*, published in 1971).[9] In it, Carey Thomas, thinly disguised under another name,[1] becomes a figure in a love triangle and is consumed with heartbreak when her lesbian lover leaves her—as it turns out, temporarily—for a short-lived marriage. The novel has been taken as fact by a good many scholars who should know better than to draw conclusions from fiction. The nature of Carey's friendship with Mamie Gwinn, as well as with Mary Garrett who has been named as another lesbian candidate, was very different from either the published fiction or whispered rumor.

9. *Fernhurst* was first published in 1971 by Liveright under the title *Fernhurst, Q.E.D., and Other Early Writings*. According to the Introduction by Leon Katz, it was probably written in 1904 or 1905.

1. The matter of her having dropped "Martha," her own first name, has been taken as a sign of her desire for male identity. As is clear (see p. 121), this is not true.

Mary Garrett moved into the Deanery in 1904, when Mamie Gwinn eloped with Alfred Hodder, and continued to live there until her death in 1915. Carey's friendship with Mary Garrett—with whom a voluminous correspondence exists—appears to have taken the place in Carey's life of the sort of relationship she longed to have with her own mother. Carey's devotion to her mother was only natural, but occasional remarks, and complaints about the excessive size of her family, show signs of an ungratified longing to be the only child of an indulgent mother. There is her recorded wish that her mother had been "born a widow" and she "her only child and [we could] travel about."[2]

In attaining this ideal relationship with a friend, Carey quite deliberately pushed out of the way Mary's childhood friend Julia Rogers. She then had all to herself (with not even a token "sister") the devotion of someone capable of helping to gratify her wishes. Mary was older than Carey and more sophisticated by upbringing. She was intelligent, an ardent feminist, and her ideas and Carey's coincided. She perfectly met Carey's need for someone Carey could respect and to whom she could unburden herself and gain approval for her plans. It is significant that the correspondence between the two doubles in volume following the death of Carey's mother in 1888 and again doubles after 1894 when Carey Thomas became president of Bryn Mawr and assumed that position's attendant responsibilities.

On the other hand, Mamie Gwinn was an only child in search of a surrogate mother, since her own continually rejected her. Mamie was useful as a traveling companion to Carey during the years of study abroad, but four or five years after their return Carey appears to have begun to feel saddled with Mamie. Like a waif, Mamie spent years running from her real mother to Carey, seeking refuge from the one and then the other, not entirely welcome in either home.

2. See p. 10, footnote 7.

After 1890, Mamie became even more of an unwelcome obligation to Carey. Mary could not abide her, and after a time would not come to the Deanery unless she was away. In 1890 Carey refers, in a letter to Mary, to having spent a year with Mamie she would not care to repeat. In a letter a year later she writes that she and Mamie don't quarrel anymore; the implication is that they have arrived at something of a modus vivendi, unsatisfactory though it may be.

Years later, after Carey Thomas had died, Mamie wrote a long letter to Logan Pearsall-Smith (Carey Thomas's first cousin) in which she "corrected" certain "myths" about herself and Carey she claimed he had recorded in his latest book, *Unforgotten Years*.[3] "Some women, mainly foreign, might be made like men," she wrote, "but in our minds there lurked, I think, the same division between female kinds that Kipling later formulated:

A man must go with a woman, which a woman can't understand./ Or if they understand it, they're not the marrying brand.

We were the marrying brand, and didn't want to marry, and were rather smug about it."

The gossips, of course, knew none of this, and myths have continued to flourish. Perhaps not so accidentally, "Fernhurst" was the name of the Pearsall-Smith enclave in Sussex where, according to Carey's late nephew Harold Worthington, "Aunt Hannah like a Queen bee gathered her brood about her as she did wherever she moved." Gertrude Stein was acquainted with the Berensons, and the Russell-Berenson connection kept the gossip about Carey and Mamie alive on both sides of the Atlantic for some time.[4] Bertrand Russell's widow, the former Edith Finch who wrote Carey Thomas's authorized biography, told me that she had no doubt Carey was a lesbian; that

3. Logan Pearsall-Smith, *Unforgotten Years* (Boston: Little, Brown, 1939).

4. See p. 7, footnote 6.

everyone, including Lord Russell, knew it.[5] Carey Thomas's lesbianism, Edith Finch told me in 1975, was in her opinion a foregone conclusion because several of her own and Carey Thomas's mutual friends were so inclined. Although Finch mentioned names (they did not include Mamie Gwinn or Mary Garrett), she failed to note that these women had merely accompanied Carey Thomas in her travels after her retirement when she was approaching old age.

Some of Carey's executors, perhaps taking note of the effusive declarations they discovered in the correspondence which follows, as well as a number of letters written two decades later to Mary Garrett, kept the papers well guarded and thus served to promote the notion that there was something to hide. It is true enough that until recently such effusive expressions of affection as can be found, here and there, in the letters, would almost certainly have been misunderstood.

In the selections which follow, passages which record Carey's smashing on any number of attractive young women (she was decidedly fickle) should be read from the perspective of an exceedingly conventional young woman, anxious to be one with the crowd: if smashes were "in" and she and her family did not consider them wrong, she was not to be left out. They must be seen, as well, as an outlet (the only one open to her) for an emotionally charged young woman and a profoundly romantic one, who was inhibited from virtually all but the most formal contacts with men both by her upbringing and even more by admonishments upon leaving home.[6] (An exception appears to have been her ice skating with men, which neither she nor her family found disturbing.) Indeed,

---

5. Lady Russell added: "I made that perfectly clear in my book." Careful scrutiny of Edith Finch's *Carey Thomas of Bryn Mawr* (New York: Harper and Brothers, 1947) indicates nothing of the kind.

6. For example: "We miss thee much dear daughter and shall be glad when thou art through and ready to come to us again. I am glad that thou hast firmly adhered to thy own and my convictions and avoided all society (except what study requires) amongst the gentlemen. . . . " Letter from her father to Carey Thomas at Cornell, 9 March 1876.

aloofness from male students seems to have been a condition of her having been allowed to leave home, and there are indications that she was made to feel that lapses in this regard would jeopardize the chances for all those women for whom she was professing to be a pioneer in coeducation. Her letters home from Cornell make a point of mentioning her difficulty in refraining from attending dances (Quakers were forbidden to dance). She did dance, she confesses, but hastens to add that it was with girls. Her mother and Aunt Hannah had been through the "smashing" phase themselves and found it enjoyable, if somewhat distracting from the work at hand. As with Carey, it was the only sort of courtship permissible without the requisite of impending marriage and sexual submission.

Some physical contact unquestionably played a part in these romantic emotional attachments; just as unquestionably, for reasons already set forth, in Carey Thomas's case I believe sexuality did not. At the same time I cannot ignore her very human need for companionship and affection, and in her case a superabundance of devotion. After her retirement, when she was given to clipping articles that spoke her mind, she saved a letter to *The Woman's Leader* (undated), evidently one in a spate of letters following reviews of Radclyffe Hall's *The Well of Loneliness*. A portion of the letter reads:

> There are thousands of women: independent, vigorous, capable, temperamentally rich and mentally alert, who are restless, hampered, frustrated, warped, according to their various degrees, because they are denied a proper emotional life. . . . Marriage, for a variety of reasons, has been denied them. . . . The physical side of it in many women's cases plays a very insignificant part; it would be developed, no doubt, in marriage; it is sublimated out of it—in any case it is relatively unimportant. Their yearning is the multiple and complicated need of a complex human being. They could find it, many of them, with equal success through man or woman—many of them, out of human disappointment, turn to dogs for something of that companionship they could not find elsewhere. . . .

86

Carey Thomas's niece, Millicent McIntosh, tells of her aunt's sadness in the late 1920s after having seen a play about homosexuality. "She was grieved," Mrs. McIntosh says, "that this was the sort of thing that would make it difficult for women to develop the warm and close relationships some of them needed so very much."[7]

In her last days at the Deanery, emotionally quite alone in the midst of fourteen servants, Carey turned to her dog for affection. "Oh, she was tough!" said Mrs. Katie Gaffney who (as Katie Doyle) had been her personal maid at that time. "She was difficult. It's hard to explain but there was a softness and a sadness about her too. That dog—name was Ching—she treated him like her baby. Hugging and kissing the thing all the time. And she was always taking him driving. She would be in the driver's seat and Ching beside her and the chauffeur in the back seat.[8] Now that *was* a sight!"

This image of Carey seems entirely in character as we come to know the young author of the following journals, which in this section I have interspersed with some of her letters in order to fill in the extensive gaps between entries. I have also inserted a letter from Miss Slocum that shows the extent of her influence on Carey's choice of a college and career.

M.H.D.

Howland School
October 13, 1872

Dear Grandma [Whitall],

Here I am sitting by the window in our room writing while Bessie is lying on the bed reading. We had an

7. That is to say, such widespread publicity about homosexuality as would inhibit people of the same sex from living together for fear of being labelled. A notation in her diary dated 26 January 1927 reads: "Saw 'Captive' about infatuation 2 women—vile play all people horrid."
8. According to her friends and relations, she loved to drive, drove badly, and took the chauffeur along to get her out of ditches, fix flat tires, and take over the driving when she tired. To have put him beside her would have struck her and her circle as socially incorrect.

elegant journey here and arrived at Howland School about 9:30 o'clock Fourth Day night. Mother and Father and Cousin Frank stayed at a hotel all night and came and helped us unpack and then went in the morning. It was pretty hard to see them drive off and leave us and the teachers looked as if they expected us to cry but they looked in vain.

Now I know thee'll want to hear about our room, it's about as large as that little room next to the one Bessie slept in, in your town house, and has a great big closet where we keep our wash-stand and we have a lot of pictures hung around among others two pictures of thee and Grandpa so the room looks quite home like. We created quite an excitement among the girls as we were the first Baltimoreans that were ever here, but they really are the nicest girls I ever saw, perfect crowds of them have come in our room to see us and the other night we found a bundle of grapes and cake and pears with a card of one of the girls wasn't that kind of her?

They have been speculating as to Bessie's and my relation to each other and one of the girls asked me if we weren't twin sisters.

Now I have something to tell thee that I'm sure will delight thy heart. We have to *make our own bed and sweep our own room* and get up at quarter past 6 o'clock and go to bed at 9 o'clock ain't it too dreadful for anything? Just think in winter the girls say we have to eat breakfast by lamp light. This morning we went to Meeting and it was just the other extreme of Haddonfield [noted for its short "paltry few" sermons] for I never was in a meeting where so many people spoke. Seven sermons and three prayers. However it was very interesting. David Uptograph's daughter is here and is right nice and Caroline Ladd's daughter is one of the handsomest girls here. . . .

But we have the awfulest things to eat—tell Grandpa that it is as good as going around Cape Horn. . . . I wrote home a most touching letter to Mother begging her to send me something to eat for really Bessie and I are almost starving. I can't bear to think of the elegant dinners we used to have at the Cedars. . . . How is Uncle Robert [Pearsall Smith], have they gone to Clifton yet, and how are my darling grandpa and grandma and won't they write to their poor lonely granddaughter whose mother hasn't written to her for three whole days and who must now stop to study her lessons?

P.S. We have to make our fires too.

[Journal]
October 26, 1872
Howland School

Here I am way off at boarding school. Rex [Bessie King] has come home and here we are in Eastern New York. It was dreadful hard for them to let me go, but there was no school at home and Bessie was going and so here we both are rooming together on the third hall at Howland. She has come home just as nice as ever and we both are working like the mischief. My lessons are Latin . . . Greek (Bessie and I are beginning together), Geometry (I don't find that so awful) and literary—that is, we read books and then tell Miss Slocum what we've read. These are all I study and yet Oh journal, would you believe it, I'm so busy that I haven't one moment's time to read and Oh it's such a grind to learn anything and to think that it must last for at least four years more. But then think of the end Oh "Eureka." Sometimes the grindstone stops, though, and we have jolly fun Friday and Saturday and Sunday for we have the gayest set of girls here; Oh, I do love fun so much and I do really like study too and they don't all, I'm afraid.

Spring 1873 [undated]

Howland still—it is just now the spring term. I have been home twice since I last wrote. Frank's namesake[9] has been added to my brother's. Frank's life is out just as

---

9. New brother, Franklin Smith Thomas, born 15 February 1873.

I am beginning to look forward to another summer and to think that last summer we were everything to each other and now—but I am no different only may be able to understand more what sorrow means.

I took up my journal today though with the intention of writing about a friendship of last term in case it should never be renewed that at least I may have *some* remembrance. It was with Libbie Conkey—we got acquainted, how I hardly know. The girls said we "smashed" on each other or "made love" I don't know—I only know it was elegant. She called me "her boy" her "liebe knabe" and she was my "Elsie." We used to see each other oftenest in Professor Satterthaite's room in the gallery of the gymnasium hall and there after supper we would sit and talk in the twilight. Then after all the classes I would wait for her and we would walk over together—we studied Latin—she was reading the Fifth book of Virgil and I read it with her for fun (I think we learnt something else except Latin, at least I learned to care for her more than I knew). Always in fact *every* Sunday evening last term, after tea, we would talk and at last I cared so much about her that my lessons were a secondary matter. Well, the end of the term came—I wrote her a piece of poetry—we said "Goodbye"—she went to Rochester, I home—that is all about the very pleasantest friendship that I have ever had. Of course she may come back next year and we have letters, but her "boy" is very lonely here. There is nobody I care about that *way* now—Oh Journal why is it that when you get to care so much about people life is nothing but Goodbyes, some longer, some shorter—But now my own "sweetheart" goodbye once more on paper, and if we should never meet again this page of my journal will always call up "Memories and Remembrance sweet" of my darling Elsie.

Thanksgiving, 1873
Howland—It is a cold snowy day—the girls are off somewhere and in the quiet of our room I have sat down to write a little for sometimes I think in after life it will be nice to look back and see a peep here and there of my life.

I have entered the senior class and the long long summer has gone and I am here for my last year. Last night Alice Hicks and I sat up until a quarter to three and read Paly. . . .[1]

August 1, 1874

Atlantic City—This quiet Sunday afternoon with the noise of the breakers alone breaking the stillness I have sat down to write a little in my long forgotten journal. On the seventh of July our class graduated. Everything went off well and now that page of my life, the page Bessie and I were so anxious to turn, is closed. On the whole Howland has been an experience I would not have missed for much. It has been a first rate place to study and an elegant place for fun—My two pleasantest friendships almost, have been formed up here, the one with Libbie Conkey—we have written to each other and I visited her in Rochester, she was at school commencement and every time I have seen her our friendship has been nicer. The other with Carrie Ladd. When Libbie went home at the close of the winter term of '73 we began to know each other. We were in Astronomy together and almost every night would trace out the stars. Betelgeuse was my star and Rigel hers—both in Orion. We used to play and romp and discuss and argue and have such good times. In the summer we both got up to look at Orion, and from twelve till six as I sat on the porch and saw constellation after constellation pass by, I wrote her [a poem]. Last year was a busy one at school for us both. Carrie is as practical as a Yankee and has an original way of looking at things and we used to have the nicest talks. For a half an hour a day we used to read Emerson's *Essays* out loud. I hoped our intimacy helped us as I'm sure it gave us a great deal of pleasure. Bessie King from the first never approved of it entirely, I think, but I don't think she understands Carrie. Carrie is a dear darling friend and I love and admire her extremely.

1. Perhaps William Paley, English theologian (1743-1805), author of *A View of the Evidences of Christianity.*

Dr. Test has given us some noble lessons which we will remember forever, I think. He has given me a love for Latin and Greek which I will never lose. He has given us a glimpse of a grand and noble theology which will remain with us. He has my earnest love and gratitude for the many many helps he has given me. But there is one who stands higher than all—Miss Slocum. From the very beginning she seemed to like me and helped me in every way. She is a noble woman and lives an unselfish life. She said to me lately, "Minnie, I wish I had the chance you girls have—it is too late for me to begin to study now—all I can do is to give you what thoughts I have and help you all I can and then send you out to do what I might have done."

Sometimes I have thought she let me come closer to her than the other girls, for when I would go to bid her goodnight she would draw me to her and kiss me and tell me my love helped her more than I knew. It is a noble thing to help girls as she has helped us, to see her day after day talking to us, trying to show us the worth and importance of life. Our class was her favorite and she said to some one we were the smartest class that had ever graduated. While I was writing out my Political Economy examination she watched me in a very peculiar way and as soon as I went out she followed and asked me to come in her parlor as she wanted to speak to me. Then she said as nearly as I can remember these words—I want to put them down so that they may be an inspiration to me—

"I don't want to flatter you but I don't think it ever does harm to tell people the truth. I have watched you carefully ever since you came—I have been pleased with your recitations and with your examination papers. Both have showed that you go to the root of things and understand them. You would be surprised to know how few girls do. You have good habits of study and now I think I have found out what you can do. You are the only girl I have seen who has the power and mind to do this. What we want in the cause of women are not doctors and lawyers (there are plenty of those), we want scholars. You have, I think, as fair a start as any boy of seventeen in the country and now I want you to be a great scholar. I don't think you will be content to merely receive and not originate. You have a great deal of time and none of it is lost if you work steadily for your end. I want great things of you."

What could I say except that I cared more for her opinion than any one else's, that the thing she wanted was the one thing I had dreamed of—that I would try and show her that I was worthy of her confidence and trust. And so I will devote my life to study and try to work some good from it. There is no use of saying any more—this book is filled with enthusiastic rhapsodies but God help me to be true to what is best! When I kissed Miss Slocum goodbye after commencement she put her arms around me and said "Goodbye precious, remember I shan't ever give you up."

Atlantic City
September 8, 1874

My darling Aunt Hannah,

Ever since I went back to Howland I have been intending to write to thee and tell thee how much I love thee and miss thee, but somehow the time has slipped by. It is First Day afternoon. Father has gone with Isaac Sherman to preach to the fishermen on the wharf, Mother is asleep and the children are down at the beach, so in the quiet I have sat down to write to thee. I wanted to write to thee yesterday the anniversary of Frank's death [in 1872] but could not find time. Oh, Aunt Hannah, I miss and appreciate him more every year. We used to have such fun down here as long ago as I can remember.

So at last Howland is over—Father sent thee an account of our commencement I believe. . . . Everything did go off nicely. I did not mind speaking at all. Father's address was really splendid, the end, which was the best, was not reported. Does thee remember how a long while ago thee saw the notice of Howland School in the *Friends Review* and sent for a catalogue? That catalogue first put Bessie and me in the idea of going there. I am very thankful for it, for it has done us both a great deal of good, I think,

Aunt Hannah. Miss Slocum has had such an influence over me from the first. She was so kind and the last term before we graduated she was more with me than ever. Next to thee and Mother she is the noblest woman I know. She was very much pleased with Father's speech and one of the girls heard her say, "I know the reason Dr. Thomas could talk so grandly about women. Look at the women he has known. Look at Mrs. Thomas!" . . .

I look forward to Cornell now, as that is the highest place open to ladies. The more I study the more I care about it. I should love to spend my life in it—that was what Miss Slocum wanted me to do.

Thus far, Aunt Hannah, my letter has been all about myself, but I thought Aunty Hal and Mother would keep thee informed of all things of general interest. Thy letters are so interesting, Aunt Hannah, they used to send them to Bessie and me at Howland and we and Bessie King used to be so interested in reading them, sometimes I would read them to Carrie Ladd.[2] Also, I read thy article about the will in the *Pathway of Power* and was interested in that. Thy Matthew Arnold is a great pleasure. Last week Father took it out on a sail and read it to us.

I have just been reading *Wuthering Heights* by Emily Brontë. Has thee read it? It is a powerful, wild, uncanny story and somehow reminded me of some of those thee used to tell us. What intense pleasure thee used to give us that way.

I expect there is one thing more thee would like to hear, Aunt Hannah—that is that I am consecrated to the Lord. But I can't tell thee that. . . . However I do think I believe in Christ and it is as much as I can do to hold onto that sometimes. Dear, dear Aunt Hannah, I do love and admire thee so. And I thank thee for thy kindness to me more than thee can ever know. From the time thee used to call me the "light of thy eyes" till now I have loved thee next to Father and Mother.

2. Both her cousin Bessie Nicholson and her friend Bessie King attended Howland Institute with Carey Thomas.

[From Miss Slocum]

Union Springs, NY
October 15, 1874

My Precious Minnie,

Your nice long letter came today and delighted my heart
. . . I have so longed to know what you were doing and
planning for the future. . . . I understand how hard it is to
study at home and sympathize with you, while I think it
very important that you should learn to overcome just
such difficulties as you are meeting.

I do not wonder that Cornell seemed rough to your
father after Harvard. One institution embodies the culture
of America from its earliest history—the other is just
struggling to express the future of the nation. One con-
fines itself to literary development, the other recognizes
Mechanical Art and Agriculture as legitimate forces in
the national progress. Doubtless ladies would find the
surroundings of Harvard more to their taste than the
associations of more modern institutions. But unfortunately there is no choice in the matter.

I can appreciate your father's feelings and do not wonder that he hesitates. . . . I have too full a sense of my own
fallibility to venture to give you "the advice" which you
ask. I can only tell you what I know of University life
from observation. . . . I think you will eventually find it
necessary to avail yourself of the help of some University
in order to attain to such scholarship as your aspiration
will lead you. And I believe that you will more and more
see that the work which you are called upon to do for
womankind and for the world is in the direction of sound
scholarship and true culture. But one year, even, will
bring about many changes and you can certainly trust
fully to the wise sympathy of your parents. We will talk
this over from every point of view when we meet, for I
mean to accept your kind invitation and join you next
vacation if I possibly can. . . .

Lovingly, Jennie S.

[Journal]
Thanksgiving 1874

I am sitting in my room which I have fixed up to study in. I am preparing for Cornell and it requires hard study— I have nothing that is a real positive pleasure—not anybody I care to be with particularly—of course I like to talk to Bessie for half an hour or so after our lessons—but "the old order changeth giving place to new." Study indeed is its own exceeding great reward but as yet I know so little and then after it is attained "cui bono?" I have not come back from Howland as happy or as *"faith-ful"* or as confident as I went. How vehement and headlong and positive I was two years ago! I think I am as *vehement* now perhaps more so, only it is a *stiller* kind. As trusting I am not—How well I remember my half distressed delight when I read the first infidel views I ever met with in Shelley. Yet such thoughts are very familiar now. In a sort of dream I go to meeting and hear talking of Christ and his love and nearness. They believe it—and, unlike Bessie, I hesitate to pronounce the belief of those I love dearest and best, "illogical." Yet I know how my imagination and enthusiasm runs away with me and—may not Christianity be a deeper, purer enthusiasm perhaps than any of the rest—yet be an enthusiasm? The infatuation of Christians is no more than that of Hindoos. What have they to oppose to this—their personal delights, their lives, the nobility of the Bible—the gloriousness of His life and creed—Yet His creed teaches that all save a small portion of His creatures shall be damned. His followers carry His love down to such concreteness that all the godlikeness is gone and at best nothing but a narrow human man is left. Many of the hymns are like profanation to me—God is high as heaven and deep as hell. What canst *thou* know? How dare they speak of Him with a familiarity which His own most beloved disciples dared not use—

February 14, 1875

Today, or rather the other day, I found a sentence in Ruskin's *Modern Painters* which explains something I had often thought about—We often hear of the objective writings of the Ancients and the *Modern* subjectivity of the poets especially—their making nature express the feelings of man and describing it in terms of human passion. Of course it was explained by the fact that, e.g., in Homer's time men were as yet observing outward nature and had not introverted their eyes. But Ruskin says this principle was there just as much only they separated the two, the human or the personality of a river from the water itself and never confounded the two, as we do—It is said that Homer has left no imprint of himself on his poems but it seems to me he has left more than appears at first sight—One can tell his favorites throughout. He shows his sympathy with Hector. And every now and then a remark comes in in [undeciphered] persona. I have enjoyed the seven books of the Iliad we have read intensely. Everything in it almost is beautiful. . . .

February 19, 1875

We are drawn by a certain affinity as it were to read books that are just suited to our state—else how can we explain the fact that books reread often seem so different from our first impression? I can hardly bear to try the experiment on those I love best. This subtle law of attraction runs through our friendships and all our pursuits I suppose. The other day I picked up Keats. He was nothing more than a name before to me and I can hardly explain the effect and fascination he had for me—Perhaps it was the utter change from the steady round of study to the world of beauty of which he himself was earnest follower. A great deal of "Endymion" is sensuous—but Keats was so young, only the first and most obvious forms of beauty had he embodied in his verse. Afterwards would have come the grander symphonies. But he first led me to see the meaning of those many stories of mortals falling in love with the immortals.

February 28, 1875

How often will and character are confounded. *Will* is strength, the power of bending circumstances to our desire—*character* is will turned in a certain direction so that beforehand his friends can postulate what he will be likely to do in given conditions. The most unhappy time is when the ego becomes two—the *I* that acts and is carried away by passion and desire and unworthy motive, and the cool unbiased I which judges all the others' actions and hates and despises or approves—always a self within a self, I would like once to escape—

I have had for a long time two "impressions" in spite of its being like Miss Howland I cannot help them. One is that I will die young, of which there seems not the slightest prospect. The other—[the remaining four lines are crossed out, two so thoroughly that the other "impression" can't be deciphered at all. Crossed out, but less thoroughly, is this line: "There, I wonder how much they are worth!"—Ed.]

March 14, 1875

Last night I woke up with an undefinable start and heard a voice repeating "He is dead He is dead." Of course it only seemed and I think I must have been repeating them to myself in my dream, but now I can understand what is meant by those uncanny impressions. If there is one thing that is more glorious than another it is this fact—that though man as an individual may fail of his end and of finding the keynote to the latent harmony of his life, yet the progress of the race is ever onward from age to age, one century finds the solution to the problem the former has been working out, each succeeding one finds the cure of the diseases of the generation before. There *must* be progress. It is the one answer to the ever recurring *cui bono* of life. What a mistake it is for writers to write too soon—if they do they lose all the vantage ground of this nineteenth century and run the risk of solving over again questions of which the solution has already been given to the world. I have had a practical illustration of this in my essay. If ever any one worked out a thought independently I did the moving one of my essay—that in doing evil man was ignorantly choosing what seemed to him a good, etc., but since then that very thought has started up before my sight everywhere. It was the germ of Socrates' philosophy and of countless Socratians. I am not so sure now that it is perfectly true but at any rate I have the consolation of saying—

March 15, 1875
. . . Because a person is stupid debars him not a whit from pronouncing whether another comes up to his idea of smartness. We give our opinions, as a rule, independent of our life. I find myself doing it again and again. This is one reason why I deny Bessie's proposition that a man's thoughts are good for naught unless worked out in his practice. . . .

The one wish and desire of my life is for an education—not such a one as we see all around us but one that will enable me to pierce a little below the surface of things. Nothing but knowledge will help to do that and sometimes I wonder if even that will, but at least knowledge, study, wisdom, is the highest thing I know. I cannot believe that all girls' lives are like mine. I am unhappy, I do not understand things and sometimes I think I have begun upon those problems of "equations and unequalities of life" too soon. I do not think it is the happiest thing for a *girl,* especially, to get interested in study—it is like the [word crossed out]. The sweetness of its voice lures on and on. And then the misery of knowing so little!! I would rather die than anything else I think—for there is so much opposition to the only thing I care for and—it is so impossible to get the highest culture by one's self. And I have to see thousands of boys enjoying and often throwing away the chances I would give *anything* for.

Baltimore
May 10 [probably 1875]
My dear Anna [Shipley],
. . . President Gilman[3] was here to tea the other night and he and Father and Mother and I had the nicest evening. Besides being everything they want as the head of the University, he is a delightful man. His ideas about

3. Daniel C. Gilman, first president of the Johns Hopkins University.

the University are just what I want above all things to be done here. He talked so nicely about Cornell and promised me a letter of introduction to his friend Mrs. White, President White's[4] wife. And said the classical teacher Professor Peck was one of the most learned men we have. There is going to be a grand opening of the Sage building on the 16th of June and so we will probably time our visit for that.

Do tell me about thy arrangement with Bessie Love—I say President Gilman and Father are "smashed" they are devoted to each other. He is a widower of about thirty-five, I should think. I describe him so particularly because I am so perfectly delighted at having such a man here. This is a rather superficial letter is it not, Anna, but 10 o'clock on a warm evening one does not feel like going into the depths. I am struggling to have girls admitted into our new Friends School here—it is the one chance for a sound education for our Baltimore girls. If there is any one thing that heart and soul I am in for, it is for trying to help girls along. There is nothing like a little experience of your own to fall back upon.

[Journal]
July 16, 1875

Well, it is *done:* on the 13, 14, 15 of last June I passed the entrance examinations at Cornell University for the Admission into the Classical Course. This last summer it seemed impossible. But the whole of this year with a steady, unalterable determination that surprised myself even—I have been working for it. Father was terribly opposed and last Christmas when Miss Slocum was at our house, said he never while he lived would give his consent. Many and dreadful are the talks we have had upon this subject, but Mother, my own splendid mother, helped me in this as she always has in everything and sympathized with me. Again and again last winter did the old difficulty of deciding between "duty to ourselves and others" come up—for it was not a religious duty of course

4. Andrew White, first president of Cornell.

to go to Cornell and sometimes it seemed as it ought to be given up. I know all the Grove people thought so—but I *could* not. Then too the difficulty of preparing without knowing how they examined and of getting teachers, but, above all, Father's feeling so about it. For I love him dearly and cannot bear to disappoint him. How it was done I do not know but if it had not been for Mother I am sure he would not have consented. But about three weeks before, he gave up and I began to prepare for the examinations.

I never did such terrible studying every moment for those three weeks. . . . However, it is over with—Professor Peck said I passed a splendid examination in Latin, ditto Professor Oliver in Algebra and Geometry. . . . Almost all the professors complimented Father and Mother upon my passing so well. Mr. Howland when he saw me said he was proud that a *Howland* graduate, etc., etc. The strain was terrible because I could not have endured failure. And it was an inexpressible satisfaction to pass well. Father and Mother were up there and explored the university while I was getting examined. Mother was delighted with it and I think Father was pleased. The last night he said to me, "Well Minnie, I'm proud of thee, but this university is an awful place to swallow thee up."

If I can help it he and Mother shall never regret having yielded to me in this thing.

Cornell
September 14 [1875]

Dear Father and Mother,

I have just come out of Latin examination—from half past two till seven o'clock. I think that any more such examinations will be too much for even my nerves. About fourteen young men came in from other colleges—one from Amherst the freshman year, to be examined for the Sophomore, and *all* of them failed and had to go into the freshman. You can tell from this what an ordeal it was. He examined me on every book I had read except Livy and in Allen's *Prose Composition* because I had studied Arnold, he said. He asked questions about formation of verbals, etc., things I had never had, but at any rate I am not as hopeless as the fourteen boys. My geometry comes Thursday and Greek. Professor Flagg has been sick and says I may enter Junior and be examined afterwards. . . .

There is a *rara avis* staying with Professor Russel[5] till the Sage is open—Miss Ruth Putnam, daughter of the great publisher[6] and sister of Dr. [Mary] Putnam Jacobi. The [sister is the] great New York lady doctor who has just had a baby and it is five weeks old but she receives patients and gives courses of lectures as usual. She and her husband, also a doctor Miss Ruth says, are wild over it and when *she* sees patients, *he* kneels down by its crib and looks at it and vice versa. She—Ruth—is a sophomore and has a room right by me, is short and stout and jolly-looking, short curly red hair, bright brown eyes, worships her sister and came here because she wanted her to. She asked me about my family tree before we had been together two hours, expressed great amazement because I was a Friend on account of my voice which she says sounds like a lady who had been out a great deal in society. She evidently thinks Friends are cooks or something. . . .

Nothing could be pleasanter than everything is made for me by Professor Russel. He took me to the Casquadilla, a local restaurant, for the first time to introduce me to the proprietor and I enjoy staying here very much. . . . The students call President White "Prexy" and one of the young ladies suggested that Vice President Russel should be called "Proxy" so he goes by that. . . .

I am very tired and they are talking in the next room. Every now and then Miss Putnam comes in to address a few words to me. She is really very interesting—is a cousin of Julian Hawthorne's. Thinks him simply horrid . . . she said no distinguished men had distinguished or talented sons—I mentioned Julian H. as an example which she contradicted. . . . This evening a succession of

5. William Channing Russel, vice president of Cornell and associate professor of History.

6. G. P. Putnam.

students have been in.[7] I have been writing here and have not appeared and shall not.

Cornell
[No date 1875]

My dear Father and Mother,

I have been to all my classes today. We go in our hats and gloves, just like a lecture.

I am delighted with my rooms—I consider them the prettiest ones here. By taking the two, I have two bureaus and two tables and two bookshelves, so I have plenty of room for dresses. . . . My articles of vertu are all set around and I wish you could see how cozy we look. Yesterday President White came up and stopped in by the door a little while and asked me there to tea at six. I wore my light silk and nothing could have been kinder and more perfectly lovely than Mrs. White. . . . AFTER TEA we looked over engravings and Mrs. White said she had heard my rooms were such pretty ones and wanted to visit after we got fixed. . . .

This morning we had to report to all our classes. There are three hundred boys in the present Freshman class. I saw President Grant's son sitting on the steps today. There is nothing disagreeable here about the men except that they collect by fifty's on the steps of the different buildings and to pass between them into the lecture rooms is quite an ordeal. They stare so—usually I find myself perfectly crimson by the time I am past them. Besides this, nothing could be more polite than they are, I think. I really do think that this university is going to be what I want. The girls whom we see at the table are mostly as we expected: teachers and poor, struggling girls, but not all by any means, and up on this hall we four girls form a coterie by ourselves. We sit together at table etc. . . .

I think I will have to go down to Howland tomorrow. I want to have somebody call me "Minnie" again. . . . You must not direct [mail] to "Minnie" for I shall not get your

7. She stayed the night with Professor and Mrs. Russel while Sage was made ready to admit students the next day.

letters. . . . Give my love to the children and Nell—tell Frank "My dear Carey" sends her love. . . .

Cornell
First Day 10th [1875]

My dear Father and Mother,

It is half past four this First Day afternoon. . . . I shall have to break a piece of news to you gently—I mean to Father. They allow anyone to take their meals at the Sage and a good many gentlemen have come. Among others the Sioux Society, fifteen men who have turned a large house halfway up the hill into a club and room there and take their meals here. Also they scatter gentlemen among the ladies, without saying by your leave. I have taken a seat at the end of one of the tables and barricaded myself with Miss Putnam on my left and Miss Hicks on my right hand. . . .

Cornell
October 3 [1875]

[To her parents]

I was in the slough of despair last week. I made a bad recitation in Tacitus, and by the way his Annals are the hardest Latin I have ever met with. Then I got so confused reciting before so many men in the German class. [I spent] yesterday morning at Professor Flagg's house and he has admitted me into the Junior Class. He said he had to look over my paper to see if he should have me make up in Greek Composition. But now I am happy for I have entered full junior which seems to be rather an unusual thing for anyone to do. . . . One anecdote to illustrate Professor Oliver's absentmindedness. The other day in Miss Putnam's class he dropped the blackboard rubber on his *own* foot. In great confusion he turned around and said, "Oh I beg pardon, beg pardon". . . .

Cornell
[No date 1875]

My dearest Parents,

The chimes are playing for the close of recitations for the day. There go the students two and two, tramp, tramp, down the hill, with here and there a girl or two scattered in between. Professor Russel has just passed; soon will come "Beauty and the Beast," university parlance for Professor Wilder and his big black dog . . . and then the dinner bell will ring.

I have no recitation this last hour so I always study my Greek at the window and watch the moving panorama. The autumn foliage is glorious. The trees scattered over the hills opposite and along the shores of the lake look like so many little bonfires. So much for the world outside. Within my room is so comfortable and warm and furnished, in contra-distinction to most of the other rooms here, that it is a pleasure to be in it. Withinest of all in my mind, there is a seething mass of thoughts none of which will condense on paper for my composition which is due tomorrow. So in despair I have begun to write a letter to you by way of lighting the "lamp of genius". . . .

Yesterday I forgot about the men and went into the parlor to waltz with Miss Hicks, when in they came, and in a few minutes Professor Boyesen[8]—he takes his meals here now—came up and presented another tall, rather handsome, youth and I was fairly cornered. But there was no help for it and we had a very pleasant talk. Professor Boyesen's poem, illustrated by that wonderful lady engraver—who is it?—the one who illustrated Longfellow's *Hanging of the Crane*—is to appear in January *Scribner's*.[9] Then they all gathered around the piano and began singing college songs and among others a Yale song adapted:

"Here's to Prexy White

8. Hjalmar H. Boyesen, professor of German literature.

9. *Scribner's Monthly,* Vols. IX, X, XI, XIII, include a number of poems and stories by Hjalmar H. Boyesen.

Drink her down, drink her down
He treats us all so right. . . ."

and so on. It is perfectly absurd. Then a favorite one is "Vive la Companie" and each lady and gentleman shouts her or his respective class—"Let every old bachelor fill up his glass, Vive la '76 or '77, '78, '79," and it is perfect discord. I wanted to give you an account of an evening down here as it is probably the only one I shall have a chance to describe and it is such an unexpected phase of life here.

Nothing could be more deferential and polite than the way the gentlemen behave and that funny Mr. Harris, who used to wear a flannel shirt and a grey coat when he first came to our table, now appears resplendent in a white shirt and black coat. "Refining influence of women!" . . .

Cornell
[No date 1875]

My darling parents,

. . . As yet, I expect I have told you before, I feel as if I were at a little disadvantage in my classes except perhaps in Greek where in the highest class in the university Miss Bruce and I are alone. . . . Oh, about the result of my Greek examination! On Second Day I went to Professor Flagg in fear and trembling—but he said in his terse way, "Miss Thomas, your examination was satisfactory, you are admitted without any conditions." Was not that splendid? . . . I am going to write Uncle Allen [Thomas] to thank him, for a great deal of it is due to his kind interest in preparing me. . . .

The atmosphere is a different thing here from Howland and there was Bessie always and the class and Miss Slocum, but here . . . you are absolutely on your own responsibility. I like it and yet it is lonely. Our position here is *perfectly* nice—the faculty one and all, behave to the ladies as if they were out at a party together and think of not the least impoliteness or familiarity. Their wives meet those they know more than halfway in advances. The students who before would not even be introduced to the university girls, are now quite the other way. And as far as I can see it is not considered in the *least* derogatory to ladyhood to attend the university. Even Doctor Wilder, Mrs. Wilder said, encourages his young sister-in-law to come next year and one of the strongest "anti cos" [anti-coeds] as the term is here, sent over an invitation to the young ladies of the Sage to come and take as many pears as they wanted from his orchard. I wanted to make this statement for Father's benefit.

Cornell
November 21 [1875]

My dear Zac [Anna Shipley],

. . . Oh Anna it is worth everything to be here. I must just rave a little because I know thee sympathized so with my wanting to come. The classes I am in come up to all my ideals—it is only I myself that fall below. . . .

The gentlemen students treat the ladies with the greatest deference and respect. They will even wait in the halls to open a door for you. And in Analytical Geometry, I happened to get there the other morning before the recitation and there were about fifteen men talking and laughing rather loudly, and immediately every hat was taken off and their whole manner changed. This is a sample. I am a complete convert to "Coed," as the term is here. And even when last week I stood up on the platform, gazed at by eighty masculine junior eyes, and read my essay, (though it was a severe proof) my belief did not waver.

How do I occupy my leisure time when I have any? Take a look at my center table! Two volumes of Roman History I am reading in connection with Tacitus, English Literature and *Canterbury Tales*, for Corson's[1] lectures on literature which are grand, Sainte-Beuve's "Causeries du Lundi" Professor Russel lent me, and on top of all *Music and Morals*, which Mr. Gardiner, the champion skater of Cornell, brought me the other day. . . .

1. Hiram Corson, professor of literature.

Well I have been and gone and done it—I may as well confess. Ever since the first I have struggled against it. I made up my mind that up here, at least, I would not have a friendship that was in the least absorbing. It takes time and I don't approve of them. . . .

I knew from the first that I should like Miss Hicks very much but not one advance did I make. Indeed the first week we were here, it came up in the course of conversation and I said that I had made up my mind not to have any more intimate friendships and she took that as a hint and carefully avoided showing that she liked me. So matters remained in this interesting state and if the fates had not made her fall in love with me, I should have kept my resolution. It was dancing and Swinburne that did it. . . .

Cornell
[No date 1875]

My own Mother,

. . . Oh it is such a perfect day, and everything is fun and more fun than all is the thought of getting home to you. Perhaps what made me like Beecher's sermon today so much was what he said about the nobleness of Fatherhood and Motherhood and the way the parents sacrificed themselves in order that the children might have education and everything. I often think of how many pleasures you don't have because you give us everything and I do hope we will be worth it. . . .

Cornell
January 23, 1876

My dear Father and Mother,

. . . My lessons are really such a pleasure that the time goes faster when I study them. . . . Romney's and Aurora's characters in Professor Corson's readings afford a grand field for discussion. Miss Putnam, Miss Hicks and I had a fierce discussion on that point. I held that Aurora's mission, that of a poet to raise the few and inspire them with heaven-sent visions, was higher than Romney's to be a raging philanthropist and give soup to the masses. For the few of course in turn can go and work out the thought inspired by the poets. . . .

Yesterday I wasted. I went skating with Mr. Gardiner all the morning and in the afternoon was tired and went to sleep on my lounge. . . .

Cornell
February 20 [probably 1876]

My dear Parents,

It is another glorious day—it snowed last week so the hills are covered. It seems impossible to get a sleigh ride as we six girls all went downtown last Sixth Day to get one and the livery men just laughed at us—then six gentlemen—Mr. Gardiner, Tolkman, Randolph, etc., invited us to go sleighing yesterday afternoon, but the livery men were unmoved by masculine as well as by feminine entreaties. The trouble is that it drifts so that there is hardly any continuous sleighing.

Also did I tell you that the [Greek Fraternity] had invited us six girls to visit their chapter house which was quite an honor as nobody but the faculty ladies have been inside it. But in talking it over—and I very strongly argued this—we thought it would be just six gentlemen to receive us and the rest would be hiding in the closets—no depth is too low for their curiosity to stoop to. Then without any older lady to be entertained there, for they do things in style, and be presented with bouquets and discussed over their ale and cigars after we left, it would be better to refuse. So we did. The gentlemen seem to draw a distinction between us and the rest of the girls and several remarks have been repeated to us, as "Oh, their table is the aristocratic table," "The Third Hall clique would not think that proper." Do all rank distinctions come as unsought?

The grand affair in everyone's mouth is the Navy Ball which took place last Friday. Miss Tilden went with Professor Boyesen and wore a shimmering green satin dress which Professor Boyesen said looked like the "sea foam of the Mediterranean now milling into blue, now shimmering green," and one looked all the time to see handfuls of seaweed starting up under his hand. As Mr. Gardiner sagely remarked, the waist was "terraced in puffs of lace," and when we reviled him for not giving a more exact description, he said he had done all a man could, he had even stepped on her dress in attempting to examine it. Poor Professor Byerly had to take Miss Latimer, Miss Tilden's lame friend who doesn't dance. Such are the penalties of love. Miss Hicks wanted to go very much to the Ball but Miss Kimball refused on the score of propriety, being in a public hotel and without any matron, and so greatly to Miss Hicks' grief she had to refuse too. I was delighted. . . .

I am delighted the boys are taking boxing lessons. Of course you have heard of the engagement of Sam Hillis and Amy Tatum. "So much of *her* and so little of *him*" as Anna remarks. . . . The latest joke on Sage is that a letter came in the post directed by some simple-minded papa whose daughter sought women's higher education: "Mrs. Sage, Principal of Cornell Seminary, Ithaca, New York." Now goodbye. I must meditate upon my essay, "The Respects in which Men are Born and Unequal," and try to upset the equality basis of our glorious American Government. Oh the crime of forcing mere tyros in literature and thinking to grind out their premature thoughts in essays. I love you dearly and am your loving daughter
Carey

Cornell
[Winter 1876]

My darling Mother,

. . . I must tell you of something so dreadful that it seems as if I never could forget it and as if Latin and Greek could never be the same again.

Right over the way next to that little brick house of Professor Shackford's thee remembers is Professor Morris's and Emil S——has boarded there. He is that wonderful genius and I was in classes with him ever since I have been here and many and many a time thought that there was nothing like being able to study as he did. Last First Day night at ten o'clock he shot himself with a little pistol

110

that he had bought at the Centennial and left an explanation saying that he had lost his health and life was worth nothing. . . . I don't know when anything had such an effect on me and on Third Day of our special Latin class went to Professor Peck's and by accident it happened he had given us Hamlet's soliloquy to put into Latin and it seemed so terribly appropriate and Professor Peck was utterly overcome. . . . Every time I wake up in the night I see Mr. S——sitting there in his little armchair and filling the pistol. . . . Is it not terrible with all he knew and could have done?

Yesterday I spent most of the morning over my Latin verses and in the afternoon Professor White asked me to go skating and so I went. . . . We had a glorious skate from half past two until half past six and got home late to supper and just filled a table and had a very funny time. We eat up six dishes of hash and seven or eight plates of rolls and I don't know how much else.

Professor White has the reputation of being very smart. He has been abroad and is going again in '78 and knows [James Russell] Lowell and [John] Fiske and all those Harvard Literati and what is still more important he skates better than anyone else here now Mr. Gardiner has gone. . . .

Cornell
February 26 [probably 1876]

My own darling Mother,

. . . There is to be a dance and sociable of the Curtis Literary Society and I have had quite a time getting out of going. Miss Bruce said that as a personal favor she had something to ask me. She said a gentleman had asked her to ask me to go to it and that he thought that I would be more likely to go if she asked me and as a personal favor to her. Miss Bruce said she knew I would not go alone, but she thought maybe I would go with him and her. Of course he was Mr. Lucas, a senior and very nice smart fellow and I would like him even better if he would not profess to "admire Miss Thomas" so much when he never

111

has the *least* ground, for I never see him. But I refused because if one once begins to go out here, it seems to be impossible to stop, though I must confess I would have liked to have gone better that way than any other. As I have told you once before—I think it is considerable of a sacrifice to cut myself off from all of these things and I stand *absolutely* alone. There is not another girl in the university who refuses to go and especially it is hard when the girls on this hall all go and beg me to. Not that I care about the gentlemen, though they are all as polite as can be and more interesting perhaps because we have very much the same work in the university, but it is having the girls go and being left behind. But of course your wishes and especially what Father said when I came, are enough to make it rather a pleasure than otherwise to do what you want, and then I think it is best anyhow. My only fear about education is the social parts engrossing too much time, but the intercourse between the ladies and gentlemen is so perfectly frank and natural. . . .

Oh our Bible class[2]. . . the girls attack me and ask me point blank about Christ. They are serious but without a bit of reverence. However we have interesting talks and I hope they will lead to some good. Now for instance I hardly like to tell this but I want to give you some idea of how different they are. Something was said about Christ's brethren and the girls expressed the greatest surprise and I said, "I suppose they were the children of Mary and Joseph," and Miss Mills with the most contemptuous tone asked whether I did not consider Christ the son of Joseph. There was a dead silence and I suppose she saw from my face how irreverent I thought the question and begged my pardon, but she really wanted to know. I said "no" and we passed on.

I could wish that my faith were a little stronger and my knowledge a little more definite before being passed through such a mill as this. . . .

2. An earlier letter explains that in deference to her parents' wishes, although with little enthusiasm ("I don't think it will do much good"), she initiated an informal Bible class among her friends.

Cornell
[No date, probably 1876]

My darling Mother,

It is a most glorious spring day. . . . There is a *rara avis* here, she came this last week—a tall, sad, poetical-looking woman who droops her head and looks up at you with her dark languishing eyes. She came here to take the course in Journalism and we knew there was some mystery. On the fly leaf of her notebook was Sarah S and the last name scratched out and Sternes written over it. We knew her as "Miss Sternes," but finally she told Miss Johnston and she told me, as she tells me everything, that she was a divorced woman, though her husband adores her and is "physically and intellectually her ideal man." She has come here because [she is] not strong enough to practice medicine, though she graduated from Edinburgh Medical College. She writes really very pretty poetry and is a sort of wonder to me. Miss Johnston persuaded her to correct the mistake about *Miss* as I believe it is against the law for a divorced woman not to keep the Mrs. She came to my room by mistake last night and talked about everything. She is an "adorer of Tilton," the gentleman she was engaged to "at that time" was his groomsman. She likes Friends "because they believe in the spirit, in fact they are spiritualists, you know" and so on. I shall be very careful about not getting intimate with her but she is a study. I'm afraid she may be a believer in free love but at any rate her views are decidedly revolutionary. . . .

Cornell
[No date, probably 1876]

My dear Father and Mother,

It is a lovely spring day. . . . Well, the whole university was in a laugh of amusement over Professor Boyesen's and my contretemps. The way it got out was this: Mr. Noble, a Kappa Alpha, went down in vacation to visit a friend of his at Williamsburg and saw on the books of the hotel, "Professor B——and Miss Thomas." He returned in a state of delight and announced the fact to his secret society while they were all at dinner and of course every-

113

body thought it too good a joke on Professor Boyesen to keep quiet a moment. He tells everyone that he is very much mortified, that it was too bad for me, but that he himself had an elegant time, which I suppose is the only thing he can say under the circumstances. . . .

Cornell
[No date, but probably 15 October, 1876]
My dear Mother,
    . . . Last evening President White gave a Senior Reception. No one else at all was invited except the professors who had senior classes. There are senior ladies. . . .
    Mr. Milford, the class president, waited on me to supper and is I believe the best talker and most agreeable man I have met here. We talked for an hour. Then there was a rumor that President White was going to address us in the library and we went in and stood while he gave us the nicest farewell talk for about three quarters of an hour. He was so sorry to have to miss knowing the Class of '77, he said, then went on to talk over the university and its success and its troubles. Said that on the seniors depended the success of this next year and wanted us to stand by the faculty and when we graduated and went away to stand up for Cornell first and last. He then bade us Godspeed and goodbye.
    In the first part of the evening he talked to me very nicely. I told him of the adverse criticism of Huxley's speech and he was very much amused at Gilman's catching it when he himself had been stormed at for so many years. Professor Shackford walked home with me and there were four of us each with a gentleman. . . .

Cornell
October 15 [probably 1876]
My dear Anna [Shipley],
    I have tried to answer thy letter sooner but could not. A little while before thy letter came, I received one from Mother telling me of Sarah Cadbury's death. I was so shocked to hear of it. I do sympathize with thee—a sudden death is so terrible. I hope I may not die in that way. But

except when it is sudden I think death is a splendid thing, though Anna, I wonder if it always is so when one grows older. I am getting to care to live so much more than I used to; especially in this fall weather when the air is like wine and the trees and haze like fairyland. As I wrote home today, I am just enamored of my life here. After the do-nothing summer, it is glorious to be at work again. Latin and Greek, Sanscrit, Philosophy and Literature and Essays are my studies and they are all congenial. Then thee knows what fun it was to be a senior at Howland and it is great fun here. I went to a senior reception given at President White's last night and it was quite agreeable. The class president waited on me in to supper and was devoted, even though violently opposed to coeducation. It was a curious feeling—six ladies besides Mrs. White and her daughter and eighty gentlemen. . . .

Miss Hicks is of a most practical turn of mind. I tell her the one unreasonable romantic thing she has done in her life has been to fall in love with me. . . .

Has thee read Mr. Boyesen's story in the last *Scribners*—it is the most powerful short story he has written I think. I had a long talk with him the other night. He does talk so nobly and truly about genius and his aims and longing to do some good in his works that I am always carried away, while I talk to him in perfect sympathy with him. We fairly raved together over *Daniel Deronda* and George Eliot, but when I go upstairs and think over him I do not trust what he says, somehow. I should like so much to believe in him and in his genius but there is something so—I can't tell what—about him. . . .

Cornell
[No date, probably 1877]

My darling Mother,

. . . This is the programme for commencement week. On First Day the seventeenth of June, James F. Clark delivers the sermon to the graduating class. On the Second and Third Day evenings there is speaking, Thomas W. Higginson being the principal speaker. On Fourth morning, the twentieth, is class day and on that evening a grand concert provided by the senior class, and on Fifth Day commencement. . . .

Yesterday Miss Hicks and I studied in the woods and it appeared to be an ant holiday for wherever we sat they swarmed but except that it was lovely.

Today I went down and spent an hour with Miss Bruce. She is very nice and says she has no idea what will become of her now. She must look for a situation. And I want Father—I am afraid it will be a trouble—but I want him to do this much for my friend—to ask Mr. Newman, principal of the Normal School if there is any opening for Miss Bruce. She taught in the Normal College in New York and got $1800. a year before she came to Cornell. She wants to teach Latin or Greek, History or Mathematics. I think she would take $800. and she is an experienced teacher and could get the highest references. She wants to come to Baltimore where she could attend the university afternoon lectures and be south. Miss Bruce has been extremely kind to me and such a slight thing as this I would like to do for her. I suppose there is no chance in our school of course. . . .

I love you very dearly and in spite of my desires after independence I am rather glad I have such a home to go to instead of having to make my own way as Miss Bruce has to. I am going to try to be very satisfactory next year, to try and make up.

P.S. Do if it is possible let the boys come. I have set my heart on it and it would be such fun for them. I must have some money. . . .

[Journal]
June 12, 1877

Sage College, Cornell University. It is almost two years since I have made an entry. I have now finished all my senior examinations and have nothing to do for the next nine days except wait for my degree. . . .

At last the object of my ambition—the one purpose that runs through my journals has been attained. I have graduated at a university. I have a degree that represents more than a Vassar one.

I wish I had kept a slight, at least, record of my experience here and now it is too late to recall it. The first two years I had a difficult time to get into the new methods of study and especially in Latin I entered behind.

Altogether I have learned a great deal and it has been thoroughly profitable to be here—it has given me a new outlook. Though I feel very far from a good Latin and Greek scholar, yet I do see light somewhat. My life here has been very hermit like, except seven girls. I have seen very few people, half the men here are uncultivated and Cornell misses all that glorious culture that one reads of in college books. The girls are for the most part of a different social station and I have seen very little of them as they have nothing to counterbalance that fact.

I want to write about my fifth friendship, for in spite of myself I have one. When I came here I made up my mind that at Howland I had wasted a great deal of time with friends and that it amounted to very little except pleasure and that especially away from home the pain of being separated more than overbalanced the other.

The first girl I saw was a young lady in Algebra examination—lace-dressed, in gray with a brown hat with a wing in it. She was up at Pres. White's to tea and we had a little talk. I thought she was smart and well prepared in the examinations next day. I "rather hoped" I should see her again next fall. Next fall came—she was the first person I saw as I drove up to the Sage College. Her mother was with her and together we chose our rooms on the same corridor third hall. Miss Mills was to room with Miss Hicks and would not unpack until she had heard from her examinations. Miss Putnam whom I had met at Prof. Russel's chose a room on the same floor. It was lonely at first—my only consolation was going down to Howland every other Friday and seeing Carrie [Ladd]. At first I rather looked down on the girls in our hall. Miss Hicks, Miss Putnam, Miss Mills, Miss Head and Miss Mitchell—they seemed more interested in fun than anything else. And not one of them was smart except Miss Hicks; the other girls in the Sage were good enough students but not ladies, and the gentlemen, except Prof.

117

Boyesen, were second rate, "half cut" Bessie would say.

Well, I began to see more and more of Miss Hicks. She got in the habit of coming and reading me her mother's letters and of bidding me good night. We used to go and study some time in Casquadilla woods and when it would get dark we would sit under her blue shawl and talk. Then we came across Swinburne's "Atalanta in Calydon" and Miss Hicks would come in her wrapper after I was in bed and we would read it out loud and we learned several of the choruses. One night we had stopped reading later than usual and obeying a sudden impulse I turned to her and asked, "Do you love me?" She threw her arms around me and whispered, "I love you passionately." She did not go home that night and we talked and talked. She told me she had been praying that I might care for her.

That was the beginning and from that time, it was the fall of '75, till June '77 we have been inseparable. I put this all down because I cannot understand it. I am sure it is not best for people to care about each other so much. In the first place it wasted my time—it was a pleasure to be with Miss Hicks and as I cared to be with no one else, I would have spent all that time in reading. It was different with her—as she likes a great many people and liked the other girls and would have wasted her time anyway. In the second place it was almost more pain than pleasure because we quarreled so. All our ideas were opposite. Miss Hicks' mother I think is rising in society and there is not the least bit of fastidiousness in Miss Hicks' nature. She likes everyone. She cares for everyone's opinion. She would do a great many things I did not think suitable. I would object and say more than I ought to and Miss Hicks would fling herself on the lounge in a passion of tears and sometimes we would both cry—altogether it was dreadful—yet all the time we cared about each other so much that we could not give up our friendship. Again and again we gave up in despair and then we would care and have such lovely times that we began again and the whole thing was over again. Often I prayed that I might stop loving her.

This high tragedy seems ridiculous written but I know I shall forget the possibility of such things unless I do. It seems rather too bad when one goes to college to study to be distracted by such things. It was not Miss Hicks' fault but I know I did not study as well because of her, but I could not help it. I was mastered by it—one thing that made our friendship as unpleasant as it sometimes was was my feeling that I ought not to give way to it. Miss Hicks has no generous abandon in study—her companionship did not help me, I think, in an intellectual way. I tell her she ought to be obliged to me. I taught her to love passionately and to be passionately angry. Neither of which she had experienced before.

She is lovely in many ways. She has a sweet simplicity and straightforwardness about her, an utter faithfulness—I would trust her absolutely with any secret—she is naturally very smart but I think, at least until she came to Cornell, she studies because she had nothing else to do and because of her love of approbation. She wants to be an architect and seems very fond of it but I do not feel as if she would make a success. She seems to me to be easily turned aside by people. It is hard to talk to her—I never feel except when she is angry as if she were really saying what she feels with all her heart. In her manners she wants a certain quiet self assurance. I think she will probably get married. These are almost all unfavorable things but I leave out all her prettiness and her traits of character that attract me—in fact I just fell in love with her and I did it gradually too (not that adoring worship I had for Libbie [Conkey], nor the equal fun and earnest loving devoted friendship Carrie and I have) but, that Atalanta night I knew I did not care as much as she did and so it went on, I getting fonder and fonder of her until it was as I say—all the time against my better judgment and yet I cannot tell why it was. She is lovely, in many many ways much better than I am.

September 2, 1877

The day after my last entry I was telegraphed for, to Philadelphia. Grandpa [Whitall] had died at Atlantic City on the 12th and was buried on the 15th. All the older grandchildren were there and it was sad and yet glorious— to have him die at the end of a completed life. I graduated on the 21st, went with Harry and Tom to Niagara and the summer has been between Anna Shipley's, home, the Cedars, and Atlantic. The Cedars seemed doubly dreadful now without Grandpa and Frank. Today little Dora[3] is to be buried. She died very suddenly on the 31st [August].

She had had quite a cold for two days before but we were not anxious. At one o'clock on Sixth Day Father came in and from that time she grew worse, but at dinner we all went up in the front room and she lay on a pillow on mother's lap breathing shorter and shorter and afterwards with a little moan at each breath, and then stopped very quietly, her eyes were half shut and just as she stopped breathing she opened them wide with the most beautiful fixed expression—her beautiful dark eyes—and they remained that way till Mother closed them. Poor little Nellie and Frank, they just leant on mother's shoulders and sobbed. Death is perfectly dreadful. It completely fills my imagination. I do not think I can stand another death without dying myself—if only one don't see them die, but I never can forget Frank and now to have the breath just stop while Dora's sweet little lips were red, it can't be borne! We know so little about the other world— there must be one—it seems to me or all our struggles here and our real intellectual life go for worse than nothing— but I do not believe separate individualities are known.

September 23, 1877

Yesterday I made application to the Johns Hopkins University to study for a second degree. Mr. Gilman was very polite and it will come before the Trustees in a month and I (oh I hope there is some chance for ladies!) am in great anxiety. . . .

I am glad I went [to Cornell], I learned far more than was possible at home. I broke away from old rules and mingled with different classes of people; but there was no real earnest intellectual companionship, not much earnest heartfelt study. When so much could be offered so little

3. Her mother's last child, who had been born on 12 June of the same year.

was given. I suppose I expected too much; the other girls seemed satisfied. . . .

There is much that is very hard for a *lady* in a mixed university and I should not subject any girl to it unless she were determined to have it. The educational problem is a terrible one—girls' colleges are inferior and it seems impossible to get the most illustrious men to fill their chairs, and on the other hand it is a fiery ordeal to educate a lady by coeducation—it is impossible to make one, who has not felt it, understand the living on a volcano or on a house top—Frank Heath's story and that horrible cartoon were samples—yet it is the only way and learning *is worth it*. This summer at Anna's when I heard Mr. Cadbury and Mr. Gummere talk of Harvard it filled me with envy and yet Mr. Gummere himself told me that he found no earnest companionship there. I do wonder if Mr. Gummere will accomplish anything—the majority of people I feel sure will not but I do think that there is a chance for him. We had one very nice talk this summer—a continuation of one two years ago and he is full of enthusiasm for all my favorite things—poetry, literature, my literature books are his favorites and altogether we are very congenial on literary and other logical subjects. I hope he will persevere and go to Germany and I wish I were a man for that; because *Germany* is shut to ladies along with the J.H.U. and a few other of the very most glorious things in the world; yet I would not be a man.

October 4, 1877

Have been reading *Pendennis* and I do like it so much . . . . In this book I think I found Thackeray's idea of women—Pen says to Laura—You women are beautiful, etc. and pure, we shudder before you, etc., the highest eulogy but—if you had reason you would not love us men—You do not eat of the fruit of the tree of good and evil. There it is, that is the keynote of his treatment of the sex. Oh, this year does look very pleasant ahead and life seems a very delightful thing. . . .

Baltimore
October 31, 1877

To "Zac" [Anna Shipley]
[No salutation]

. . . In reading over thy letter I am utterly disgusted that I have left it so long. . . . The Executive Committee of the J.H.U. passed a vote last week—the motion proposed by the very gentleman who opposes women most fiercely, "to admit Miss Thomas to study for a second degree." The Board [will] act upon it next week but of course it is virtually decided. Oh, Anna, I am so delighted and yet it makes me a little sober too when I think what it means. I had a long talk with Gildersleeve, the Greek Professor in his *sanctum sanctorum* and he said that they meant that a degree of the Johns Hopkins University should count with the German ones, that he had two students who had graduated at college, studied three years, one of them in Germany, and who will have been two years under him when they try to take their second degree next summer; so, he said, from that I might see the amount of work he expected; he said I *might* be able to take it in three years . . . . Well, thee sees a little what a terrible undertaking it is; especially the German. I feel a mild curiosity as to how I shall succeed in *mastering* the German language by Christmas. So the die is cast; if I enter upon this I give up medicine forever and become a scholar. . . .

[Journal]
November [?], *1877*

They admitted me to the J.H.U. and I am now studying three mornings in the week from 9 to 3 with Bessie. . . . I am very much discouraged now that I have entered upon a three years' course of work, I feel the recoil and I feel how absolutely impossible is my knowledge of Greek and it does seem hopeless and then after all—there seems to be something degrading in the minute study classical notes require. What difference can it make if a second *a* is used once or twice in a certain writer? I cannot bend my mind to it and yet I *must*. I must now be a good scholar or nothing. . . .

November 25, 1877

Today I found a *new* poet, Wordsworth. He spoke right to me especially through his *Preludes*. I was almost frightened as I found thought after thought there that had come to me so often. He gives real spiritual help which I do need so much and I am so glad to have him to turn to now.

December 2, 1877

Today during Esther Tuttle's sermon I gave myself utterly up to believe God's promises and I am going to live a life of faith—a thing which I have not done for four years. . . . I am sure in a true Christianity there can be nothing *opposed* to reason though on the other hand it cannot be proved by reason. . . .

December 16, 1877

I am writing in my wrapper lounging back in my easy chair, with my feet to the flue. Things don't seem to go very right. Bessie's "each one must fight his own battles" is true. Our household is not constructed right. I do not think there is ceremony enough observed. Everything goes at loose ends, of course I cannot help it and I am going to make up my mind to stand it. Things are continually neglected—little things—that to me are more important than great things. I am determined if possible to be more careful than ever about personal habits because there is nothing that drives away love sooner. I am *sure* that there is a possibility of everything about a house being managed; things cooked properly and dusted and proper behavior at the table, without precluding all outside interest. If people realized that to have more children than they can afford to train and support properly was a greater crime than anything else I am sure it would be better. Nobody can tell—people are more magnificent frauds than anything else. How little sympathy can be hidden by apparently pleasant family relations.

January 20, 1878[4]

As this is rather a melancholy manner to close the old year I must add a few lines—though of course there is mirth in the above, yet after all I suppose there is always some skeleton somewhere in each household.

Miss Hicks paid me a lovely visit Dec. 21-31. I was as fond of her as ever and we had some lovely times. She is more of a friend to me than ever.

I spent a little time in Philadelphia and Anna did not seem as nice . . . it is so hard to do anything but talk about commonplace matters when we are alone. After all people are of less and less account to me, I suppose it oughtn't to be so but books are so satisfactory. . . . I must now close this journal of five years. It opens with *Frank* and an account of our pranks—what fun they were! It embraces Howland and Cornell and a year of study in between. It covers my friendships with Anna and Libbie and Carrie and Miss Hicks—I do not believe I shall make any, or even keep all of these during the next five years—what an amount of tragedy I have wasted over them. Five years from this time I shall be twenty-six, I shall know then if I can do anything of what I long for. I do feel very humble and *utterly* dissatisfied with myself and my past and do trust with the little faith I have, that I can begin a *new* life and it will be *all* right! "Wait, I have large faith in time and that which brings it to some perfect end."

4. She appears to have closed her journal for 1877 on 20 January 1878, the same day she began her first entry of the new year.

"MR. GUMMERE"

After her graduation from Cornell, Carey Thomas returned home—estranged from her religion, uncertain of her direction, and confirmed only in her resolve to obtain a higher degree, to what purpose she did not know. Miss Slocum's influence, however, is once again felt in a letter from her dated 23 February 1877, a few months before Carey's graduation from Cornell, in which she writes: "I have been thinking lately that you are the woman who must fit herself for a Chair in some university. That is the next thing to be done."

In the fall of 1877 Carey enrolled at Johns Hopkins University, an enrollment that was to an extent in name only, although she aspired toward a higher degree. She was offered a syllabus and attendance at certain lectures, and such assistance as she could obtain from an individual professor, but was not permitted to attend classes. (The legend of her having been permitted to attend classes but behind a curtain so as not to distract the male students is not corroborated in her papers.) She soon found the arrangement unsatisfactory. As Edith Finch has accurately described in her biography, Carey was dissatisfied both with herself and her studies. For her, scholarship was a means to an end—an end that was not just then in sight. She was not, at heart, a scholar and solitary scholarship was therefore all the more ungratifying. She was frustrated at being once again in the restricted Quaker environment and annoyed by her parents' large brood and her lack of relative privacy.

The years 1877-79 were nonetheless crucial in determining her direction. In the fall of 1877 Carey met Mamie Gwinn and Mary Garrett, each of whom was to have a lasting influence on her life. Carey joined a group consisting of those two, Betsy King and Julia Rogers. ("Carrie" — probably Ladd but possibly Cadbury—mentioned earlier in the following journals was simply passing through.) The five regulars met each week at one or another's home, discussed life and letters, men, women, education, marriage, and books. They wrote poetry and stories for practice and for each other's enjoyment.

They were an unusual group for those times or for that matter for any time. All were dedicated feminists and three of the five were to make substantial contributions to women's education. (Mamie's feminism was of a more philosophical than practical bent.) All five were to be instrumental in founding the Bryn Mawr School and all stayed on its Board for several decades, transcending the rifts in their various friendships. Julia Rogers would become a benefactor of Goucher College (its new library, built in 1953, is named for her). Mary Garrett would in time inherit one-third of her father's Baltimore and Ohio Railroad fortune (her brothers were by then invalided or dead and the widow of her brother Robert inherited the other two-thirds), and become estranged from her surviving family—chiefly sisters-in-law and nephews. They evidently resented her attachment to Carey Thomas and the fact that she gave the bulk of her estate to Bryn Mawr and other institutions, as for example the Bryn Mawr School and The Johns Hopkins Medical School, and went to live with Carey Thomas at the Deanery in 1904, on Mamie Gwinn's departure. Their resentment increased when, at her death in 1915, she left Carey what remained of her estate, which by then was far less than had been rumored.

The accusation that she was under Carey Thomas's influence is not only inaccurate but does Mary considerable injustice. She had a will of her own and freely exercised it, and her feminist inclinations had been formed before she came to know Carey. Some time around the year 1872 (the exact year is not clear) Mary noted in her diary: "Ruskin says that a woman's knowledge on higher subjects should merely be elementary (not superficial) just so that she may be able to help her husband; but to leave *him* to climb the scaly hill of knowledge. No! Knowledge is power and I, for one, am going to do my best to gain it. . . . " Carey Thomas mentions in her autobiographical notes how much she admired Mary for disobeying her father when he refused to let her study Greek. She took lessons in spite of him, "and when he received the bills he had to pay. This seemed to me splendid bravery, this act of defiance."

Mary was compulsively organized (most of her letters bear the notation "Received" with the date and time, and "Answered" with the date, a habit that makes her a delight to archivists), and she was thoroughly capable of managing her own affairs and philanthropies as well as selecting the latter. She had been brought up in the stratum of society Carey aspired to join. As a child during the Civil War Mary had witnessed the comings and goings in her father's house of important men of state (control of the B & O was crucial to Union victory) and she has recorded, "I was my father's confidante." Her few pages of autobiographical notes are scant, and they are typed; I suspect they were dictated during her last illness at Carey's urging. At any rate Carey had found much to admire in Mary's background and person, and her early letters to Mary have a self-conscious edge and a note of uncharacteristic deference otherwise found only in her letters to her Aunt Hannah.

Of the members of "The Group," Mamie Gwinn appears to have been the most genuinely poetic and creative, and Julia Rogers the most genuinely intellectual, the steadiest in temperament, and the most free from flights of sentimental excess. According to her friends of later years, Julia Rogers was a woman of gentle wit and quiet charm; intelligent, well read, accomplished in languages, art, and literature. In 1879 Mary and Julia passed the entrance examinations to Harvard presumably to prove that they could. Julia subsequently studied at Newnham College, Cambridge (1881-82), and went on to publish articles in *The Atlantic* and *The Nation*.

There is no question that Carey was the most aggressive of the lot, driven to prove herself, manipulative and determined. There is evidence that even while abroad with Mary Garrett during the years of study in Leipzig she set out to break up Mary's friendship with Julia Rogers, and, though it took many long years, eventually succeeded.

Julia and Mary were almost identical in age (born in 1854, they were three years older than Carey and six years older than Mamie) and had been friends from childhood. Julia's mother had died when she was three years old, and her friendship with Mary Garrett had evidently meant a great deal to her; judging by the few letters from her to Mary which remain, she was perplexed and hurt when it was terminated.[1]

For Carey, perhaps the most fateful aspect of these years was her encounters (there seems to be no other word to describe the tragicomedy) with Francis Gummere.[2] Had he offered his hand the history of Bryn Mawr might have taken a different turn, for there is Carey's significant notation that his prospects at the impending college would be enhanced were he to propose, and there is evidence, too, that for a time he was a candidate for the presidency. Put off by Carey's coldness toward him—which she attributes to her nervousness in his presence—he went off and became engaged to Amelia Mott, "the little Providence girl" as Carey somewhat patronizingly refers to her rival. Carey followed Gummere to Leipzig and seems to have made some effort to break up the match. While this is not to suggest him as a motive for her going abroad to study, her desire to compete with him if she could not marry him undoubtedly made the prospect of going to Leipzig all the sweeter. In 1879 (undated) Bessie King was warning Carey to be careful: "Thee may say thee doesn't care for Mr. G. and I believe it, but how long will it be so if thee carries out thy philanthropic design of disillusioning him? Don't do it. Thee will burn thy fingers and besides, is it fair to Amelia? Thee knows he cares more for thee than

1. In 1889 Julia and Mary signed an agreement allowing review and destruction of any letters by either party. A few bewildered and wounded letters from Julia to Mary remain. All subsequent correspondence from Julia is restricted to business matters such as Julia's medical dispensary and the Bryn Mawr School. They are signed "Yours truly."

2. She herself has acknowledged as much in adding the title "Mr. Gummere" (in her adult handwriting, undoubtedly after her retirement) to the segment of her journals covering the years 1878-79.

her, and she probably is much in love with him, and her whole unhappiness may result from thy influence unconsciously. I must say I did not see this so strongly till Mary talked to me, and she says she has written thee on the subject, so I will say no more, only it seems such a risk for thee. . . ." (Much of this passage is heavily crossed out and had to be deciphered; probably it was Carey Thomas who attempted to make it illegible when she was re-reading her letters before writing her autobiography.) There are milder warnings from Carey's mother in response to passing references in Carey's letters to skating with Mr. Gummere.

Francis Gummere spent the better part of his life as professor of English (specialist in Anglo-Saxon), most of it contentedly at Haverford. He was offered the chairmanship of the Department of English at Harvard and declined. In his field he is among the most eminent scholars, and was devoted, above all, to teaching.[3]

His grandson, Mr. Richard Gummere of Columbia University, gave me the other side of the picture which he had stumbled on while staying with his grandmother, at Haverford, after his grandfather's death. She seemed visibly upset whenever he frequented a concert at Bryn Mawr, and it occurred to him one evening to ask her to accompany him. She declined, firmly. He was curious why she did not, like the other widows of Haverford professors, receive notices of concerts and other functions on the Bryn Mawr campus. "*She* had me taken off the mailing list when your grandfather died," was her reply. Then she added: "She followed your grandfather to Germany, and she set her cap for him. But she *did not get him!*" Amelia Mott Gummere was herself a writer of some consequence, especially of books on Quaker history. According to her grandson she was a strong-willed woman; in her own way every bit a match for Carey Thomas.

3. See Houston Peterson, ed., *Great Teachers, Portrayed by Those Who Studied Under Them* (New Brunswick: Rutgers University Press, 1946), for an essay by Christopher Morley on Professor Francis Gummere.

On Carey Thomas's autobiographical lists of "Lovers," which include some unlikely (though distinguished) candidates, Mr. Gummere appears simply as an initial: "G——."

M.H.D.

[Journal]

January 20, 1878

Never did a New Year come in with such a want of resolutions—in an agony of sleepiness during the ¼ before 12.

I am also twenty-one and as you know studying for a second degree in the Johns Hopkins. Prof. Gilder[sleeve] has laid out my work for the ten weeks to April 1st . . . enough to keep me busy.

January 31

I am utterly discouraged. For the last week I have been trying to study ten hours a day—six in the morning and four after tea. But in my reading Greek it is dreadful to see how often I mistake the meaning and then the terrible thought comes again and again. After all can I possibly get any more infinite shades of meaning out of the Greek than the translator—is this trouble after all worth it? Is it not a waste of one's life? Then the amount of study necessary. I am absolutely at the threshold: inaccurate, badly trained, not able to write a sentence of correct Greek. To give myself all this without a teacher, without even a guide—it seems like a labor of Hercules. I have no time to read, no time to see people—not that that amounts to much but still it is a kind of living death; but then if I had my choice this moment I know I would choose nothing else . . . my precious Agamemnon—the one inspiration to study when I lose all heart! The pleasure I had from that, the sweet echoing of lines from it that fills the pauses of dressing and eating almost is worth it all— Perhaps my studying is all a mistake—if I *only* were more master of the subject I could tell better. . . .

130

February 2, 1878

Last night our Friday Evening [group] met here (Mary Garrett, Julia Rogers, Mamie Gwinn, Carrie, Bess and I meet every two weeks at each other's houses and write two chapters of a novel and an essay or two each night).

Miss Gwinn wrote a remarkable chapter which brought up the whole question of marriage. She believes in free love according to Godwin's view, but now in the Malthus theory and therefore refuses to consider the bringing up of children. Says that if a man cared enough for her to wish to be her intimate friend, she would consider him a beast if he did not agree.

This started the whole question and we discussed it till eleven o'clock. We all concluded there *is* something wrong about the present relations of marriage and yet none of us accepted Miss Gwinn's views. . . . I said and think that as for a few words in church or before a magistrate making all the difference between right and wrong, of course that is nonsense. But we must judge this question purely on grounds of expedience on what will lead to the best moral results. Now it *does* seem to me that free love will (and platonic friendship I think is not possible with men) degrade matters and above all women. . . . I do wonder what will become of us all. I really think that I personally do not know what to say about this matter and must wait till I see and know more to decide. I am afraid I could, if I let myself, be devoted to Miss Gwinn—she has a strong fascination for me. Have I time?

February 13, 1878

Last night I went to the theatre for the first time. Father and Mother of course disapproved but I was twenty-one last month and I went entirely on my own responsibility. Mary and Julia and Miss——[4] and three gentlemen and I. The play was *Camille* and Modjeska acted it. It came up and went beyond anything I had imagined. I utterly lost all idea of locality and just saw Camille in her magnifi-

4. Usually an indication that she could not remember a name or date.

cent longings after a better life. The play might have been made a disagreeable one but the whole thing was raised by the purity of the passion and I could see no imaginable harm in it and oh it is such a mighty pleasure! . . . I feel deprived all these years.

Mary and I talked till eleven o'clock and had an elegant time. I like her very much—there is a sort of sweet strength about her. There are so many points we have in common sympathy. There is something horrible about being separated by this thought life from other people. Mary says she feels it more and more. We discussed the whole question of women.

There seems no solution of the question of marriage, for it is difficult to conceive a woman who really feels her separate lifework to give it all up when she marries a man and yet I think—a fact which I used to ignore—that it is and must be a giving up. Then a man, I should think, would not care for that sort of a wife. Bessie asked me whether I would refuse a man I loved for that reason. . . . Oh, it is a real question and Julia and Mary and Bessie and I all feel it. Will the solution be that we will be four old maids?[5] If a woman has children I do not see but what she will have to, at least for some time, give up her work and of all terrible things taking care of children does seem the most utterly unintellectual. But then one talks of "doing" and "life work" and yet after all what is it to be! I *do* feel as if I could do something but then every young person feels so I suppose. And think if everything were given up and for *nothing*!

February 22, 1878

Libbie has been here since Monday. Before she came I read over what I wrote about her in my journal and my poem, and all my eager, passionate feelings of grief at parting with her came over me. The next day I waited as coolly for her to come and kissed her and etc. without one pulse beat the faster. How can such a thing go so utterly? I have been amusing her and giving up all study. . . .

5. Carey, Mary, and Julia never married. Bessie King in middle age married a cousin named Ellicott, an architect.

I have to put the wax in my ears and with my own hands keep myself to the mast—a living death—and do nothing but devote myself to Greek. But I have been putting it off too long and I shall *fail*—and I who care so much for women and their cause—will *fail* and do them more harm than if I had never tried. But it is so hard.

Well, about my girl friends: Mary Garrett I like more and more but Julia I am disappointed in. She is oh, I do not know, shallow and not *soulful* somehow. I cannot have deep confidence in her. Miss Gwinn I really like and trust and find a pleasure in her. If she would once break down the barriers and care for someone and be broad enough to comprehend another, the thing needful would come. She is now too self-centered. Bessie has something lacking for a perfect friend. She is not perfectly dependable. She sometimes defends a side unexpectedly which she does not believe. She cares too much for admiration and young men I think. She wants abandon and a largeness of vision. Who does not—I myself lack everything and am contemptible, but then we judge from an ideal standpoint. I have been thinking for some time about Friendship and analyzing my feeling toward it:

Friendship

For the most part we go along on the level of every day affairs with a feeling as if we were, as it were, feeding our individualities. We are stirred out of ourselves by generous impulses but always falling back into loneliness. But there is one loop hole through which we escape into an upper region. A new breath seems to come into our life; a rare, intimate devoted friendship between man and man, woman and woman. We are carried out of self and see through another's eyes. We understand another's nature as we never can unless love unbars the way. Not of such a friendship as this can it be said, "Come down, oh maid." In love between a man and a woman there must be more or less of coming down. There is an element of selfishness, of self gratification in it; but girls know that they are each other's for only a little while, as long as each is worthy and love lasts. It has not the commonness that possession gives. . . .

I *worshipped* Libbie, she was lovely and far above me in my thought of her. I have been different ever since from the mere feeling. Of course now I see her as she is and all that passionate devotion has gone but I hate to miss it.

Carrie I loved too, though never quite that way. Now I see she was not what I thought her and everything except a calm liking and sense of obligation is gone.

Cornell is just full of Miss Hicks. The pine forests and the falls and glens and walks. . . . Our friendship was an absorbing one—everything we did or read together is impressed with her image, or rather my idea of her. She came to see me Christmas—thought I cared for her—yet now the feeling has gone. How perfectly unaccountable! I can give no reason for it. This does not speak well for perhaps the very thing I am longing to prove—friendship. . . .

Now, for the first time since I went to Howland in '72 do I feel perfectly free to give myself to study without the desire to see anyone except, of course, as an ordinary friendship requires, where companionship is an aid, pleasant but not necessary. But then I can never pour my very thought out to anyone now, when complete sympathy of love if not of abstract thought and clasped hands and loving eyes and close kisses and admiration, bowing before another's spirit . . . all join in making thought and your soul life a real thing and make you feel noble and generous living in another, not selfcentered. This is what I imagine friendship could be.

March 18, 1878

Just home from Meeting. As I said to Bessie afterwards are we fools or are we idiots that when we can't get time to go to really instructive lectures or to read splendid books we sit there and listen to a discourse about "cows and twenty-four Indian princes" prolonged anecdotes, mere exhortation to believe in Christ. I am in a perfect maze theologically. I cannot help thinking there is something in religion and yet upon my word, between dogma and narrowness it seems as if all the divine primal inspiration had escaped between the lines. . . .

Mamie Gwinn I do like very much. She is a terrible temptation to me as I tell her—she represents all that side of my nature I am trying to suppress, the roving through literature and study, seeking out whatever the bent of my fancy leads to—the dilettante spirit, the complete contradiction to the steady working spirit I am endeavoring to summon. . . . But life is so full, and Greek life after all is only a part.

My interest is now in the first part of present century; Godwin and Shelley, etc. Miss Gwinn introduced me to Godwin and his *Political Justice* has really changed my thought very much. How could I have been so blind to all the sufferings and miserable unequality of people around?

March 23, 1878

Have just come in from a ride with Mary Garrett. She is lovely. I do not know when I have admired a girl so much—her fearlessness on horseback really gives me a sensation of real, warm admiration. I should so like to have an earnest friendship with her.

March 24, 1878

Last night, instead of studying, I wrote a sonnet to Mary Garrett. It was the first sonnet I had ever tried and it took me till ten o'clock a.m., of course not steady work. Oh I do wonder if I can ever do anything with poetry. I seem to have a certain little power, not by anything I have done but by what I feel. Work years I would give if it were possible—to be a poet has been my dream of dreams. . . . If only I knew!

. . . Then too it seems conceited, perhaps; but Heaven knows if anyone purposely deceives himself in his own thought, there is no hope for him. In writing these stories for our Friday nights, I have felt that perhaps I could write. Other people have told me so too, but the uncertainty and then the long preparation it requires—my style is *wretched* and if I thought I could, I would, and I think I shall, upon the chance, devote myself to improving it and reading. . . . Everything seems secondary to my desire to read. . . .

Now I want to write down something that has been quivering on my pen every time I take it to write in my journal and I hope if anybody takes up this book they will have the honor not [to] read it. I write it because I want an account at the time. Last summer, after coming from Anna's that something came, at least the suspicion of it against which I have always prayed. In the summer of—— (at Atlantic City) I think I first saw Mr. Gummere. We went on a sail together and one evening he and Dick Cadbury and Aunt Mary[6] and I talked on the porch; then I think he came to see me one afternoon. He sat on the sofa, that wretched green sofa, and I sat in the little cane rocking chair in front. His head had just been shaved (that is, almost shaved) and he looked very funny, I remember it as if it were yesterday. We talked of our plans. He was sick of law—the study he said was noble, but the practice degrading and he felt as if he must go to Harvard to study and after all that was worth more than anything else. I told him of my dream of going to college. We had a talk upon study and men and women's work. He said Tennyson just expressed it. I got him my green, long copy and he read that part "not like in like but like in difference," etc. We agreed of course.

I saw him once at a party at Anna's. I remember we talked about books and stood by the mantlepiece. It was their Filbert Street house and I had a fan. I can't remember what we said. Then that winter he and Mr. Cadbury wrote that "Bells" to Bessie King, Anna, Bessie Nich and myself at Howland. I have it.

Sometime the spring of that year (I have an awful time getting the chronology straight so perhaps it was not then) I was at Carrie Cadbury's and she asked me to stay to dinner and said Richard Thomas, Mr. G. [Gummere] and Mr. C. [Cadbury] would be there. I said thoughtfully that then there would be too many and went home—of

6. **Sometimes** referred to as "little Aunt Mary," her father's young half sister.

course having come about dinnertime I did not like to stay. Sarah [Cadbury] (poor Sarah, *requiescat in pace*) told Mr. G. the moment he came in that I had said I would not stay because he was there. He became very much excited as both Richard and Carrie told me afterwards—said he knew he had talked about his devotion to me, that of course he had had no right and I was angry with reason, he would never see me again. They reasoned with him but it did no good. He did not come to see me that time.

In the summer Uncle Allen spoke his "Mystics" before the Alumni at Haverford and Anna and I went out together with Johnny and Whitall. We were sitting talking when Mr. Gummere came through the car and passed us with a fierce bow—I thought of all his anger and the wretched misunderstanding and my heart stood still with excitement, I guess. I can remember how I felt. He offered to hold an umbrella over Anna as we left the car but she refused and went with me. Mr. G. sat over to the right by himself "glaring" at us as Anna kept whispering to me. Afterwards I was talking and saw him coming nearer and for a little while we talked each to someone else with our backs to one another. Then he turned and held out his hand. "Miss Thomas, I want to congratulate you on your examination and admission at Cornell." He asked if he could walk to the station with me. I was about to refuse but Anna whispered "Go Min" so I went. It was pouring rain and Mr. G. in talking would forget the umbrella every now and then and I remember the lightning flashed very much as we were going down the steps under the bridge and Mr. G. was telling me what to study at Cornell and we both walked off the board walk.

That summer he and Mr. C. were out at "Windon" for two days while I was there and Sue was somewhere else too. We had a long talk one moonlight ride, Mr. G. and I, while Anna and Dick drove in the buggy behind. Mr. G. had only ridden once before when he had been thrown and his disregard of his horse was magnificent. He let the reins hang so loose I remember that my foot caught in them once or twice. We had a lovely talk—the nicest we have ever had—about Harvard—he told me all about it, and Cornell, and I told him; and religion, he was in great doubt and perplexity—I of course was too and oh we talked perfectly freely about it! and then poetry—he said something that shocked me about Shelley but it was in such innocence that it made no difference. We got home before the others and went in the dining room to get some water and Mr. G. said he could not tell me what a nice ride he had had. That evening we tried that putting on of hands game and later sat on the porch in the moonlight and the fountain dripped on the lawn and planned a camping out for next summer. Then Anna and I tried to say "Intimations of Immortality" and failed utterly, Mr. G. said "The Garden of Proserpine" and "Hymn to Proserpina" which haunted me for two years until I found them last year. Then they insisted on a poem from me and I said "The Last Ride" of Browning's and got intolerably frightened in the midst. Afterwards, two years afterwards, Anna said something that made me think Dick had thought I might have intended some allusion (How horrible! the thought of Mr. G. had never entered my mind but it was too unfortunate). I pretended to Anna I did not understand—I could not endure explaining even to her.

Then Anna and Dick (he is in love with her by the way) wandered off and Mr. G. and I talked very late on the piazza about everything—religion mainly. We then walked down the path; it is so amusing to see the way I remember all these little things though at the time I never thought of them—I can see the trees shaking, and the water, all as we looked at the rockery. In the morning the boys were going and we drove to the station by way of Hazards and in the parlor I was looking at their elegant books and Mr. G. followed me and we had an enthusiastic comment upon them. Mr. G. and I shook hands at the station and wished each other success—he me in Cornell, I him in his first attempt at teaching at Providence.

I did not see him at all the next summer but in June, that is June of '76, he wrote me a very splendid letter regretting his not being able to join the camping out, which afterwards was given up, on account of going to

138

Germany for the summer. I hesitated but concluded not to answer it.

Then I did not see or hear of him much till last July when we four were again at Windon for one day and a half. And Miss Shin was not even here this time and it was horribly embarrassing; so we only let the boys stay one night. They came at 11 o'clock one day and then we sat and wound hammock-cord for a hammock which helped us through; that hammock was an unfailing source of relief. Mr. G. held my cord and we got in a fearful tangle neither of us knowing how to manage it, and Anna and Dick got through and went off. Then for the first time I felt embarrassed. It was such a ridiculously novel-like position and for the first time I think I felt conscious. It provoked me so, that I should have allowed—though I could not have helped it very well. Father had objected to my coming and that, and the thought of the way Mr. G. had looked up on me before, made me resolve to be as cold and careful as possible and show him that I did not care about him, which indeed was true.

That night we talked, discussed Wordsworth and Pope, and Mr. G. and I agreed so it was fairly funny and then Anna and Dick went off and I felt again the position I had placed myself in, for it was evident Dick and Anna cared most to be together and there were Mr. G. and I left. I determined again but Mr. G. (he sat in a great big rocking chair and moved it nearer and nearer as he talked) was so splendid that every now and then I would forget; but I think probably he was disappointed a little. Then at ten we went in and made lemonade and then I proposed going up stairs. It was dreadful to me to stay there. Mr. G. frightened me a little though I don't know why but I felt as if it would be a relief to get away. The next morning we drove—Mr. G. drove the double horses to—oh somewhere—an island in the Wissahicken—and we had a picnic and sat up on a bank and Mr. G. and I looked over a Tennyson and I showed him one or two poems he did not know and it was embarrassing because Anna *would* leave us together, and I was not like myself.

That afternoon Dick proposed to Mr. G. to go in swimming. Mr. G. made some objection. He had said last evening that he had a letter he wanted to show me, but of course I could not help him out and would not, so they went and did not come back till just tea time. Tea was disagreeable. Anna and Dick must needs both leave the table to speak to the coachman and Mr. G. and I sat opposite each other. He began a sentence and stopped in the middle when they came back which necessitated my explaining it and asking their opinion. After tea we looked for the little time remaining at my Cornell pictures. Mr. Cadbury asking me about Mr. Boyesen (to whom Mr. G. had heard I was engaged) and I gave him a full description and yet all the while I was conscious that I wanted to make up with Mr. G. though there was nothing to make up. Mr. G. barely shook hands when they left.

A week afterwards I met them both accidentally in the Philadelphia library and the moment I saw Mr. G. I felt that I blushed and knew that I felt a little differently toward him. He had just spent a week at Atlantic City and I was going down the next day. I did not even dare to say I was sorry we missed each other. I tried to get courage to tell him I received his letter and thank him for it but I could not bring myself to mention it. They went but not before I had completed my indifferent role, though this time unconsciously by telling Mr. Cadbury I remembered the sail on which I saw him, and though it appears Mr. Gummere was on that same sail, I deliberately told him I did not know he was there. I had not time to see what he thought, for they went then.

After that all last summer and this fall and winter and spring there is no use in denying the fact that I do think about Mr. G. and the worst of it is I can't help it very well—in the midst of study, there is limitless time to think between the turning over of the leaves of a Greek dictionary, and whatever I am doing, when I go to bed at night. My theories have given way, positively. I cannot help thinking about him. . . . I am just irresistibly controlled and feel this way. I think most probably things were so unfortunate last summer and I certainly must have shown him my coldness and constraint that he will think I have changed and get engaged to some other girl. (The way with men!) And I do not think it would be a trial to me. Because, and this is the second thing I think—I do not think I would marry him anyhow (that is the reason I tried to show him last summer and yet I forgot so often that I cannot really tell whether he saw). I would have to give up I am afraid my dearest work that has lain next to my heart from my childhood. And yet it is so indefinite; but then at least one can try. Then one third thought—I *know* and this is most certain of all, that I have lost my interest in all other men except as studies and to amuse myself with—I know that I will never find one who is as splendid as Mr. G. He is literary and enthusiastic, a passionate worshipper of poetry and a writer of it. He is interested in the same things as I am, he is struggling with the same old problems of life and religion, he is brilliant and so cultivated in many ways that I am not—I feel a continual admiration for many things in him and yet I felt that I can give him some culture too—I love to talk to him. The thing I most regret is that I would not let myself this summer, because fate is a blind goddess and after all I might as well have.

I see his faults but still they are faults I like . . . he has a little of the divine fire I think and hence is utterly removed from all other people I know.

Now it has struck two a.m. and I must finish since I have begun and after all, I presume by thinking out all these circumstances I have undone the work of weeks of struggling to stop thinking about him. Then too my journal will be a great care for fear people might see—this is the reason I have not written all this out before. And then too I did not face the fact till this fall. It was an awful trial. I cried and cried myself to sleep often because I could not stop thinking about him. You see, I never came to anything before that I could not, partially at least, manage. . . .

If I only *knew* that he understood me last summer and it was all over, I would be glad of the experience because he is very splendid and certainly did make an ideal of me

141

until I stepped off my pedestal myself. And I am glad to have the feeling, in spite of the efforts I am trying to make to quench it. Then I don't believe a person, even Mother, guesses the way I feel which is best in any case. No, the thing that troubles me is that it being so uncertain. I cannot dismiss this from my mind until I know. I have an intolerable desire to know if I will see him next summer (and yet I positively am going to refuse to get up the camping because I don't choose to put myself in his way) though why I want to see him is beyond me. . . .

I am utterly at a loss—I have prayed about it with all the little faith I have and struggled against my foolishness (and yet it is not foolishness and I like it and that again is the worst of it) but it is no use and now I am going to wait and see.

April 7, 1878

Last Monday April the 1st Mary and Julia came up to tea and afterwards, at eight, came up to my room. I had gotten Mrs.———[7] *What Women Should Know* and about fifteen of father's medical books (he was in New York) and we began and read till 11:30. The reason we wished to was it seemed to us we were old enough to know all about the different forces of life and for myself I felt that if I do care and I do, to work for the good of people, and to try in my own life to do no harm, I must not be blindfolded and if passion and sensuality are sure factors I wanted to understand them. Otherwise what can be reasonably done against them? And then I thought, to the pure all things are pure and after all in purely natural phenomena what can be degrading? The other girls thought the same.

But positively after we had done we did not say much, we could not, the revelations of vice and hateful disgusting things that we had not the faintest conception ever existed were too much, but I went to bed sick. Absolutely—I had eaten of the fruit of the tree of knowledge of good and evil and it seemed as if there was no such thing

7. Eliza B. Duffey, *What Women Should Know* (Philadelphia: J. M. Stoddart & Co., [1873]).

as ever believing in purity and holiness again, or ever getting my own mind pure again. It seemed as if everything in the world was governed by this one hateful beastly impulse of men and as if it was impossible for the human race ever to become higher—philanthropy, religion may as well cease beating their heads against this wall—*sense* remains and apparently *men are made so.*

I was talking with Mary today and she said she felt just so but now we both of us have reasoned ourselves a little out of it and are not sorry for reading through it—it is a crucial test after all. Positively for the first day or two I was in despair. Thoughts of the things I had read kept coming up in spite of the perfect abhorrence with which I regarded them. But I think that must have been the utter shock I received for now I am just as usual except I shall never forget and I do not wish to. I am sure it is hard, inexpressibly hard, but I am sure it is every woman's duty to face things in women's knowing all about it and being pure and noble themselves and restraining, as they only can, therein lies the only future salvation. There is one thing that also has come from this. It is very hard for a woman who does not care for the only field open to women—social success—not to feel herself hopelessly weighted in the race for intellectual prizes, but this knowledge makes me more thankful than ever. A woman by the mere fact of her womanhood seems higher morally and physically than a man and therefore the time he has to spend in struggling against his lower nature she has to advance in. . . . One other thing, it had always seemed to me possible if a man and his wife chose for them to live as friends in a beautiful companionship and pure and lofty things and for *no other element* to enter; but I believe, I am afraid, I am convinced, that this is not possible.

Easter Sunday April 21, 1878
Anna Shipley has just been paying me a visit of a week. We have had a more intimate time than ever before. She told me of a love affair. I had long guessed and it is so sad. I gave her advice that I am sure is best but I do not think she will follow it. Almost everyone has something of

that kind. There is Bessie King. I am still surer from little signs that she cares about Mr. Dana, though I think she has refused him. Libbie is in love with Mr. A. though I don't think she fully knows it and is afraid he is not in love with her. Mariana's life turned to temperance and religion on account of that wretched man. Mary Garrett I think is in love with Dr. Murray—Julia's romance and Carrie's and Bessie Nicholson's are yet to come, and of course Mamie Gwinn's.

Well, Anna and I had a long talk about Mr. Gummere and she told me what I had guessed—that he has and does admire me, but looks at it as something unobtainable and is prevented from asking me to write to him by a sort of awe.

It does seem too bad. . . . If I could only see him and have a long talk with him and tell him my plans, as I have never let myself before, I could tell if it would be possible to have a friendship. . . . I would make the attempt if he gives me a chance. I cannot bear to have him go to Europe this summer without making the attempt, at least.

May 2, 1878

I never had such a fit of the blues in my life. Yesterday I walked with Mary Garrett and it was insufferable, I could not say one word. Then to tea at Mamie Gwinn's and it was worse. *Richelieu* in the evening. Booth is grand. I never enjoyed anything so much. I saw him in *Hamlet, Macbeth,* Lear, Shylock, Petruccio last week. It just carries one away, but the inferior actors are so wretched it would soon spoil my pleasure, I think.

May 3, 1878

It does seem as if fates conspire to bring up Mr. Gummere's name. Just as I think I am getting along so nicely and not thinking of him at all, almost every week this winter has come some incidental mention of him; even to Father's calling Frank Allinson Frank Gummere. Today came a letter of congratulations to Richard which Tom

Worthington to whom he sent it must needs bring here. It says he sails June 27 for nine months in Germany and throughout Mr. Morris's paper on the time of Herodotus' composition, as a wretched undertone, came the thought that of course I would not see him—I write this all down because it is too provoking. I had made up my mind that I had completely stopped thinking about him and now I discover that it is not so. . . .

All this winter when things went wrong and I got discouraged and provoked with myself I would say, "It don't make any matter, nothing amounts to anything, I will think about Mr. Gummere," and after an hour or so I would emerge very much disgusted with my strength of mind and go on and perhaps not think of him again for a month. *Nous changeons tout cela.*

May 5, 1878
I feel better by dint of idleness and Hamlet and Iago and like work tomorrow. "Richard is himself again." Mamie and I had a nice time Saturday. I don't know—I think I might really get to care about her. I felt more like it yesterday than ever before. . . . I do not like Carrie, the revulsion of feeling is dreadful. We have no subject in common and yet I feel as if our love had the greatest claims. How despicable it is to change, and yet I cannot help it. If people are naturally very attractive and have no personal habits one objects to, then love fades into a cool liking and a loving remembrance like Libbie, but Carrie— every now and then offends my taste and then liking passes the boundary line. I wonder if it is utterly base to let little things make such a difference.

It cuts us off from half the world. When I see Father eat with his knife or when Mother does something I don't like, it takes me hours before I feel like going near them. Like Iago I am afraid "I am nothing if not critical." But I struggle against it and it does no good. I have not cared to talk to Esther Tuttle since I saw her put fish into her mouth with her knife. Yet these are mere accidental circumstances. . . .

145

May 8, 1878

Another distracting letter from **Miss Ladd**.[8] Mr. Gilman's contemptible, mean treatment. He told her he could not say whether she would receive, after her examinations [at Johns Hopkins] a degree or a certificate. Wretch, he *knows* the motion stands "Resolved that Miss Thomas be received as a candidate for a second degree" and of course her case is the same. . . .

I think I am now determined to get the degree in spite of them. It will always be useful to me, Ph.D. is not to be despised, if I write, and especially if I teach, or if I take any distinguished educational position. . . . I will take the degree in their teeth if I only have FAIR PLAY.

June 26, 1878—Atlantic City

Mr. Gummere sails today I think. For the last three days I have thought maybe he would come down and I have cared very much to see him. Now all chance is gone. Perhaps it is best as I do not know why I wished to see him. Now I hope I can dismiss all thought of him from my mind.

July 6, 1878—Atlantic City

. . . I am here alone with Grandma [Whitall] and have much time to think and though I am not unhappy and do listen to dear Grandma's little stories and sit a wondering spectator at her friends and her talk about people, people, people, in a sweet cherry round with a kind and tender touching upon the death and illness of so and so—a curiosity about this and that affair—a *certain* faith in all old beliefs and in Christ and God, a reverence for the Bible that sinks the tone into an *awful* chant in reading— never a word of abstract thought, utterly untouched by the throbbing needs of the day. . . .

August 25, 1878

Mamie came to pay me a visit of a week. The old story over again. We talked, and read Swinburne and I was

8. This refers to a second Miss Ladd who may be related to but is not the aforementioned "Carrie."

146

miserably unhappy about religion. Sunday 14 July we sat out on the balcony at sunset and read his "Hymn of Man" in *Songs Before Sunrise*. It is a paean of triumph over the vanishing of the Christian religion. To Mamie it was elixir, to me poison— though I could not help the bewildering beauty of it carrying me away. . . . She (Mamie) is the cleverest, damnably clever—I used to think; now, I think gloriously clever—girl. . . .

Aunt Hannah and I talked and she is the most completely honest woman. She is grand and noble in many ways but she is without a grain of useless and false sentiments—marriage, love, all. She holds on to two things in slavish devotion and real selfishness: her children and her Christianity. Uncle Robert on the contrary reverses it. . . .

One night about eight o'clock I got in one of the light canoes and rowed out in the middle of Long Lake, then down the lake. I was over a mile from shore. The sunset glow had died away and it was a clear starlit night. The little waves broke against the keel. I was thinking of the fact that I had wasted this year in struggles to believe in Christianity, useless[ly], hopelessly so. I was in horrible doubt about the university—it is quenching soul and spirit to go on; it is risking all upon my being able to write if I stop. A horrible blank. No God to pray to, no shrine of Apollo to go to. A life of rasping at home if I can't believe and that is impossible, at least now. Suddenly, as suddenly as a possession, came over me the temptation to upset this boat. Suicide was here removed from all its objections—no one would grieve over my damned spirit. It would be thought accidental; many accidents happen in the lakes up here. I shall never forget how the waves sounded and the stars looked. I came so near doing it. I tremble to think of it. "Suddenly thy shadow fell on me." There seemed to come as a stealing melody some use and beauty into life. All the old fighting to believe died away . . . . All religions are "part of the hunger and thirst of the heart" good and noble so long as they do not shackle, but only notes in the chorus: Godwinism—its core, the heavenly secret of Shelley "to fear himself and love all hu-

147

mankind," the secret of Christ "A dying daily—self re-
nunciation" are all one. It is worth working for, worth
living to work out that. I rowed back. Though I have been
disloyal very often the inspiration has not failed yet. I am
happier than I have been for a long time. I will try to be
good and work it out— Ah God, if I had genius to dedicate
to it!

August 27, 1878
. . . I could not help telling cousin Frank that I thought
Mr. Gummere would make the best president for the new
Taylor College.[9] I can do that much for him at least. After
I went to bed I felt as if talking had undone the work of
this summer; though to tell the truth Bessie Nicholson's
engagement to Frank Taylor aroused the whole thing
again, and I spent all last First Day meeting thinking
about him.

September 1, 1878
I have been reading Aunt [Hannah's] journal the whole
of Sixth Day. I read from her sixteenth to her thirty-fourth
year and it a revelation. Here are excerpts:

October 20, 1852:
I am too young to be married—the cares of life have
come upon me so soon that they have crushed all the
joyousness of my spirits and except that when I would
have more strength of mind to bear me up I feel as if I
were 40 instead of just 20 and I wish I were indeed 40 or
rather 60. [Later] I am too apt to chafe at my duties to
feel for instance as if the time spent in household
affairs or in rocking and fussing with my little tot were
wasted.

9. The tentative name for Bryn Mawr College. Carey's father and
other relatives were on the Board of Trustees. Dr. James Taylor, the
benefactor and founder, drew his will in 1877 and died soon after. The
ground for Taylor Hall was broken in 1879. The College accepted
students for the first time in the fall of 1885.

Nov. 24, 1852:

I must fully realize that it is my indispensable duty to submit myself entirely to my husband and I must do it without any lingering thoughts towards my old notions of independence . . . I am convinced if this is not speedily done the happiness of our intercourse will be materially lessened, perhaps wrecked. . . . I want to accustom myself to think when there is any difference of opinion that he must be necessarily in the right and I in the wrong and even if I feel confident that I am right it would be better for me to give up the point.

12 mo. 20th:

I am very unhappy now. That trial of my womanhood which to me is so very bitter has come upon me again. When my little Ellie is 2 years old she will have a little sister or brother. It is all the more heavy a trial because my husband agreed with me in thinking that I am too young for such cares and such suffering and he promised I should not again be so tried at least until I was 25. And this is the end of all my hopes, my pleasing anticipations, my returning youthful joyousness. Well, it is a woman's lot and I must try to become resigned and bear it in patience and *silence* and not make my home unhappy because I am so. But oh, how hard it is.

September 14, 1878

. . . I feel as if a crisis had come. This room is so filled with last winter's struggles and dreads that involuntarily I drift into the old channels—I long to plunge myself in university work. I dread the indefiniteness of my other plan. Places have a tremendous influence upon me. I wish it were not so. . . .

To the Board of Trustees of
the Johns Hopkins University
Gentlemen,

A year ago by your kindness I was admitted into the Johns Hopkins University as a candidate for a second degree. I naturally supposed that this would permit me to share in the unusual opportunities afforded to post graduate students under the able instruction of Professor Gildersleeve.

But the condition "without class attendance" has been understood to exclude my attendance upon the Greek Seminarium and the advanced instruction which is given to the other students of the University. I have thus found myself dependent upon such assistance as Professor Gildersleeve could give at the expense of his own time, which, notwithstanding his great personal kindness, I hesitated to encroach upon.

My object in entering the University was not so much to obtain a degree as to profit by the inestimable assistance Professor Gildersleeve gives to his pupils.

A trial of a year during which I received no help other than advice in reference to my course of reading and the privilege of passing an examination, has convinced me that under the present regulations, the assistance referred to cannot be obtained.

I make this explanation to you in order that my withdrawal may not be prejudicial to any other applicant, and because, so far as I have been informed, the only official recognition of my relation to the University exists upon your Minutes.

Respectfully,

s/M.C. Thomas

Baltimore. October 7, 1878

October 8, 1878
Much has happened. I wrote to the Board of Trustees of the university. I had a talk with Mr. Gildersleeve. There was nothing more to be obtained than last year. It seemed the only thing to do and yet as I sat in Mr. Gildersleeve's room it almost broke my heart to be so near and yet so far from all his inspiration. . . . There is a sense of freedom, the first in six years. . . .

October 18, 1878
Rebecca Smiley is staying here. She sits by me at table and today was the third meal. I was sure she would speak

150

about Frank Gummere—I scented it from afar. She spoke of Anna. Then Richard—"Richard is an intimate friend of Frank Gummere, is he not?" She looked at me. I do declare it is too provoking. She then talked about his marriage to a German *fraulein*,[1] wished he could get a splendid American wife. I announced that no one should marry till he or she was forty. A discussion followed. I know she knows about his having cared a little for me and it is like living under a spy. I am afraid I showed an unbecoming disgust at his marriage "so young." Now it makes me feel as if I cared again. What shall I do—if it were once certain if he were married or dead. Until he is— I do not believe I will be entirely happy—worse luck!

October 30, 1878

I read over what I have written of my novel yesterday and it is wretched. I am so discouraged I feel as I could never write. Surely this is some test and it has failed. I am lost. What shall I work upon? I am nearly twenty-two and know nothing, almost. So much of my work has gone for nothing. . . . I am not generally agreeable. I can not take the trouble even if I could be. Mamie criticized me so much yesterday. She said I swung my arms very much. Bowed too low—pushed away a person's hand, did not look at him, that is, half-turned away; sat with my legs crossed and my arm over the back of a chair and threw my head when I talked. Could there be a longer list? Then if I can do nothing—Oh I would like to go into a desert and try— here I am distracted by so much. People come to tea, stay in the house, I never get a fair chance to try. . . .

November 21, 1878

The best thing of all: Anna wrote saying she had found out that he [Mr. G.] cared about another girl. I was sure he would as soon as he found it was impossible for me to care about him. I am so glad now. It is the one thing I wanted to make me sure. I can be sure now that nothing could turn me away. I consecrate my life anew. I am thankful for this certainty. I sing paeans of joy—

1. She means the possibility of his marrying a German fräulein.

January 11, 1879

. . . Mamie said, "I love you dearly, more than anyone else, but I do not love you all I can love." She was reading me to sleep but that waked me up like a thunderclap. It was the expression of what I felt. . . . I have just had a talk with Mother and I do believe I shall shoot myself. I almost think I will. There is no use of living and then Mother would see in the morning that she had been cruel. She says I outrage her every feeling, that it is the greatest living grief to her to have me in the house. A denier end defamer of the Christ whom she loves more than she loves me, that I am merely selfish, a cipher or worse, a finder of fault in the house; that she has ceased to love me except as a child; that I make the other children unbelieving, that I barely tolerate Father, and that I am utterly and entirely selfish, I use the house of which I take the best of everything and Father and herself for my purposes and then care no more in them. . . . Oh heavens what a religion that makes a mother cast her daughter off! . . .

March 24, 1879

Last week I received a letter from Ed Allinson saying Mr. Gummere would be in Philadelphia and could I not come on and have a conference upon Allinson affairs. I was completely disconcerted by this letter, and my slain enemy returned. I discovered that I was as much in a turmoil about Mr. G. as ever. I wrote back asking them to come down here and they are coming the 28th. I suppose it is natural even if I am over caring about Mr. G. to be rather distracted. I tried two days to work on Greek but found I must have something to occupy my mind so read history furiously all last week and even yet I find that I had better not resume my Greek. For I cannot help thinking about Mr. G. My greatest comfort is that he is in love with that little Providence girl but still I am so anxious to meet him, naturally, and yet if we could have one long tête-à-tête and I could once show him that I am as friendly as we were before that hateful summer. The whole thing is a test of my firmness. To meet a man whom I am in love with—a little—after nearly two years when he has stopped caring for me, in the presence of two men who know all about Mr. G's former preference for me and who will watch me attentively . . . I cannot help thinking and dreaming about him. I have done it for four nights. . . . The whole conjunction of Mr. G's visit strikes as fatalistic. I am hopeless in regard to going abroad, unless I myself make the money . . . living at home is intolerable on account of being such a distress to mother and father in religion. It would make a difference in Mr. Gummere's prospects in the Taylor College if he were engaged to me. If he should still care about me there could be no likelier time for me to accept him. . . .

March 27, 1879
Been sick with one of my dreadful headaches all day and lay on the sofa and read Trollope's *Is He Popenjoy?* Mamie came to see me and spent three hours. She is devoted and sweet and good but I do believe I am out of love with her. I thought so Sunday and now I am sure, almost. Maybe it is the near prospect of seeing Mr. Gummere. Tomorrow they come. It is the most profoundly exciting event that can happen to me and after this I hope all will be level work. Yet I do have a cowardly hope that he may care a little.

March 30, 1879
Received letter from Ed. Allinson. Mr. Gummere has been called to Cambridge by a telegram, sends "his regards and very deep regrets." *Cela va sans dire.* . . . I shall never believe in constancy again. Also, talking to Mr. Cadbury has made me believe that I should not like Mr. Gummere so much. He was dithyrambic and in crude colors and now I have escaped from that. . . .

153

II

STUDY IN EUROPE

Once Carey Thomas (with her mother's invaluable assistance) had sufficiently quelled her father's objections to leave home for two years at a coeducational, nonsectarian college, it was almost inevitable that the pattern would be repeated by his allowing her to travel to Europe for a higher degree, after her unsuccessful attempt to break down the barriers against women at the Johns Hopkins University.

The year before her departure had undoubtedly been a difficult one for her parents as well as for Carey. Her faith wavered beyond recall and theirs remained deeper and more abiding than ever. They could hardly have found her to be a proper example to the younger children. Nor could her moodiness, her demands, and her outbursts have been easy to live with. I have no doubt that her mother, devoted as she was, saw her daughter leave with some relief.

The question of a proper traveling companion was crucial; without one it would have been nearly impossible to secure her father's permission to go. Mamie Gwinn was the only prospect, and until the very last moment there was the unsettling question of whether she would be able to leave. Her situation was quite the opposite of Carey's. An only daughter, she had a mother who was every bit the martyr Mary Thomas was not. A fragment of a play, obviously autobiographical (even to the author's forgetting herself and unwittingly inserting her own name at one point), written by Mamie in middle age,[1] portrays a scene in which the mother does everything possible to make her daughter feel guilty. In doing so, she demolishes her daughter's looks, her clothes, her friends, not to mention her plans. It is no wonder that Mamie had a decidedly neurotic personality.

"When I was going to Germany," Carey Thomas wrote at a later age, "and she [Mamie] wanted to make her parents let her go, she fell in dead faints that lasted for hours, and her temperature was often at 102° or 103° and even 104°. Finally the doctor said she would end by killing herself, so they let her go."[2]

Mamie was several years younger than Carey, pale, fragile, and somewhat lazy, though gifted. Her lassitude complemented Carey's energy, and she was in at least one sense Carey's ideal companion for she did all the readings, attended lectures when she felt up to it, and could discuss the scholarship with Carey. (After Bryn Mawr was underway and a graduate school was set up, Mamie

1. Found in the Papers of Alfred Hodder at Princeton University. The Papers of Mamie Gwinn Hodder, also at Princeton, are closed until the year 2000. Both in the fragment of the play and in letters to Hodder ("Beloved Playmate"), Mamie refers to Carey as "Sabina." In a summary of the play, she writes: "Mama gives an account of her interview with Sabina who called on her in her last flying visit to Aislake [Baltimore]. 'You will be amused, but *I* was quite fascinated by Sabina. She looked *dressed:* and her eyes were beaming with animation and she was so full of energy and talked apparently with so much interest during the little time that she stayed, and I looked at her and thought she really was a very attractive and remarkable woman and sure to succeed in what she undertakes and to have things her own way.' (Valentine [Mamie] noticed with displeasure the note struck that always indicates in her mother the fear of having any contest with Sabina. . . .)"

2. Carey Thomas's note goes on to say: "She used to manage me by getting ill for years until I understood. The last time, she was determined that Father should not come to the Deanery, and gave herself such a high temperature that she became delirious and I thought her out of her mind and called in the first doctor passing. He told me that it was nothing but acute hysteria, and told her so, and told her that he had told me. This was the last time it happened." Interestingly enough, Carey's other close friend, Mary Garrett, records having had attacks of hysteria as a child.

was awarded a Ph.D. from Bryn Mawr for a dissertation based largely on work she had done abroad.) Yet at no time while Carey was in Europe striving to outshine her fellow students, as she ultimately succeeded in doing, did Mamie represent competition.

After returning from abroad Mamie went to live at the Bryn Mawr Deanery with Carey and visited her mother on weekends. When she left for the weekend or a summer holiday, Mary Garrett would move in and stay until just before Mamie was due to return.

Bertrand Russell, whose comments on Carey Thomas and some members of her clan are more caricature than penetrating, has given an amusing eyewitness description of these comings and goings in the Bryn Mawr Deanery, in the first volume of his autobiography.[3]

Mamie had the unenviable choice of living with a domineering friend and, as time went on, feeling less welcome, or going home where she would never be permitted to forget that she had chosen to leave her mother and was not especially welcome back. There is more than a hint in the letters from abroad (see page 257) that Mamie would have returned to the States earlier had her mother not made it plain that, having made her choice, she had to stick to it.

Contrary to the fiction, not only was Carey Thomas *not* consumed with grief when Mamie finally left the Deanery to marry, she felt considerable relief, albeit mingled with some temporary guilt at having driven her friend, through her indifference and abandonment, as she saw it, into what she felt sure would be a disastrous match. The friendship had been wearing thin, as has already been mentioned, for well over six years before Mamie and Alfred Hodder (with whom she eloped in 1904) had even met. Hodder had come to teach at Bryn Mawr in 1896 and stayed two years. The affair continued when he left to become assistant to District Attorney William Jerome of New York. Judging by the few references extant (Carey doubtless destroyed more pointed references in the course

3. *The Autobiography of Bertrand Russell,* Vol. I (Boston: Atlantic, Little, Brown, 1967), pp. 193-95.

of reviewing her correspondence) she was aware of the love affair for some time and knew of their plans for elopement before it took place. During the year after Mamie's marriage, she and Carey kept in touch by exchanging birthday notes and gifts. All contact appears to have been broken off in 1906 when Hodder's common-law wife brought suit for divorce and made his marriage appear to be bigamy. Ever conscious that a breath of scandal could hurt Bryn Mawr, Carey was faced with one involving a close friend and former member of her faculty (Mamie had been a professor of English)—and indeed two faculty members, since Hodder, too, had taught there— that must have surpassed her wildest nightmares. Hodder died suddenly (and rather mysteriously) in 1906 before the case came to trial.[4]

In this section more than any other, qualities of character that are less than admirable come into focus. Carey's letters show traces of snobbery, pretentiousness, and an overbearing urge to have her way. This streak had been chillingly forecast in a letter written to a friend just

4. Alfred Hodder's papers disclose that the woman (Jessie Donaldson) who had at various times been presented publicly as his wife, was an acquaintance of William James, whose student Hodder had been while at Harvard. A draft of a letter (virtually a howl of outrage) from Hodder to James, written in 1906 shortly before Hodder's death, accuses the distinguished professor of "attempted blackmail": "You have been trying to gain by menace of scandal points for your protegée to which you were openly conscious you had no right in law. I think of no ethical element wanting in such a position to bring it within the definition of attempted blackmail. . . ." The James's had evidently placed Hodder in the position of representing Jessie as his wife on various occasions over a period of time sufficient to safeguard her legal status under common law. She had followed him to Germany, where he had gone to study after graduating from Harvard, and there she had had a child conceived in the States. The James's had arrived on the scene and, Hodder claims, forced him into the first of a series of introductions wherein he was compelled to present Jessie as his wife. He acknowledged paternity of the first child—the daughter born in Germany—but not of a second-born, a son, who subsequently became a ward of the James's. A tantalizing roadblock in tracking down this story is the fact that certain of William James's papers at Harvard are closed until the year 2025.

158

before going off to Howland: "I have got two real pretty pieces of crimson Brussels for mats to take up. Mother is not quite resigned to my taking them yet and looks longingly at the two parlor doors in which they fit so prettily but I hope soon to reduce her to a becoming resignation. What a great thing submission is!" In the last sentence Carey's syntax is askew, but her meaning is all too clear.

Carey's attempts to manipulate friends and family by mail would be more amusing if it were not for her occasional cruelty. Her letter to Miss Hicks shows how needlessly brutal she could be.[5] There are hints, in letters to Mary Garrett with whom she was striving even then to develop a closer friendship, about "Julia's conduct," implying misconduct. This and other letters show Julia to have been a victim of unpleasant innuendos that Mary withstood for a long time considering the tenaciousness of their source. In her attempts to manipulate her parents and relatives on the Bryn Mawr board, Carey met her match in her invincible Aunt Hannah, who quite cleverly manipulated *her,* as Hannah's letter attests.[6]

These letters from Europe have been selected from many hundreds. She wrote at length, at least once a week, sometimes twice, to her family and various friends, for a period of over four years. I chose those that struck me as the most interesting in content and the most revealing of Carey Thomas's character and the development of her career. Excised portions are largely repetitive or have to do with costs and prices. She was restricted in her budget while by nature self-indulgent, and this condition, combined with a mild sense of guilt that could not have been diminished by her mother's reminders that other family members had equal claims and needs, made her loquacious in defense of her expenditures. Those eager to learn of the costs of railroad travel in Europe, the prices of food, clothing, lodging, books, stationery, and almost anything else on the continent and in England circa 1879-1883 will

5. See p. 222.
6. See p. 284.

find a wealth of material in unpublished portions of her letters from abroad.

The last item in this section is the very last entry in the final volume of Carey Thomas's journals. It was evidently written some time after her return from Europe. It is so enigmatic as to invite speculation. She appears to have changed her mind after a provocative opening and decided to omit what was to be a confession. Whether "the temptation" had to do with another "smash," or a love affair with a man, is the tantalizing question that remains.

M.H.D.

CHRONOLOGY
OF
CAREY THOMAS ABROAD

September 1879   To Leipzig, by way of Antwerp, Brussels, Stuttgart
1880   Study in Leipzig. Side trips to Italy, Germany, and Austria during holidays
1881   Study in Leipzig. Summer in England and on the continent, as parents and youngest brother and sister join her
1882   Study in Stuttgart and Zürich. Ph.D. received at Zürich, November 1882
1883   London, Paris, Channel Islands. Home to U.S.A. in November

June 7, 1879

My dear Girls,[7]

In Phila. I was so busy that I did not have a moment to write, and besides there was no satisfaction in writing before I was decided about Germany. . . .

7. The "girls" are Mary Garrett and Julia Rogers.

Yes, I can go to Germany if I can live on $600. a year. Grandma [Whitall] offered to help me before I said a word. Mr. Jones's account was the most complete I have yet received. He says there is no difference in a lady being alone, for his wife, who looks as young as I do, stayed there all last year and found no difficulty. He says I can live easily on $600. and probably on much less after I know the "ropes." He also says if I will come with him, he will take me to Leipzig or Hamburg for $80 via National line and first class passage. Of course I cannot and do not wish to go immediately. Julia, what do you think? Will you come?

Mother and Father are away for a week and what with you and Bessie away it seems lonely. Mamie and I are going to console ourselves by the Park Monday. Mrs. Gwinn now says that I am the ringleader of the whole Friday Night, that my going to Cornell started everything. It was in vain Mamie declared you were already steeped in the iniquity of study before you had seen me and appealed to your testimony as to my trying to modify and civilize her (Mamie's) opinions.

I saw a great deal of Mr. Cadbury in Phila. and Thursday afternoon we got caught three miles up the Schoolkill [Schuylkill] in a light rowboat by the most tremendous storm—hail, lightning, thunder, etc. We stayed under a bridge until 8 o'clock when in desperation we started on our three mile row (I had on my gray hat) and reached home drenched of course. He was really splendid, and said among other things (which of course added to his charms) that I had quite as much ability as any man he had met at Harvard. I knew he had had the slenderest opportunity for judging, but (when one is in the depths of melancholy over three years exile from you girls and mother) a straw is snatched at. He sails for Paris on the 13th to live there and in Italy for at least a year. Happy man. He does not have to stay rooted like a vegetable!

No, in my innermost heart I am truly delighted but I did not realize the terrible self control it would take to soberly decide to leave everyone I love for three years. When it seemed uncertain it was much easier. Now, unless Mother and Father lose their resolution, it is sure. . . .

161

If I go I shall probably sail on or before Sept. 1st. I grudge this year to that Harvard examination, because you might almost as well have been in Germany and you may be—married before three years.

I cannot give you warm enough congratulations upon the result of the Harvard examinations.[8] I do not know when I have been so delighted as when Julia wrote me about it. It was splendid, Mary, to do so well when you were feeling as you were. I suppose I am sorry for the other girls, but I am so glad you and Julia were the only ones who passed in all you tried. Our Friday night group should crown you and Julia with laurel when we meet. . . .

Devise some plan for freedom on your voyage over. At least I shall expect you to radiate the new culture and help you have obtained during your reprieve. Till then, and in fact whether you do or not. . . .

[To Mary Garrett]

[No postmark]
Thursday, June 12, 1879
. . . My going away is even surer than when I last wrote because Father and I had one tremendous talk over it, he saying he could not stand it, that it was wrong to let me go alone, that it was horrible to think of the anxiety of knowing I was out of reach and help if anything happened, etc. Mother threw herself into the breach and took the whole responsibility of my going and afterwards Father was lovely. It made me see even with Father's liberality how tremendous a sacrifice it is for him to let me go—sacrifice of paternal responsibility, authority, traditional feeling about women, etc. Mary, before I die one book shall be written to try to protest against the misery and oppression of a girl's life. There ought to be invectives like those of the French Revolution and we must all try and work there. If we can do nothing else, by influence and writing we can help, if ever so little, to change things for succeeding generations of girls. . . .

8. In 1873 the Women's Education Association of Boston prevailed on Harvard to offer examinations similar to those extended earlier to women at Cambridge and London universities. See *Old and New*, Vol. 8, p. 371.

Atlantic City, N.J.
July 24, 1879

My dear Mary,

As my postal told you Aunt Hannah has decided not to go. I received your letter to Mamie and myself which was very nice if it was not necessary as a goodbye. Your letter to which I promised an answer is *not* a very nice one, please—it is so general and has so little of *you* in it and you see if I am to be separated for three years from all you girls we must write intimate letters or I shall come home an alien to you all. . . .

Nothing has passed since I wrote except some glorious baths and sails and talks with Prof. Corson of Cornell who is here. He is a man I could talk to for a month at a time and in these few hours has explained me poems, taught me things about verse and men that would have taken me a long while to work out. Father and Mother half disapprove and are half amused at our intimacy. Oh Mary if we had a few such men in Balto! He is going to read "Maud" for us this evening in Grandma's parlor. . . .

Father received the nicest imaginable letters from Pres. White this morning promising his assistance to help me enter Berlin if I chose and affirming what we had heard as to Leipzig's being already practically open. . . . I do mind so much going away from you before I feel that I know you half as well as I want to, that I am rather hungry for any chance of seeing you. . . .

[A. D. White[9] to James Carey Thomas]

[holograph]

American Legation
67 Behren Str
Berlin
July 4, 1879

My dear Dr. Thomas,

Thank you for your kind letter of June 20th just received. It will give us all very great pleasure to have your

9. In the spring of 1879 President White of Cornell was appointed to Berlin as United States Minister Plenipotentiary.

daughter and her friends in Germany, and to do all in our power to make their stay here pleasant and profitable.

My judgment is that your daughter, in the Department to which she has devoted herself, could use a year or two in Europe to great advantage. As regards learning German, I think the best way would be to settle down first in some German family to familiarize herself with the language, and then to go where the advantages are greatest for her peculiar studies. As to admittance to lectures, there are some subjects on which ladies are quite freely admitted to lecture rooms. I remember that at the Polytechnikum at Stuttgart ladies attended Professor Lübke's lectures on Art, and probably some of the others, but in general it would make a great uproar if a lady were to go into the lecture rooms of any great University. I have never heard of any lady in a lecture room here, but will take pains to find out whether attendance on any lectures is possible by them.

For students in English literature, Anglo-Saxon, etc. I have an impression that Leipsig is the best place. I know that Kennedy (a graduate of Cornell) selected that University on account of the excellence of the instruction in that department. But allow me to say that I do not much care about the studying of specialities by Americans in Germany and France. English Literature and Philology can be studied to excellent advantage at home, but a familiar acquaintance with the two great languages of Continental Europe is certainly a very valuable acquisition for any lady and that can be obtained only here. While students are thus engaged they can by reading in those languages, attending some lectures, and by travelling add very largely to their general stores of information.

I will look into the matters regarding which you ask more closely and should I learn anything of use to you, will at once inform you. . . .

Yours faithfully,
A.D. White

[A. D. White to James Carey Thomas]

July 5, 1879

My dear Dr. Thomas,

Since writing you yesterday I have more information regarding instruction to ladies at the German Universities. It is hardly likely that a lady would be admitted to the University of Berlin, although it is not impossible. But at Leipsig there is already an American lady, Miss Eva Channing, attending various lectures, among others those of Curtius and Lange. I understand from Professor Buck, who is Professor at the Boston University, that he saw Miss Channing in the lecture room, and that all seemed to go perfectly natural and easily, her coming in attracting no attention. It requires possibly some little fortitude, but it is probable that Miss Channing will remain another year, I understand.

Of course, we would be greatly pleased to have your daughter here, and I would do whatever lies in my power to aid her to enter the University; but in any case Leipsig would seem to be open to her.

As to learning German, it is not a very easy matter to find just the right family with which to live. Still, it is not as very difficult when some little time is taken for it. The main difficulty lies, I think, with the food, which is not the sort generally to which an American girl well brought up is accustomed. But this might be remedied by some special arrangement.

I remain,

Yours faithfully,
A.D. White

[To Anna Shipley]

Atlantic City, N. J.
[No date]

My beloved Zac,

At last a letter. How many wretched letters, business letters, have I now written within the last month—letters about Germany, escorts, letters to dressmakers and coat-

165

makers and hatters and steamer men—and yet no letter to thee. I waited a week or so to tell thee definitely about my plans. It is arranged now. We sail the 22nd of August with a large party of Beavers whom we know of and who will be a safe escort to Stuttgart. "We," I say, for wonder of wonders, Mamie Gwinn is going with me. Her doctor and herself accomplished it and even now they may bear her off the vessel but as far as being all ready and partially packed before she goes to Niagara counts for she is going.

However that may be, I am going certainly. And Anna, now that it is all arranged, I am melancholy to the last degree—to leave Mother and home and all of you girls for three years is not realized until one is within a month of it as I am. No, I am sure it is best and right, but one cannot help having roots, even the most would-be philosophical person.

I follow mother around and am unhappy with her because I know I shall so soon be hopelessly away from her but being yet more unhappy away from her. I am lounging away my days—the days that ought to be devoted to German—looking at her. . . .

[To Mary Garrett and Julia Rogers]

[No date]

. . . Julia, while battening in the delightful Mercantile Library in Philadelphia I came across a book that contained some useful and interesting information on marriage than we have ever yet found. The book is clarion peal to lead all to purity. The mere fact of such libraries are an enlargement after our Peabody. . . .

Girls, it wakes me up every time I go to Phila. We get in grooves and think that because we are circumscribed, no earnest work is being done. I saw some of the Cornell girls and heard of all those I knew most intimately hard at work—girls and men—at law, political history, philology, art, etc. Even the comparatively stupid are *working*. We are cursed by a dull show of refinement and custom, which forcibly stops the moving springs of power. We can and must wrench ourselves free. . . .

[To Mary Garrett and Julia Rogers]

August 18, 1879

Your letter came just after I had been dreaming about you all night—or at least it seemed like all night—and now though there is only a little time I must write you a few words for there will probably be no other chance. . . . Today I went to my last Meeting and it almost upset me because both Father and Mother prayed and every word was meant for me, I know. They are both as nice as possible about my going and I am so repentant and sorry that even when Father in a talk—the only one he and Mother have had with me—told me he was sure I was a Christian if I would only realize and confess it I—SAID NOTHING. There was no use. . . .

Mother and I have been talking and sewing all mornings. You would be surprised to see how fast I have learned and I must confess it has been a real pleasure. In the afternoon I drive mother in the phaeton. I have had her all to myself as Frank and Nell are the only ones at home, though Harry has returned now. He is threatening to adopt an elder sister. I tell him he can take one of you if he will promise only to see you once a month—Julia, will you accept him?

I must tell you about Mamie, I suppose. I had not seen her since Tuesday when I had too bad a headache to remember anything she said. Yesterday I stopped there and found her looking absolutely worse than I have ever seen her. She had not been unwell since July 5th or longer and it seems that in the midst of my headache I had recommended a hot bath which Mamie accordingly tried Thursday night. At 3 a.m. that night she was taken with violent cramps which lasted five hours. Dr. Smith quieted her with opium but she was violently ill and of course has subsisted on beef tea ever since. All the medical books say that it is harmless [a hot bath when one is "unwell"] and Father says that a mere hot bath could not have caused it. . . .

She says Mrs. Gwinn is lovely and only says such things as this: "Mamie darling this is the last Saturday we shall probably ever spend together," and when I think that my only salvation is having nothing of that kind said, I do not see how Mamie can hold out (in health, I mean). Even now, though her trunks are all packed, I do not feel certain she will go. She may be sick at the last moment and if going is almost too much for me what must it be for Mamie who is so delicate? Personally it will be a very great, terrible, disappointment; how great I did not realize until yesterday. And then to leave her to that life!!! . . .

After tea—in my nightgown 10:45 p.m. Mother and I had the nicest talk this evening, indeed we have had all along and if I am to go I am going with the very memories of all others I would wish. Only Mamie—I know it does not trouble you to talk to you about her—I am utterly unhappy about her if she stays, and if she goes I cannot possibly help feeling that it is my fault if she should die or anything, in addition to the terrible grief it would be. Father considers her his only opening now and begs me to wait at least till next summer but of course I cannot feel it best. He asked Mother the other night if she thought I would stay if I were suddenly converted—Mother said "No" so there is no other hope [for him] but Mamie left . . . . Suppose Mamie should be sick at the time of sailing, ought I to wait or go? But she won't be, and of course I should wait if her will were still firm, though I doubt if this be not her one chance. . . .

Steamer *Vaderland*
Sunday August 31, 1879

My dear Mary,

You have taken a sure way of getting a steamer letter. Even if you had not said you wanted one, human nature even amid the laziness of this laziest of all imaginable lives, could but be generous enough to acknowledge your delightful fruit. Every night we have a fruit supper perched on the edge of our berths in our nightgowns and though Mamie expostulates, between grapes, as to the unhealthiness of eating at all times and at that time in

The Girl Friends: left to right, M. Carey Thomas, Julia Rogers, Mamie Gwinn (seated), Bessie King (standing), and Mary Garrett

particular, even her stoicism quails before your pears and peaches and grapes. It was so kind in you to think of it, Mary—it has made the greatest difference in our happiness for to tell the truth as we have neither of us had an hour's sickness, we have turned into true animals—we live to eat. All Mamie's principles have vanished—I don't dare to remark upon it for fear of their appearing again but I secretly rejoice as I see her crunching the bones of squabs and pigeons "those small birds of which such a large number are killed to satisfy man's cruel appetite when one ox would suffice." . . . There is no one on board except young Miss Beaver and her two cousins, a Miss Taas and a Mr. Smith who are neither relations nor engaged and who are going to study music in Berlin and Leipzig respectively and yet who are travelling together and very devoted, a Miss Miley who is going alone to Dresden, young and pretty and who flirts with the handsome young ship doctor, a nameless youth of nineteen, who are at all available, and all of these romp so—and though not really loud or fast, are thoroughly objectionable. They allow the Captain and the doctor and Mr. Smith and the nameless youth whom they all call "Mr." to handle them in a way that scandalizes Mamie and therefore much amuses me, as I *had* a conception that such possibilities existed. So as Mamie and I can't enter upon that fooling we are delightfully free and sit all day side by side in our sea chairs or walk up and down or stand and look at the sunset. We have plenty of books and have read *Jane Eyre* (and tell Julia, Mamie more than agrees with me—the passion makes one sick). . . .

[To Mary Garrett]

Steamer *Vaderland*
September 2, 1879

The foregoing letter was so unsatisfactory as a letter to *you* as I discovered when half way through, that I changed its character, put a heading to it, etc. So long as I had gone into such stupid particulars there was no use of tearing them up or rewriting them—ergo:

Now I have so little time and then too I have lost your letter which for more reasons than one distresses me very much, so you must take an answer from memory.

Your letter was a very nice one but I am greedily discontented to have missed your other note, i.e. if you write it. I believe—September third we land.

[To Mary Garrett]

September 3, 1879

We land tomorrow and England is in sight. It is like enchantment to be so near it. . . . Before I do anything else, though, I must clear myself. For five years I have said nothing in the least insincere to Carrie. I have always had a strong friendship for her. I am so glad you saw a little how brave she is. I don't know anyone who struggles so hard and under such disadvantages—all last winter when she was worn out from singing and school she forced herself to read Eng. Lit. and really and truly seeing me is the greatest pleasure she has. Mary, I think I took away the comfort she used to have in being an earnest Christian too. You girls care for Jenny and *you* spent time with Lettie Williams, and Julia and you go to see Bertha, and yet you find fault with me for keeping up my friendship with Carrie and Miss Hicks. Libbie, except that one week she spent with me and which politeness forced me to ask her for, I have done with. I write about every five months and then not one insincere word. Carrie I *am* friends with and she has every claim which loving one really dearly can give. As to Miss Hicks, I never do and have not for a long while, indeed never, written such letters as you might think. I only receive them. I told her before I became friends with her that it was certain I should not care after I left Cornell, that it would only be because I wanted some one to be fond of and that we were really uncongenial.

She said she wanted my friendship on any terms. For this same reason I refused twice to visit her but the last year I thought it too outrageous and went. I found as I had expected that though as far as innate refinement goes

171

Miss Hicks was a perfect lady, they lived in a different way from any I had been accustomed to. And I thereupon made up my mind that drop Miss Hicks I would not, until she had visited me, and until quite naturally it ended.

As far as mere cleverness is concerned she is the equal of any girl I know. She is working earnestly at her architecture and reads all her spare time and really except that she is in a little different circle and that I know now and knew before other girls whom I care more for, there is no reason for being unkind. I *shall* write less and less often—mere necessity enforces that.

Please, Mary, I care for your approval and I don't want you to think of me exactly as you do—about friendships. Except with Libbie and then I was just fifteen I have never been deceived, I knew exactly how much friendship I had for Miss Hicks even when I was rather in love with her. I should never let myself be placed in that situation again. I see how unfair it is when a girl gives you friendship—her deepest friendship and love—"adores the very ground you tread on" as Miss Hicks told me once, etc. and you give in return the privilege of amusing you for two years and of being cared about strictly during that time. No punishment can be as severe as the one I have, but I do want to try to bear the unpleasantness myself because she has not been to blame. Even when I do behave with the caution of a Solomon I am not better off.

Tell Julia that I received two letters from Miss Clements imploring me to let her know when I sailed so she could bid me goodbye again for a few minutes and though I was in Phila. a day before—I just went off (being utterly unable to endure an interview and having no excuse that would seem reasonable to her to give) without even writing a word. . . .

Mary, I wanted to explain this once and then not trouble you about it again. But whether you consider my friendship a compliment or not it is too sincere to be taken away for any such reason. . . . Oh Mary there is nothing else to say, you have been through it, you know how impossible it is even to get a letter finished at sea and as far as thoughts and books they spin themselves out through an eternity. If you were here—but you aren't here—so please, just telling you how much I cared about your letter and how much I shall care about them, I must stop. I think you know everything I could say. If you think I do not write as often as I want to, you will know it is because of time and not one hour of this three years shall be idle if I can help it—Please tell Julia her *letter,* her farewell note, was rather amusingly formal, was just like her and almost as nice and as much "fun" as she herself is and that I shall answer it soon . . . please write when you can.

[Steamer *Vaderland*]
4 p.m. Sixth Day [1879]

My Dearest Mother,[1]

We have all our trunks checked and the checks in my pocket book and our stateroom trunks in our stateroom and are sitting writing in our sea chairs with our stylographic pens which work to perfection. It is after lunch, which consisted of cold roast beef, tongue, ham, pickled salmon, raw tomatoes, bread and butter, roast potatoes and champagne, corned beef and a curious red peppery stuff which we think is sauerkraut. The Beavers fill one division and two men, Mamie and I, and an old German woman whom the Beavers are taking over with them to teach them German, and a young Beaver, Willie—about twelve [years old] sit at the other.

Mr. and Mrs. Beaver and all the young ladies are very pleasant. Miss Chamberlain is the nicest, she I like already. "Stewart and Minnie" are opposite us which is also nice. Stewart always looks up when the steward is called, which causes amusement. It was most fortunate Mr. Gwinn came down as otherwise our baggage would never have gotten off. He was most attentive and both he and Mamie cried. Mr. Gwinn bid me goodbye most affectionately (he kissed me) and Mamie and he waved till the ship

---

1. This letter to her mother and those which immediately follow, dated through October 1879, were found in a notebook, in her mother's handwriting. The originals (which were probably circulated) have not been found.

was out of sight. It was dreadful seeing the last of you and I sat trying to recover my composure for a half an hour and then talked to the Beavers and the little children. . . .

Mr. Gwinn was so disturbed when Mr. Beaver told him he was going to travel a month before going to Stuttgart that I acted as if we had expected that contingency, and said we would stay with them in Antwerp and telegraph for Johanne.[2] He was *perfectly* satisfied. Now—this is my plan—to send our trunks by express as the Captain said, and telegraph Johanne to send someone to meet us at Mayence, or whatever is the nearest place to Stuttgart. Then we will go to Brussels with the Beavers; he is going right there after a day in Antwerp, and there get on the Rhine steamer, and from thence it is straight sailing. Both Mamie and I feel as well as possible. This steamer is charming, you can do just as you please, and the Beavers are most free and easy . . . I am appreciating the *fun*. I do not believe we shall be sick. . . . Everyone, steward and stewardess are most polite, and one of the midshipmen, the one who handed us these chairs, has taken such a fancy to me that he hunted out and carried up *our* state-room trunks and box and basket of fruit, and the Beavers are storming about not having gotten theirs yet. . . .

Johanne's letter says she was in the Tyrol when our letter came, that she cannot take us as the rules are everyone must come for a year; she deprecates my hardi-hood in thinking I can get along and says if we come to Stuttgart she will find us a place to board where we can hear German. . . . I do thank you for giving me the desire of my heart. It is the fulfillment of all my dreams to be really on the steamer, and from where we are sitting out of sight of land. . . . With dear love to the children and the very dearest to thee and father. Send this to Grandma.

2. Johanne's last name is probably Mühlenbruch. She appears to have been an acquaintance of the Shipleys and evidently taught in or ran a school. The use of her first name indicates that she may have been known to the Thomases in the capacity of a governess, or (as we would now call her) an "au pair." Later, she is referred to as "Joan."

Steamer *Vaderland*
August 29, 1879

My dearest Darling Mother,

The reasons why I have not written before have been many and various. . . . First and most important neither Mamie nor I have had an hour's seasickness but we have had other trials commencing the moment we finished our pilot letters. We then went down to unpack and had just tacked up our curtain . . . when in upon us sitting in confusion puzzling over francs and lira, etc. came the conviction that seasickness was fast coming unless we went on deck. . . . The consequence was that during the next three days during which it was very warm and most of the time it poured in addition, we were in despair over the disorder and the impossibility of finding anything . . . the horrid discomfort of heat and smells below, and soaking rains above—why the rain just swept across the deck in sheets and all around us the hot gulf stream—until Fourth Day it cleared up and I got well and since everything has been delightful. Mamie and I have a tremendous appetite and Mamie's last scruples have vanished—she eats squabs on toast with gusto. . . .

We have plenty to read and I am trying German in good earnest. There are several German novels here and also George Sand's *Consuela* in the three volumes of which both Mamie and I are involved. It is the most delightful life imaginable, and so lazy, you just sit all day long in your sea chair and watch the sea which has been mostly the bluest blue and keep an eye for Miss B's [Beaver's] improprieties while you turn the pages of your novel. Old Mr. B. is seasick and hardly ever on deck. He seems to be in chronic bad humor. He says he hates travelling and here he is off on a two years' trip. Mrs. B. lies in her stateroom most of the time, and the coast is clear for the younger Beavers. There are [also] Miss Stuart and Miss Taas, musical, whom a Mr. Smith, also musical, waits on. . . . They are no relation, not engaged, but very devoted. Mamie and I consider it improper for them to travel together, but no one else seems to. Then there is a

175

pretty Miss Miley who is going all by herself to Dresden, a stray boy of nineteen who has introduced himself and is devoted to Miss Minnie Beaver, a very handsome young ship's doctor, and of course Mrs. Chamberlain and five children make up the number of passengers. Miss B. is jolly and handles everyone on board except us at her pleasure. She puts her hands on the Captain's shoulders, walks under the same shawl with the doctor, holds Mr. Smith's hand and so on. Mamie is horribly shocked and amuses me very much. We talk to them some, but of course don't romp with them.

So many funny things have happened that I tell Mamie her dimple will be a hole clear through to the other side when we return. She is full of fun and could not be better. Among some other misfortunes she has torn buttons off her waists, torn her coat, ripped out the kilt plaits of her silk dress. The other morning I waked up and saw her lying back on the floor among dresses and shoes holding a waist out at arm's length sewing a button on without a thimble. I believe she would rather have stayed at home than take care of her clothes, and is looking towards shopping for a seamstress the moment we get to Stuttgart. I have been much more fortunate by dint of following Mary's directions and have torn nothing. Among Mamie's other misfortunes she discovered she was wearing an ulster not her own. Hers was seal brown, this is a black with a red stripe. When and how she exchanged we neither of us know, and Mamie is rather disconcerted as she "hates a red stripe particularly."

[To Mother]

Vaderland
September 1, 1879

It is the most ideal day and today Mamie and I are so sorry that our voyage is almost over. Fourth Day we were in the English Channel and Fifth Day night at Antwerp. We sleep that night on the boat, and then we are going to stay with Mr. Beaver some days in Antwerp. Our plan is to leave the Beavers at Cologne. . . . But you will receive this after we have reached Stuttgart and unless it be too expensive, you will have received a telegram. I feel perfectly capable of managing the whole journey if we had it to take—it seems such an ordinary thing for girls to travel alone, e.g. Miss Miley. Mamie is in perfect health and such splendid company. We talk German most of the time now, and Johanne's letter to the contrary, I know I shall have no trouble after the first few weeks. Mamie has fits of sorrow on Mrs. Gwinn's account, and I think if she lets herself think of her, would be very melancholy. . . .

[To Mother]

September 3, 1879

Land! Land! Land! We are three miles from Lizard Point Cornwall and the bare cliffs show as distinctly as possible—houses where there are any and sail boats by twenties. It is like enchantment to feel between England and France. I cannot describe the fun it is. . . . A soft violet mist hangs over the cliffs and our own bright day of America is gone, and over us is a blue so faint it is almost gray. . . .

They [the Beavers] have been very nice. . . only they are hopelessly uncultivated. Mr. and Mrs. Beaver and Mrs. C. constitute the unexceptional part of the party. Of course they are going to stay at the most expensive hotel in Antwerp but we are so delighted to be able to see the pictures there that we don't complain. Mr. Beaver says we can have no possible trouble on the Rhine and for Mrs. Gwinn's sake we are going to telegraph for Johanne to meet us, or send some one to meet us at the nearest point, and as we shall explain our difficulty, and of course pay her expenses I am sure she will. . . .

[To Mother]

September 4, 1879

We have passed Dover . . . both Mamie and I had imagined the chalk cliffs so much whiter than they are, and so much higher, but the castle on the bluff overlooking the town looked just right and consoled us. . . .

177

[To Mother]

Antwerp
Hotel St. Antoine
September 5, 1879

... Here we are in Antwerp. ... Dutch streets, tiled houses that one could almost shake hands out of with one in the windows on the other side, and curious bonnets and men in blue blouses and women in short bright petticoats and white stockings and slippers. It is exactly as we imagined it—everything. The hotel is entirely too gorgeous and so full that we are all waiting in a little parlor till they get our rooms ready ... will write again from Cologne. ... I often and often think of thee Mother darling, and thy beggars and accounts and wish I could be with thee, but it makes my eyes fill with tears to write sentiment. ... Do give my love to everyone and especially my darling Harry and Nell. Nothing could equal the extra politeness we have met with so far for being ladies. With dearest love to father and thyself, ...

Hotel St. Antoine
Antwerp
September 7, 1879

My dearest Father and Mother,

The cathedral clock has just chimed 10 p.m. I am writing in a quaint little room in the fourth story by the light of two tallow candles which Mamie and I purchased (three for ten cents) stuck in the inkstand and candlestick respectively. Mamie is sound asleep in a high bed with a curved head and foot board and a white linen canopy ... a bed likewise arranged is against the wall on the other side and between is a large round table where I am writing. A curious low washstand holding two pitchers and basins, with odd shelves behind and underneath, a round bulging cabinet which holds our clothes, four chairs, a spittoon, an immense wooden boot jack and a ridiculous rack to put a waiter's tray like the one we have in the dining room, completes the furniture. Add to this a faded Turkey carpet, paper with odd little red and blue spots, and a window six feet high and broad opening in the middle by two glass doors made of little panes and looking out upon a square court set round with plants and dining tables and you have before you the cunningest little room just like the one Goethe's Gretchen occupied. . . .

Such enjoyment these last three [days] have been—through tiled roofs and crooked streets filled with little Flemish babies in the brightest and shortest of little blue blouses, clattering around playing horse and catcher in their little wooden shoes. The pavements are generally a foot wide, so everyone walks in the street—women in bright purple and blue and red dresses reaching scarcely below their knees, and stockings generally striped green and yellow with the foot and ankle some solid color and darned on the heel with a patch of the brightest scarlet which shows at every step as the wooden shoes reach the pavement. . . . They either wear muslin or white dimity caps, and all knit as they walk—always stockings . . . and running here and there among the people are dogs—sometimes six, sometimes four, sometimes one harnessed to carts of all sizes, mostly though milk carts filled with bright brass cans. You mostly see four dogs abreast the size of Madge Nicholson's coach dog, trotting along as merrily as can be. At every tenth house, which on account of the sharp turns of the streets comes sidewise like the YMCA, is a Madonna or a Christ in plaster of gilt built into the corner with a canopy over its head and sometimes a taper before it. . . . Every open place is filled with old women knitting and offering for sale immense posies of tulips and some large white and red flowers—no bouquet is less than a foot in diameter. . . . All [of] Hans Anderson and fairy tales are realized. Mamie and I have wandered over almost the whole of it in search of different churches and can find our way very nearly as well as Baltimore. . . .

The people speak French but can't understand German, and Mamie is perfectly at home and I find no difficulty. There are innumerable churches—six at least besides the Cathedral, full of old Masters, mostly Van Dyck and Rubens, and all rich and curious . . . and the Museum . . . yards of Rubens and Van Dycks, one Titian and one Fra Angelico, two Giottos, four or five Murillos and the quaint old Flemish painters of 1400 and later who are so sweet and funny that I could spend hours over one picture. . . .

Mamie is a terrible companion, she sits and munches innumerable rolls—seven one morning, with perfect contentment when two literally make me sick. Not having had her years of practice in bread eating, consequently I fare much worse. Today we both concluded never to touch another currant bun however. The B's are very kind but as they hate pictures we see nothing of them except at dinner. They throw away money in royal style and drink unlimited wine. . . .

[Antwerp]
Morning September 8, 1879

Great hurry starting for [Brussels]. So many funny things have happened I will tell you next time—and fleas! I have twenty great bites . . . camphor after one bite is a comfort. One bed is so infested that Mamie and I have fled to the other—a single bed in which we both sleep. All this letter from Antwerp and not one word about the Cathedral where we heard the most glorious high Mass . . . they have chairs with broad pieces on their backs on which you put your elbows as you kneel on the chair, and Mamie and I perforce devoutly kneeled as the Host went by with the tinkling of silver bells and incense. Rubens' "Descent from the Cross" more than fulfills my expectations. . . . We went all through a house of the year 1550 that has been kept untouched, and also through the old Antwerp castle where the Inquisition was held and saw the dreadful dungeons and tortures. After all, though there is the other side to Catholicism, yet Art can never pay its debt to it for its cathedrals and lovely madonnas and Christs. If I wanted to convert a skeptic I should send him to Europe. . . .

Mamie is in perfect health and we get along perfectly. She is really white—her jaundice seems to have disappeared. And *fat!* I feel as if I were repaid just by Antwerp. I do thank you so much for even this and for the three years of study and pleasure that are coming. I hope you don't miss me too much, but except for being without the sense of a "heathen Greek" as Julia says, sitting upstairs, I am afraid you don't. Our expenses at Antwerp for three days and three quarters were hotel $6., guide books and extras $3.35 so it is not too expensive, you see. I never got so much pleasure out of $10 before. . . .

Brussels Hotel
September 14, 1879

My dearest Mother,

. . . We arrived yesterday the 13th, were met by Joan's lady teachers and driven to Moserstrasse 12 where in the prettiest little library surrounded with busts and filled with books and engravings Joan received us most warmly. Owing to the telegram not arriving before two guests of "Misses Grüneisen," three stately maiden ladies who are to receive us, they were not ready, so at great inconvenience I am afraid, Fräulein Prenzel gave us her room which is right opposite Joan's and this morning, Sept. 14th, we are writing in it, having just eaten breakfast Joan sent across to us. . . .

Joan said Mrs. Gwinn had written to her. She seems to think she knows of a lovely house in Leipzig and a number of introductions to give us but we do not yet clearly understand. . . . Joan is cultivated and comfortable and altogether jolly. We are so sorry she cannot take us. She says every room is full and her parlor boarders engage their rooms three or four months beforehand. . . .

Later 11 a.m.

Here we are temporarily settled in a room that is not ours, in the Grüneisen's. Two of them we have seen and they are rather prim but very kind and are going to talk to us all the time we wish. . . . The trunks will arrive Tuesday. . . . President White was right about Stuttgart, it is beautifully situated. The town lies in a basin and all the more handsome houses and villas are built up the hills on all sides. The King's palace is in the centre of the town with charming grounds and a beautiful park. . . . Joan's and Fräulein Grüneisen's are far up on one of the hills and have a charming view. Nothing could be more satisfactory . . . except the expense, probably $40 or $50 for our month, but Joan says it is well worth it to get started in such cultivated German and to meet the people we shall meet here. She says we shall learn more than six months in an ordinary family who pay no attention to our German. Joan treats us amusingly like children, as she does everyone else, teachers and all. She arranges and orders people around in the most good humoured and brightest way. She says we can travel alone everywhere, especially in Switzerland, that it is most common, which brings me to our journey here. I think you will admit that we have piloted ourselves with a success that deserves further fields of action.

We were a day and a night with the B's at Brussels and it is not very interesting. It is so modern and fashionable, like Paris I suppose. The Wiertz Museum was the most wonderful thing there. A very peculiar man named Wiertz painted the pictures for his own pleasure, and one picture is marvelous—the canvas covers the whole side of a room and represents Christ's head against the background of the cross. . . Satan is like a wonderfully beautiful, defiant, half man half woman, with floating dark hair. There are also awful pictures of dead men, and at one place you look through a hole in the wall and there is a man apparently buried alive and struggling to get out of his coffin. Mamie says a lady she knew of looked in and went crazy for years.

From Brussels we went to Cologne. Mr. B. said we could have no difficulty and recommended us an hotel. We met two charming English old maids who told us of one near the station . . . it seems perfectly a matter of course for girls to travel alone and indeed much more so than in America, for all the first, second, and third class cars have separate carriages for ladies alone. We reached Cologne at four o'clock Fourth Day afternoon and spent the time till supper in the Cathedral. In my wildest imagination I never imagined anything so beautiful. I could have spent a week there feeling the "dim religious light" and the wonderful shooting arches that were so high and

182

yet so perfectly proportioned. . . . And the Rhine! . . . And castles! . . . Frankenberg near Aix-la-Chapelle where we stopped over a few hours was ideal. It was a castle of Charlemagne's and the lonely tower stands in a tangled wood of trees and moss and ivy surrounded by a moat of stagnant water of the deepest green slime. Therein his wife Fastrada dropped her magic ring and after her death Charlemagne sat there for months and mourned. The day before we visited it a peasant woman fell in the moat and was drowned. . . .

Stuttgart
September 16, 1879

My dearest Mother,

Now at last we are settled in our room, writing. . . . The Grüneisens live on a flat in what we would call the second story, but here they call it the first. They have a kitchen, parlor, dining room and library opening out on a dear little porch with an awning and table where they sit, and three other bedrooms besides ours—stairs go downstairs to the street and upstairs to a balcony that leads into the most German garden extending up to a street that runs along the top of the hill. It belongs to all the different flats, and each family has its separate part and summer house and every part is a mass of green trees, grass vines, and a great deal of crimson Virginia creeper here called "wild vine."

Mamie and I passed a delightful morning yesterday reading German in the arbor. From our having to ascend from the second story to get into the garden, you can see how steeply the hill slants. Our windows look right out on it—a sloping wall of green. Stuttgart lies right at the bottom of a cauldron and is the prettiest little city I have ever seen. They say it is called the Florence of Germany . . . . I can give you a much better idea of the family now . . . all genius and brilliancy are centered in Fräulein Mathilde, the companion of her father, the writer of reviews for the Athenaeum, the correspondent for German papers, the intimate friend of Lübke, the corrector of his manuscripts, the friend of Prof. Ebers, Sanscrit prof. in Leipzig, the former intimate of Schleirmacher, etc., etc., etc. She is the most thoroughly well educated woman I have ever seen. Art is her "leibling" (darling) as she says, and from Lübke's consulting her so much from the way she talks it must be. Philosophy she also knows from having read it with her father. . . . She says Strauss had an almost unbounded philosophical influence until the "old and New Faith" appeared which ruined his reputation. Hartmann is now the reigning influence.

She knows all our American reviews even to the *Galaxy,* indeed she knows entirely too much about America, and submits it to us for confirmation, much to our confusion as we have never even heard of much. . . . The disgust, politely concealed though it was, when we could not describe California! They have a curious custom of shaking hands before each meal—each separately and each says *"guten Mahlzeit"* this is four times a day . . . . Fräulein [Mathilde] reads to us some of Lübke's Art lectures to accustom our ear to the University lectures and talks to us about it afterwards. She seems thoroughly interested and is going to invite a Prof. who is librarian here to tea to talk over plans with us and also I believe the American Consul Mr. Potter whom she is intimate with. She says Curtius[3] of Leipzig is the great friend of the women and that it would be a great help could we have an introduction to him. Could not Father when he writes to Prof. Child for an introduction to Bernhardt ten Brink ask if Goodwin knows the Curtius at Leipzig, or perhaps Gildersleeve does. . . . Fräulein Ida is decidedly the least nice [of the Grüneisens] but she is the story teller of the family and tells funny stories of which I sometimes miss the point, and a question discloses my depth of ignorance. . . . Every spare moment I am reading Art. . . .

3. **Georg** Curtius (1820-1885), leader of the conservative school of philology according to Carey Thomas. He was professor of philology and classical languages in Leipzig, and according to published sources pioneered in basing classical philology on comparative philology.

[Stuttgart]
September 27th [1879]

[To Mother]

... Tomorrow is the great Volksfest—a yearly fair for the whole of Wirtenburg. The King and Queen, Crown Prince of Sweden and Prince of Weimar and the court will all be there. We have gotten tickets for the grandstand. . . . The slavish adoration of the Kaiser and Bismarck is absolutely degrading. The Grüneisens know at exactly what hour he is precisely at what place, and the weather is discussed each morning with reference to the reviews he may be holding. They have three times rapturously told us of a great occasion on which they were "as near to the Kaiser as that tree there." Also from the time we entered the Rhinish provinces, those charming provinces snatched from France, busts and statues of the Emperor and Bismarck burst upon our view—even the curtains of the steam cars had the Kaiser's crown stamped upon them . . . [his] bust is always laurel crowned and with the fierce marble moustaches has the effect of a tiger's head. The paternal government descends into the least particulars—every servant maid and mistress must register their names and are bound to their engagements. The instant a person dies and always within the hour comes his imperial majesty's officers and seal up everything, down to each handkerchief and pencil. Until a month they remain so when the court adjudges the effects to the rightful heirs. They tell amusing stories of families left in such utter destitution that even money and clothes had to be borrowed from their friends until the month was up. . . . If Mamie or I were to die, you would have to come over to rescue our things from that red seal or appoint some representative here or in Leipzig. . . . The present King William of Wirtenberg washes the whole upper part of his body in Cologne and changes his entire apparel six times daily. His groom of the chamber has to wear different colored trousers each hour of the day, and the king is in a horrid humor all day if the color be not chosen appropriately to the hour and weather. Fräulein Mathilde asked

185

the first gentleman if this were true, and he answered, "only too true." Their father was in favor of a united Germany and this displeased the present king, who dismissed him from his first chaplainship. The Kaiser after the union had been effected invited him to Berlin to take the position of first court Chaplain but Karl Grüneisen refused on account of his age. . . .

Did I tell you of the overpowering strength of family ties in Germany, at least here, and of its curious manifestation in busts and reliefs? The Grüneisens have their father as a young man—marble bust—as an old man—marble relief. They have his cast taken from his face after death, and the other day showed us his hand in plaster—a splendid nervous hand it was too. They have their brother taken in Rome—a life size bust, their mother, cap, frills and all. Their brother's wife, life size bust, and two mysterious little life size baby busts; the babies are certainly not a week old and stand side by side, each in little frilled dresses under a glass case on a stand in the dining room. We are consumed with curiosity but do not dare to ask. . . . You cannot imagine anything more ridiculous than this baby nothingness of expression being perpetuated in marble. . . .

We have our times, Mamie and I, but they are generally nice ones, only it is a trial having this one little room. . . . of course everything is always lost but now I make it my duty to remember where everything is and am Mamie's index. . . .

We went to Joan's school Second Day and heard her teach her teachers' class—(eighteen girls from ages twenty onwards and very ugly) history. First one girl read an essay upon Ludwig the Bavarian, then Joan made each member criticize it. The remaining half hour she delivered a most impassioned lecture upon the history of the time—plague etc. She is a capital teacher, tell Anna, most splendid. . . .

Just back from *Volksfest* which was a fraud—no king, no queen, no crown prince, no peasants, only a Prince Weimar and some prize cows and a crowd. . . .

Stuttgart
[No date, 1879]

My dearest Father and Mother,

. . . You must imagine us every day between four and seven taking walks. . . . They walk so fast here and then put the final drop of gall in our cup by apologizing for not being able to walk as fast as the Americans, whereas we are always out of breath. Mamie's appetite is increasing . . . . Our meals continue quite as nice, everything is most delicately cooked. All German girls at eighteen after they have finished their education, serve an apprenticeship of three months in some public hotel in order to learn the most delicate modes of cooking. Fräulein Mathilda as an especial favor was taken into the Palace kitchen. From 9 to 12 and From 2 till 7 she used to stand by the head cook and watch. Is it not a curious custom? I don't believe even Grandma would approve of such a severe training. . . .

Fräulein M. took us to talk over plans with Herr Prof. Winterlin, the royal librarian here, and he was most kind in advising us what courses to take. He says as yet Leipzig is closed on the matter of degrees, but that it prides itself upon being the most advanced of all the universities, and in three years it may be possible. A lady has already tried for a degree there but there were only three voices in her favor. Zürich of course is open. Fräulein Mathilda has also talked over the matter with Mr. Potter, the American Consul, who says he received a distinct refusal from the Dean of the University in the case of two other American ladies and that we ought to go unofficially. Best of all Fräulein M. has written to her friend Prof. Ebers in Leipzig (author of all those German novels that have been such a success—*The Egyptian King's Daughter, Homo Sum,* and *Uarda)* to ask him if he knows of any pleasant, cultivated family where we can get rooms in the third story and provide our own breakfasts and suppers and eat dinner with the family. She says that is much the best as it gives us so much more time to study. . . .

Often and often I cannot realize that I am in Germany—everything is so homelike and it seems as if I had all my life heard German spoken. You cannot imagine how easy everything is. The Grüneisens have travelled a great deal alone and they say it is perfectly proper and easy, that except in Vienna we would find no trouble. . . .

> Care Frau Dr. Matzke
> Waisenhaus Strasse 5
> 2nd etge Leipzig
> October 2, 1879

Dearest Mother,

There is our address in full as it will be after the 15th Oct., indeed before you receive this. We have spent two days in letters and telegrams from which we have extricated ourselves with great wisdom. . . . Thy letter, dearest mother, only this morning—it was written on the 15th and took eighteen days whereas Mamie received one from Mrs. Gwinn written the 17th. After her *ship* letter had arrived. Thee must *always* put on "via Queenstown," it makes two or three days difference. Only four children at home—how charming—how I wish I were there to enjoy the sufficiency but not satiety. . . . I have never been so happy. I am sure three years in Germany will make the greatest difference in my whole power of work. I feel waked up to a new life and we are not yet in Leipzig.

Received a letter from President White today enclosing two introductions to Prof. Curtius and to Prof. Ebers, both of whom he knows personally and asking them to introduce me to Prof. Zärncke.[4] He says: "permit me to introduce to yourself and Mrs. Curtius my esteemed friend Miss M. C. T. of Baltimore who goes to Leipzig to continue her studies in Greek and kindred subjects. Miss T. has already pursued a course of four years in Cornell University state of New York with great success. She belongs to one of the most honored families of Baltimore, her father

---

4. Zärncke, whose first name and dates I have not been able to discover, was professor of philology at Leipzig and leader of the "new philology" according to Carey Thomas, who admired his teaching enormously.

being a distinguished physician in that part of the U.S. and a trustee of the new University there—the largest as to endowment in the entire Union. You will find Miss Thomas a noble specimen of an American lady and I commend her to yourself and Madame Curtius, etc." The letter to Prof. Ebers is the same except the personal part. He signs himself in full Minister Plenipotentiary, etc. Fräulein M. says it is most necessary to have such, otherwise I should think of it in rather bad taste. We are now fully equipped. I am sorry Mamie has none but of course it is all one. . . .

I am glad that you miss me a little, Mother darling, but you must think that you have given me the one thing I wanted in the world and best of all it is far nicer than I dreamed—at least so far . . . .

Ber Frau Dr. Matzke
Leipzig
October 17, 1879

My dearest mother,

On the evening of the 15th we arrived, and since it has been too confused to write. On Third Day the 14th at 4:30 a.m. we left Stuttgart. Fräulein Mathilda and Fräulein Louisa went down to the train with us after a nice warm breakfast they insisted upon providing for us. Fräulein Ida cried as we kissed her goodbye and they all seemed heartily sorry. Fr. Mathilda made me give her my picture and in return gave me hers with a little apologetic kiss on my cheek at being so silly. They always kiss cheeks not mouths here. Most of the way to Nuremberg we slept, taking turns at being abed, and at 11 a.m. were in the most delightful picturesque quaint city. . . .

But Leipzig—we reached here at 8 p.m. the 15th, and were met by Frau Dr. Matzke's servant according to arrangement. We found a warm supper awaiting us, an obsequious mother, a cunning little child "Elschen" and Frau Dr. Matzke, a rather pretty woman of about forty entirely too sweet but otherwise obliging. But our rooms!!!!! I never imagined anything so luxurious and charming. To come from that little stuffy hole in Stuttgart into this suite was Paradise. All the furniture looks like rosewood . . . the paint fairly glistens it is so white. The curtains are a sort of lace damask and reach from floor to ceiling and in the parlor blue inside stuff curtains are also added. The windows, two in each room and one in the cabinet, are wide and low and open in two sashes down the middle. The street is wide, and all the houses therein and indeed in Leipzig are gray stones and five stories high. The paper is very pretty in the parlor and here is quite passable . . . about an inch from the windows are other windows—double windows—for warmth . . . .

By four o'clock we had the empty trunks carried out, and retained two which we packed full of clothes we can't use. It seems that unless things are kept in your rooms they are stolen. Poor Mamie, she says such experiences make her wonder if one is justified in leaving a home where all is done for her. She tries her best, and is learning wonderfully, but I always get through my unpacking two or three hours before she does, and I have never had the cruelty to wait and see when she really would be through without my help. It makes me weak with laughter to see Mamie walk industriously round and round the room thinking she is fixing up. We did have a horrible day, but now you cannot tell how pretty everything looks. The rooms leave nothing to be desired. We have plenty of rooms. . . . This is the bright side of the picture—since we have come here two days [ago] we have hardly been able to eat a thing—the bread dirty white brownish stuff very sour, we cannot touch. . . the eggs. . . we have sent away each morning. . . for dinner yesterday greasy soup, some horrid pig meat, potatoes and red cabbage. *All!* . . . we have nasty kitchen steel forks and I really can taste nothing but the brass or tin whatever it is. . . . These may seem little things to you but after two days of it they assume an overwhelming importance. . . .

The University opens the 20th and I hope we shall be so absorbed in the lectures that all these things will sink into nothingness. You must not think we are unhappy in the least—it is only the stern realities of starvation that are depressing. . . .

Mother darling why does thee not write? Thy letter was four days late last week and the week before it came on Second Day and now it is Sixth Day. It makes me anxious. . . . Did I tell thee about the Grüneisen's last company where a thirty year old American Elsie G. Allen who is writing articles on Stuttgart for the *Harper* (they will soon appear)[5] took a great fancy to me and asked me to her room and told me all her history and struggles. Also an officer, sword and spurs and epaulettes and all was there, and was quite agreeable. I quite saw the reason for the feminine penchant for uniform. . . .

With dearest love my own sweet mother to thee and Father and everyone especially Grandma and Aunt Julia.

> Warsinhaus Str. 5, II
> *Bei* Frau Dr Matzke
> Leipzig
> November 2, 1879

My dear Mr. [Richard] Cadbury,

Your letter came yesterday—Now if I had only written as I intended, the day before! I came home from hearing *The Magic Flute,* a very Midsummer Night's Dream in music, and felt moved to write you the most absurdly extravagant letter—aspiration, dreams of work, all that one usually keeps in leash. Yes, I grant you I should have written sooner. But even in "Barbarous Germany" one is so overpowered by impressions—Antwerp, and Rubens; Rubens in all his color and dramatic movement, in all his grossness too, but take him all in all my education had been too puritanical for me not to bow before him for a little while. Then the Cologne Cathedral. I wonder if there

---

5. Elise Allen, "The Weibertrue," *Harper's Magazine,* Vol. 65 (1882), pp. 499-514, is the only article. It gives a history of the ruined castle in Weinsberg (30 miles from Stuttgart) called *Weibertrue* (literally "woman's faithfulness") after a legendary event in the twelfth century when the castle was besieged by the forces of Konrad III, Von Marburg, the Papal Inquisitor. After the wives of wounded and besieged town officials obtained permission to carry away on their backs their most precious possessions, the procession disclosed each wife carrying her own husband.

is such a one in Paris, if not, you have missed an experience. It sucks one like a whirlpool, into its own ethical
feeling. For the first time I *felt* what sent men on the
Crusades and into Monasteries and do you know since I
have come to Germany I have seen that to *feel* a thing is
far beyond knowledge. I think most people know things
(*especially in Germany*) but feeling is the Promethean
spark that inspires works of genius. I should place the
mead of eternity here and not in an ethical system, con-
sistent and positive. It is just because Swinburne and
Tennyson and Morris, nay Rossetti and Gautier and
Baudelaire have not felt strongly enough, have not put
themselves—their impassioned ecstasy and agony into
their work—perhaps because they could not—that their
works are "cheap show." I grant it. They are "idle singers
of an empty day." Do you not think that the ethical
systems shift ground and disappear, a feeling once powerfully embodied remains forever, magically appealing to
the same hearts as at first? . . . Entrancing as the lectures
are, I see more and more the danger of losing one's power
of original work. On a much larger scale Germany seems
to me like Scholastic Europe in the Middle Ages washing
herself upon issues which, great though they be, have a
special interest, are merely scholarly. There is such a
scramble for the truth that none has time to see and
absorb it. It may be I shall be drawn in and race with the
rest. The study of a language for its literature of course is
my greatest temptation. It is such a pleasure to attack it
with grammar and dictionary blunderingly, fumbling
with its words, when presto—its heart seems to be in your
hand and a subtle sense of comprehension comes. I remember the moment when Greek and Latin and French
unlocked themselves . . . . So you see you and I are very
differently occupied. You are braver and have tried first.
Not knowing what you are at work at, I am rather in the
dark. There is no use in my telling you how I hope you
will succeed . . . . Yes, a man and in Paris and alone with
an inspiration to work out, as you must have had before
you came, you *have a chance;* for all these reasons, more

than one. Whatever you do—to return a little advice—don't go back to America! I, a woman, in Leipzig, and not alone, feel as if my goal were ten times as near here. The glimpse of pictures and cathedrals has flashed light into what was before unformed mass. Material that in America one must laboriously amass from poetry here lies at hand. . . .

I shall feel as if my draught were very petty unless I see Greece and Rome and Venice. I am thirsty for color—I want words to clothe my thoughts. I think you should have more than curiosity about other places. Don't you think that thoughts come from every new sensation? I want to feel Rome. . . . How long ago it seems when we talked over Europe in Philadelphia. I can't realize that I ever was in America—we poor Americans that must make such efforts to get possession of our birth right. Don't, I pray you, disinherit yourself. . . .

Outside of lectures which occupy on an average four hours a day I read—the library is unlimited and in the evenings after Mamie is asleep write a little—mere spelling. Putting word and word together. I am nearer saying with Faust to each passing moment "stay thou art fair" than ever before.

In return for this prompt "fulfillment of duty" you must keep me informed of your progress and whatever be its fate—am I too presumptuous in asking to see it? If so I hope you will not show it to me.

Leipzig
November 10, 1879

My dearest Father,

Mother's and thy letters greeted me on my return from the University. . . . It is after tea—warmed soup bones, potatoes and tea. Mamie is undressing. I repent my resolution and so you shall have two letters this week. . . .

Our lectures are proceeding regularly—Curtius is minutely analyzing the Alexandrian Grammarian, Braune, tracing the Anglo Saxons, Goths, Vandals and Scandanavians in their wanderings over Europe. Zärncke is in the fableland of the Nibelungleid,[6] Wülcker,[7] stupid Wülcker whom we cut today, is over the Anglo Saxon homilies and Hermann—the philosopher—little son of a great father (the great Grecia-Godfried Hermann) is tearing Bunsen and Hegel into little shreds. . . I can hardly understand a word as he speaks all in a breath without comma or period and then suddenly gasps, ducks his head down and wipes his forehead with a red bandana handkerchief. Miss Channing said to me today, "I would have given everything to be invited by Curtius.". . . Really there is so much liberality here. Prof. Ebers said he thought women should have degrees given them. Mrs. Ebers said two years ago a woman studied here in man's dress and associating freely with the students and professors escaped detection. Just as she was coming up for her degree she declared herself, feeling in honor bound. She was married and studied to be able to support herself and her husband.

We called on Ebers at the time he fixed (12-1) and as we came direct from the University our shoes were a little muddy. We were shown into a beautifully furnished study and there sat Ebers on a Turkey rug, leaning back in an arm chair with his feet on a cushing[sic] and an eastern red rug thrown over his leg. He is lame and it was through this confinement that he first thought of writing his novels. What was our alarm when Frau Ebers, a most imposing, pretty woman, on the type of Mary Smith Marlin, swept in, in lace and black velvet, soon a young man in white cravat and gloves appeared. Apparently it is their receiving hour. They were very kind and Ebers promised to try to obtain our admission to a reading room containing all possible learned periodicals which is the El Dorado of all feminine students—it being closed to them. He said, "Don't you take any steps. I must speak to the president and tell him how you were introduced, etc."

6. Nibelungenleid, the legends on which Wagner based most of his operas.

7. Richard Wülcker, 1845-1910, professor of English at Leipzig and founder of the journal *Anglia* in 1877, and author of numerous books on the history of English literature.

. . . They immediately said they knew of a lady, a Fräulein Pochhammer (which being interpreted is Miss Door latch or Miss Door knocker) who wished two ladies as her house was too large. They said she was most lovely—a daughter of one of the profs in the University— Windisch, a Jurist. We called on her today and found her very pleasant and her rooms not as pretty as these but three in number, that is three cost only $1.25 more a month apiece and then we shall have someplace for our clothes, washstands, etc. Her price, which it was embarrassing for us to inquire and for her to tell was, as we understand her to say, $5 apiece a month for the rooms and $7.56 for dinner apiece a month—if we provided our breakfasts, suppers, light and heat. You see $12.56 apiece. Everything included it would be $24.25 a month.

If this be so, and we have written to find out, we shall give Frau Dr. Matzke warning and leave on the 15 of Dec. . . . . Think of our life here after we have announced our intention of leaving. I dislike Frau Dr. Matzke so it is important to talk German with her and Mamie and she are hardly on speaking terms (this is not to be told to Mrs. Gwinn). I have to struggle with her and Mamie sits in the parlor hearing every word and enjoys it. Yesterday I announced I could not eat another morsel of corned beef and asked for eggs—was told I should have to pay a trifle extra. I refused on the ground of our present rate being exorbitant and we compromised on one egg. Frau Dr. Matzke *tries* to be most agreeable but she is such a screw and so tasteless in her compliments and remarks. Mamie from her bed is bemoaning the fact that our "scraggly breakfast" as she calls it, takes an half hour to eat because the rolls have to be chewed so hard.

Curtius said he gets the most ridiculous letters from America—one for example from a woman, "Honored Prof. Curtius, should I come to Leipzig, *what have you to offer me?*" and another from a grocery store clerk who had become entranced with Caesar and asked if Curtius would advise him to take up classical studies. Curtius wrote advising him to continue weighing out sugar.

I must tell you about Franklin Davis's call. After my

repeated command he was shown into the parlor. It was 7:30 p.m. and as Mamie had her wrapper on I shut the door behind me. We were looking over a Gothic grammar and discussing some grammar forms when Frau Dr. Matzke entered—her keen eye took in in a moment that we were seated on her "betrothal sofa." She said to me, "If it be pleasant to see your friend often, won't he take tea with you some evening." I had of course introduced her. I murmured an assent and she walked out.

Mamie's side of the story is Frau Dr. Matzke came in three separate times: "Miss Gwinn is it *possible* you are going to leave them alone? *Aren't* you going in?" Mamie— "It is an American custom—of *course* I shan't go in." Frau Matzke in despair, "Shall I go in?" Mamie—"Utterly unnecessary." (You perceive the terms they are on.) Mrs. Curtius says this is all nonsense, that it often happens and she would advise us by all means to have calls. Of course Davis will not come again as it was only to ask me about my lectures and decide upon his course. But it is satisfactory to know we can have a call if any friend comes . . . .

Love to Mother and everyone. Tell Harry to get his steam up quickly.

Leipzig
November 15, 1879

My dearest Mother,

At last we have found a home that I am sure will be satisfactory. We called on Frl. Pochhammer again and she proposed an arrangement which she said would enable us to live much more cheaply and which she greatly preferred. If she gave us dinner she would reckon it at 25 cents a day apiece, and for everything charge us 76 cents a day or (with the third room added) nearly $24. a month. But if we could make some other arrangement about dinner she would rent us the three rooms for $10 a month, $5 apiece, and charge us the *bare* cost of our breakfast and suppers and light and heat. This $10 a month included service. She said she had but one girl and as she herself was so much interested in visiting the poor and in several large charities it would be very inconvenient for her to attend to the cooking. The dinner was the difficulty. In talking she had casually mentioned that one of the most celebrated eating houses was opposite and I suggested that we might have our dinners sent over—happy thought. On inquiring of the restaurant keeper himself we found that he had frequently made a similar arrangement and by paying 19 cents we could order any dinner we liked from his bill of fare for that day. You see by this we both get a better dinner and save 6 cents a day, besides the greater advantage of paying the bare cost of our other expenses.

We were both attracted by Fräulein Pochhammer during this visit. She must have been embarrassed before. Let me recount all the extra advantages—we have three rooms instead of two; we are five minutes' walk from the University instead of twelve; we are one minute's walk from the promenade, the great walk and park of Leipzig; we are with a prominent Prof's daughter, a perfect lady whom we can trust as much as we did the Fräulein Grüneisen, then (and most delightful) to my penurious soul we save $10 a month and if we go on trips we shall lose almost nothing while we are gone as eating is the same everywhere and it only costs us $1.25 a week to keep our rooms . . . .

[Later]

Frau Dr. has demanded her money and I went in with $60 thinking it the largest possible amount but the screw insisted upon more money for the lamps—outrageous—we pay already $7 more than any other pension we asked about. I argued but from an unwary expression of the screw's gathered that she was going to make us eat soup bones unless I yielded, which I ungracefully did . . . . I think she considers us "verwohnt"—spoiled, so she said, and what we consider her is beyond words! I hoped that in Germany at least I would be able to live cheaply and try to save money for what I really want and now by President White's letters we are forced to behave in the most respectable manner. We have to call dressed up in silk and kid gloves and here yesterday comes an invitation to a

197

party, or rather a small tea company at Ebers next Second Day evening. I shall wear my red silk I suppose. If
Mrs. Ebers is dressed more magnificently than she was
the other day she will have to appear in white satin. This
afternoon we have to call on Frau Geheimrathin Curtius
to tell her we have found a pleasant boarding place, so
that she need not look for one for us. You see we are in the
toils of convention—they seem to think money is no object
and recommend the most extravagant manner of living.
However, we have now through Ebers' own introduction
obtained board cheaper than we have found it anywhere
in all our searchings. I am afraid I am getting like Frau
Dr. Matzke who never mentions anything without giving
its price. . . .

On the street a young man dressed in fur cap and fur
trimmed coat took off his cap—he looked like a Pole or
Russian, and he said, "Pardon, sind sie Studentinen"—
are you women students? We said yes—He then explained
that a friend of his wanted to study medicine here and he
found it impossible to find out what position women held
here. We told him our experiences and walked on. It
showed great politeness for him not to have addressed one
of us in the University as he is in several of our lectures.
The students seem to want to be polite but to be afraid of
the ridicule of the others. They often do open doors, etc.
but oftener I see them hesitate and then walk through
determinedly and Mamie said a man got out of her way
the other day but expressed his feelings by "um" and an
angry shrug of his shoulders. I imagine they are much
more polite to us than the other girls because Miss Parker,
the Iowa girl, said she found them rather rude.

This poor Miss Parker says she spent her first month in
looking for lodgings and yet where she is she has weak
coffee and a crust of *dry* bread for breakfast, for dinner
greasy water with a few pinches of chocolate dropped in
or that a meat bone has been passed through and horrid
meat and potatoes and once a week beans . . . .

It is a driving snow storm . . . we are going to have a
terribly cold winter I fear—such a snow on the 15th of
Nov. You cannot think how lovely the square in front of

the University looks; one unbroken sheet of snow .... The Middle Ages are taking on a character of their own and they are as much a world as the old Greek fairyland. I never realized the enthusiasm with which people rushed from the heathendom and savagery to a religion that drew out the gentler elements ....

With dear love to everyone—especially dear Grandma. ...

After Nov. 1st [she probably meant Dec. 1] direct—care Fräulein Pochhammer, Wintergarten Strasse 7. I hope Father has written Pres. White because his letters have the greatest effect ....

Leipzig
November 20, 1879

My dearest Mother,

Thy letter from Phila. came two days behind hand .... It found me quite sick with a cold . . . I had resigned myself to pneumonia and the expenses of a doctor but this morning finds me as well and Mamie says far more frisky than ever. ... This week has been a week of misfortunes— on Second Day my cold began and feeling so wretched I dedicated part of the afternoon to mending my three pairs of buckskin gloves and helping Mamie with her shoe buttons and worst of all sewing buttons on my waists. At 5 I went to hear Wülcker on Old Eng. Lit. I had on my fuzzy gray dress. Just as the lecture began I spilt my ink stand all over the desk and my dress to the great entertainment of eighty or ninety students. At first I was in despair but happened to think of my blotting paper and while the students sympathetically watched me I blotted it up and to my delight it does not show in the least.

We were invited to Ebers that night and I wore my brown brocade which was rather a mistake as there were thirty people there. You are never asked into a dressing room but gentlemen and ladies take off their wraps in the hall. We were placed on the sofa and at first Ebers devoted himself to me. He asked about Pres. White, if it were true that he had given such great gifts to Cornell, etc. He said he had "lived" with him a month and admired him extremely. He spoke feelingly about the want of American copyright when I told him how widely his books were read there—by the way thee and Father would be interested in his *Homo Sum*. It is translated. It takes up the early period of Christianity, the church Fathers, etc. . . . All this time ladies and gentlemen were coming in and according to the German custom the whole company rose and the newcomer was introduced to every one. Prof. Zärncke had been asked especially to meet us according to Pres. White's request, but a lecture in the University which Prof. Ebers had forgotten, prevented. His daughter and her husband were there. Prof. von Noorden, a popular historical prof was there with his wife and son, two other professors and their wives, the two Ebers girls, very sweet looking, and a very décolletée girl from the Conservatory who sang at intervals during the evening in a glorious ringing alto voice, and an equal number of gentlemen. As each came in, tea was immediately handed to him or her and milk in a great silver bowl out of which you helped yourself to spoonfuls. The men all stood up against one side of the wall and the ladies sat down on the other except for Prof. Ebers. The prettiest young man played on the piano while the Conservatory girl sang.

At last a dark haired man crossed over and began talking to Mamie and me and after a move was made waited on me into supper. A tremendously long table in a long narrow room . . . . The table was lit with three candelabra holding six wax candles apiece. We had first beef tea in cups, 2. Fish and potatoes and preserves on little plates, 3. pheasants handed on immense dishes on one side of which a stuffed pheasant was sitting in a nest surrounded with its own cooked meat, 4. Raspberry water ice and 5. a three tiered dish containing first horrid little pink cakes, second figs, and lastly the greatest delicacy, *ground nuts*. They showered questions upon me as to how these grew and where, etc. The only thing in which this differed from an American supper was that the same forks were used throughout.

I discovered my companion was Dr. Creizenach, a University under prof. who is lecturing upon Goethe and

Schiller and Voltaire. Prof. Ebers told me afterwards that he was the most successful of the young men. He was very nice and told me about his degree. You must stand examination in three subjects and write a thesis which must show original research. He was examined upon English, French and German and wrote his thesis upon the comedy from which Faust was taken. He had studied here with Boyesen and of course thought him brilliant. We had plenty to talk of. . . .

After supper to my amazement Dr. Creizenach made me an elaborate bow and said "Gute Mahlzeit"—"good meal time" and everybody went up to Frau and Prof. Ebers saying the same and to almost everyone else in the room. Then a man came up who wished to speak English and it was very hard to understand him and as he couldn't understand my English at all I had to speak German. He was stupid. Then (and every ten minutes this happened) the girl sang and Mamie and I were in the midst of the most charmingly interesting comparison of lectures and hours with von Noorden when Pauline came and we had to go. It was 11—but as we were almost the first I suppose the rest stayed till one. We were both very much provoked we had to go. I quite enjoyed talking to some men again, so being forced to go was a third misfortune.

Then Fourth Day I was so sick at my stomach (which expression by the way is so refined in German that it is quite *en règle* at an evening company) that I missed my lectures again. I suppose it is the eating and to crown my misfortunes yesterday when I had hardly eaten anything for two days was sent in a curious black meat with ribs and a gizzard—tasting like game and looking like veal. Today we found out it was rabbit.

A great event happened yesterday—I forgot to tell you that we lately discovered that Frau Doctorrin had a husband who drank and so they lived apart, he in another city. Yesterday she received news of his death and came in and told us about it in such a conversational manner that Mamie nearly laughed twice and once had to cough. Luckily I was nearer to her and felt too sick to be amused at anything. She said he was a very gifted man and that geniuses were always more apt to fall than other men. Today she says she has been looking for a tombstone—oh she is a funny woman—rather clever and quite pretty, as keen as possible, an excellent character for Balzac to work up.

We have had two bitterly cold days—a foretaste, I suppose, but under our feather beds we are as warm as dormice and muffs are most necessary whenever we venture out. Father's letter came yesterday and was very nice—only you must not tell me about things to eat and civilized dinners. I want to try to forget there are such things. The other day we went to the Café Francais, the most celebrated restaurant here. The room is lovely, full of little nooks for tables behind pillars and long mirrors and in every free space fine frescoes. So different from Del Monico's. We each got a most delicious plate of water ice for 7 cents and a cake made of ladycake and pounded English walnuts and surmounted by a whole candied walnut—delicious—only 3 cents. You see how much cheaper things are here . . . .

Miss Channing is very jolly. I sit by her in Curtius's lectures. She was consumed with envy when she heard of our evening at Ebers. I often wonder how her poor mother amuses herself up in that fourth story, tiny room. . . .

It is the fashion [here] for the men to speak first, so it relieves us from all responsibility in recognizing the men we met at Ebers—a charming custom . . . .

Mrs. Gwinn writes Mamie very nice letters and sent her $20 the last time and promised another XX in her next letter. This is a secret—she wishes to send Mamie pocket money apart from the money she draws—so you must say nothing about it. Don't talk about expense with Mrs. Gwinn—I can manage it with Mamie. From what Mamie says I don't think thee can make Mrs. Gwinn believe that you cannot afford to let me travel if an opportunity should present itself.

She insists on thinking it is because thee thinks that I shall get all in Heaven anyway and earth makes no difference. I can perfectly well keep from spending more money than absolutely necessary by telling Mamie I can't do it. It is good discipline I suppose—but of course it seems hard when so little enables one to see so much. . . .

Did Nell[8] and Frank get the little dolls I sent them? Tell them I expect a letter of acknowledgement. . . .

P.S. *Thee* has *twice* sent me letters overweight and even in all my poverty I have generously said nothing about it.

Leipzig
November 26, 1879

My dear Mr. Cadbury,

Your ms. and note arrived Saturday. . . . To begin, I like your handling of blank verse—it calls up no reminiscences and is often strong and dense. Your dramatic development is forcible. I like the way the scenes follow each other. Nero is well conceived especially the manner in which you bring out his dramatic instances, his artist's pleasure in acting out his role, his love of beauty and his weakness. In your hands he is Swinburne's "beautiful tyrant." Yes, your tragedy has an undoubted raison d'être—to dramatize your solution of such a well known character—an original solution it seems to me. By such a selection of a subject you have avoided the necessity of a moral motive—our stumbling block. You have just the framework one wants. I am surprised that you have not given more time and care to the filling out. . . . Almost every scene could be shortened one half to advantage. . . . You so often have a forcible expression and weaken it by immediate expansion and repetition. . . . The muses are well conceived, I mean their entrance, but their songs are very bad. . . . Scene V is slow—though Nero's hesitating death is good. . . . I thank you very much for sending me it and I shall preserve your confidence until you spring it full statured upon the world.

8. "Nell" is her sister Helen.

203

Waisenhaus Str. 5 II
Leipzig
December 11, 1879

My dearest Mother,

Thee has received no letter in the middle of the week as usual. I want to see if thee cannot be satisfied with one letter as it does take so much time and so much of our life here is writing four hours a day in lectures. There is a mass of little things to tell thee of. First the mud of Leipzig is frightful, there is no other word for it. There is a vast open place in front of the University as large as the four monument squares in one and this is unpaved and without a blade of grass thereon—one vast expanse of dirt. When it rains, and it has rained every day for the last three weeks, this becomes a soft slimy marsh, through which hundreds of students wade and we among them. The streets are also covered with black slime and our dresses do not dry from one day to the other. We are going to have them cut yet shorter. The true German fashion is to ignore rain. Always the majority of the people have no umbrellas up and all the servant girls wear no hats or wraps. At Antwerp we often saw dozens of women in calico frocks and white aprons standing and talking together with nothing on their heads in the pouring rain and curiously enough their dresses stood out as stiffly as ever. We concluded they must have a sort of duck oil. I wish we had it! . . . Oh the sense of luxury on Fourth, Seventh, and First Day afternoons when we put on our wrappers and slippers and settle ourselves for a prolonged evening from 1:30 to 10.

I told thee I think that Mamie never puts away anything. Well now that I go early to hear Prof. Braune, Mamie has to struggle with her things alone, get herself off in time and reach Zärncke at 10. Her arrival is very uncertain; twice she has missed and twice had to run all the way to get there. Did I tell you the lectures never begin till a quarter past the given hour, but if anyone dares to enter after that time each student shuffles his feet upon the floor and when you imagine 300 or so doing this it is overpowering. So no one enters after the quarter. Miss

Channing says she was *"shuffled"* once and it was dreadful. There is an amusing promptitude of opinion displayed by the students—if the professor says anything that they do not understand they shuffle and the Professor patiently repeats. If they disapprove they groan faintly. Mamie came in late once and made a row of students get up to let her into her seat and they groaned very very softly. They always do this however when a student coughs; she coughed once and from all corners of the room echoed a faint cough. An unhappy student sneezed the other day in Braune's lecture—there were about 200 there and they hissed under their breath. This is the only amusement they allow themselves for such a studious set I never saw— they take notes without breath in between. The only conversation before lectures seems to be about notes and books. A new girl appeared in Curtius's lecture the other day, not very nice looking, and finding no seat went out. Also there is a Miss Parker whose father is Professor of Greek in a tiny little Iowa university, a Fräulein Gebsel who intends taking a degree in Göttingen, Miss Channing, Mamie and I—these are all I know of.

To pursue Mamie's adventures—I started her off to Zärncke alone one day and here is her success, as told to Miss Channing by a lady to whom a member of the class recounted it. An immense law class sat waiting, 400 or more, and every seat filled, when a young lady entered, a very nice looking lady but pale as a sheet. She walked slowly up the aisle looking for a seat. All the class were so sorry for her they hardly dared to breathe. At last when she reached the top row, she asked a student who lectured; and then walked out as pale as ever.

She is very funny and takes all her misfortunes in good part. Since we have been in Leipzig she has lost three pair of gloves, a pair of shoes, five button hooks, a gold pencil and between us we have lost five pens and six pencils. Then she has torn the sleeves out of two nightgowns and as her others are in a trunk on top of a hall wardrobe she thinks of binding the arm holes and wearing them sleeveless, as we can neither of us sew them in, nor get at the others. I am very cautious and have torn nothing. What

205

does thee suppose our washing costs us a week—it is so disgraceful and Mamie doesn't dare to tell Mrs. Gwinn. It costs us 20 cents apiece.

We were invited to tea by Frau Curtius last night . . . . As the German custom is we went immediately in to tea— a round table without either head or foot—and only bread and an ebony centerpiece that twirled around and there- upon six little plates this shape [pie-shaped sketch] fit- ting into each other and making a round dish, each filled with different kinds of cold meat and little slimy fish like those we saw in Stuttgart. The tea was handed and crab and fish salad and then the waiter left the room. The sugar was lump sugar and in a little silver jewelry box with a lock and the key in it. Every one took out the lump with his fingers.

All through the supper little sweet crackers and jumbles were passed . . . . I sat by Curtius, "Herr Geheimrath"[9] as everyone calls him, and he talked delightfully about Gil- dersleeve whom he knows nothing about except that he is interested in syntax, Whitney whom he admires, and the late Prof. Hadley for whom he has great admiration. The whole conversation was a different thing from what one finds in America. The latest book, lecture, appointment, Wagner and his music, Prof. Curtius mimicked the Latin speeches that were made at a late banquet, etc. Frau Curtius is delightful and indeed they all were most inter- esting and talked most freely about the other professors— Wülcker whom we hear upon Old Eng. and who is abom- inably stupid, Prof. Curtius says is just engaged and when anyone accuses him of being tedious, his friends reply "aber er dichtet"—"but he writes poetry." They said "guten Mahlzeit" afterwards as at Stuttgart . . . 11 o'clock came before we knew it. Prof. Curtius was more than polite and I imagine he is not always so. It was kind of Pres. White! . . .

Please give our dearest love to Father and the children and Harry. Thee must not tell Mrs. Gwinn about any of Mamie's scrapes.

9. Privy councillor.

Leipzig
February 1, 1880

Dearest Mother,

It is a most lovely sunny day—we have breakfasted and are sitting down to a cozy morning. . . . We found out yesterday about the University prison—it is in the fourth story overlooking the courtyard. You see poor, wretched men looking out through the bars. They are put in for duelling, belonging to any political society, etc. A student was put in six months for socialism. He took Italian and English books in with him and came out master of both languages.

In the last *Edinburgh Review* there is a most interesting article on Germany and Bismarck. Tell Father to read it. It coincides exactly with what we hear. For the first time I heard an authentic exposition of the views of the German Socialists. Mr. Gummere knows a student who is hand and glove with all these men. He says the belief of the party is that the government should take everything into its hands—every rod of land and all individual property— each man shall be given furniture and clothes—the old shall be taken care of by the young, etc. From the time of Plato's Republic, from the attempted community of good preached by the Apostles, down to Brook Farm—it seems marvelous that fanatics should delude themselves with this *ignis fatuus*[1]— I could not believe that the German Socialists thought this. The Universities live in fear—the great opposition to women consists in the terror inspired by the Russian women and their anarchy inaugurated at Zürich until they were banished. I really think the application of one Russian woman would be sufficient to close Leipzig's doors to women. As we get more into the spirit here I feel this panic felt by an absolute government. A paper has appeared in Dresden stating that six Russian women are studying in Leipzig and during vacation, wearing democratic colors, appeared in the students' gatherings inciting them to socialism. The Ministerium of Saxony are said to have taken notice of it. Of course it was a libel as there is not one Russian in the University.

1. Foolish passion.

If such a thing should happen as our being forced to leave—several of the most noted professors of literature are in Switzerland and I am grounded in Gothic and Comparative Grammar. This week I shall study Anglo Saxon—I have been waiting for Wülcker's edition of a grammar. Really, as I looked over the Johns Hopkins circular that Mr. Gwinn sent Mamie, and saw the young fledglings that are teaching there, I felt like a phoenix. Thee and Father care for other things—I do not think you can possibly realize the difference these three years of study will make in my life . . . .

Leipzig
February 7, 1880

My dear Mother,

It is Seventh Day evening and just an half an hour to write before I go to bed. On such days as we have been having—lovely sunny spring days like Baltimore spring. The mist bathes everything in a golden light. . . .

Some time ago we received notices from the University that we must apply to the Ministerium of Saxony for permission to pursue our studies here. Last week we talked it over with Prof. and Mrs. Curtius. It seems that the University authorities admitted women as hearers without submitting the matter to the Ministry, which being known, the Ministry sent the above preemptory order. The University took up the matter warmly and answered that ladies were only "hearers" and that the University saw no objection to any of the ladies and that further the students had made none. There seems to have been a clash between the two powers.

Prof. Curtius says besides offended authority, a fear of Russian women and socialism lies at the bottom of the movement. He told me to write to Pres. White asking for a letter for both of us stating that he knew us personally and knew that we would profit by the opportunities. He is going to write us out a formula of application and with the American Ambassador's letter he thinks permission will certainly be granted. He says if possible he will write himself to the Minister. . . . Don't say anything about this

208

trouble—Mamie has not in her letters home. We fully expect it will blow over. The other day we saw an officer driving through the streets in an open farouche waving a crimson and black flag. A crowd of people collected. We asked the man of whom we were buying a book what it meant. He said a student had just shot himself. Was it not curious? One of the lecturers stated the other day that more suicides occurred in Leipzig than in any other place. I suppose because it is a great center of commercial and intellectual life . . . .

Yes, Mamie is really a great deal better. These exercises, four hours a week tire her dreadfully; but her shoulder looks much better. She is happy and has a very good appetite. The prospect of Italy is her delight at present. Miss Parker says that if we go she will be very glad to travel with us. We asked Mrs. Curtius and she said the idea of a companion is ridiculous—that when she was in Italy she met a number of young girls travelling in pairs—that an intimate friend of her niece had done so. She says there is *no* danger in Rome at this season, that if we don't freeze we may be thankful.

I wish I knew what it would be best to take as my second subject. I shall make English literature my chief— the one on which I want to try to do independent work, but I suppose for example I wished ever to try for a chair in Taylor College? I shall certainly be better qualified than any other woman in the Society[2] and it may sound conceited, but I have not the slightest fear of my being able to teach girls of that age. I know I have a personal influence that will enable me to inspire them to care about what I do. This is after all the secret of successful teaching. I am sure I have this power and these lectures in Germany have given me the method.

I have been thinking very seriously especially since thy letter about the money you owe.[3] Study, as thee knows, and influence are the two things I care about—these I can best obtain by being a professor in some women's college.

2. The Society of Friends, Taylor being set up as a Quaker institution.
3. Mrs. Thomas had borrowed money to send Carey abroad.

Yet if I only knew definitely it would, of course influence my method of study and enable me to be a much better professor. The only two I should be at all willing to teach in would be Smith or Taylor. Of course in Taylor College I should be less separated from you and there is more hope in working out one's thoughts in a new institution. Then I do care for raising the tone and education of women and it presents a field. If I did not wish a chair in Taylor College I should undoubtedly take English literature and I am sure with my studies here and perhaps in England, I could get a professorship in Vassar, Smith or perhaps Cornell ultimately. Look at Miss Nunn without even a degree. Now of course Frank Gummere having received the appointment in English literature I must take some other subject unless I wish to cut myself off from Taylor forever.[4]

What I should prefer would be the department of general literature—working of the national literatures upon each other and the mixture of cultures—the way old Greek myths, through the Latin, were reflected in the French, German, Italian, English and Spanish literatures—the influence of form of literature. I have a very fair start for this study. Frank Gummere of course treats English literature from its Germanic side. He knows no French, Italian nor Spanish and only a college graduate's Greek. I can read Greek and Latin easily, Gothic, High German, Middle High German, and of course modern German, French and soon shall Italian. Then I should study Spanish and Provençal and New Greek and be equipped. Thee sees what a field this opens for the most wide study and investigation. I might specialize this by in addition to general lectures, giving special interpretations of Italian and Provençal. I am sure I could do good work in this and work that I hope would eventually win me a reputation.

4. As it happened, nothing was so settled as she implies. Francis Gummere's correspondence with members of the Board shows that he had gone abroad with the conviction that Dr. Taylor had a responsible position in mind for him on his return. Gummere had nothing in writing, however, and thus no legal claims as he himself acknowledges in correspondence with friends on the Board.

Ebers is capital in that department and affords the best opportunity for such study. If I did that I should study some time in Italy; all its universities are open to women. I shall then take my Dr's degree at Göttingen. I think I could get personal recommendations from the professors here by that time.

Thee sees it is really important for me to know now because I must begin to work towards a degree. I wish it were possible for father to lay the matter before the trustees of Taylor College. If they are willing to give me an appointment I would promise in writing to resign after the first year if my teaching were not satisfactory. . . .

I would not be willing to take any inferior position or at any less salary than for example Frank Gummere, because I shall have had all the advantages he has and my subject will be a most difficult one for which I should try to prepare myself even if it required six years. If this seems unadvisable, or if they are unwilling, I shall make up my mind to try for Smith and study English literature which will give me much more leisure . . . . Write me what you think, very seriously. I want this to be a complete secret, if Father does speak to Cousin Frank or Uncle James I do not want it spoken of . . . .

Leipzig
February 29, 1880

My dearest Father—

It is so soon after my last letter—two days—that thee must not expect much news. Last week we rec'd our permission to study in Leipzig "bis auf Weiteres" "until further notice." President White wrote me enclosing the documents which the Saxon Minister to Berlin had sent him. They consisted of the time honored statutes of the University—among them was this clause: "The University has the power to admit officers as hearers to its lectures." It further has the privilege to extend this to other "personnen"—"persons who are of a suitable age and culture." Under this, the University has admitted women. The Minister of the Saxon Government has lately heard of and appointed a committee to investigate it. Pres.

White also sent me the proceedings of the Landstag—
Parliament of Saxony—to which this report was presented. The Committee reported that the University had
no right to admit women just because the framers of the
statute had neglected to use a word which was distinc-
tively masculine whereas the possibility of women had
never been considered. Thereupon followed a discussion
curiously Americanlike: three against women and one for.
One man said that thank God very few German women
wanted such training and that to open the University to
educate a few Russians and French women could not be
expected. The President of Education—I think he was—
spoke repeatedly in favor urging that the University
should at least have the privilege of deciding upon each
individual case. But Minister Gerber closed the discussion
adversely. So the power of admitting women is taken out
of the hands of the University and each special application must be made to the Minister. This Minister Gerber
both wrote our acceptance to Pres. White and at the same
time asked the Saxon Minister to Berlin to tell him that in
deference to the University he admitted all the ladies—
ten—now studying here but that in future he should refuse
any other applications. Is not this too provoking? The
University as I wrote before did its best to prevent the
matter from being taken out of its hands and is now
deeply offended. Its influence has only saved those who
are now here from being turned out.

Of course it depends upon the disposition of the Minister and theoretically is an advance for coeducation because the University has declared that it causes no dis-
turbance and that there has been no exceptional behavior
among the ladies studying here. Experience has justified
it here as elsewhere—the Minister is a mere outsider and
is prejudiced against it.

The Russian women are looked upon as a scourge. I
hope I have made it clear. I wanted thee to understand the
exact facts in case it might be heard of and quoted in the
J.H.U. Otherwise it is not necessary to say anything
about it I should think, as only from that private letter to
Pres. White do I know that the Minister had decided to

refuse every other woman, and indeed he may be won over. Then the decision of the Landstag will only mean a little more red tape. How glad I am that we came this year—next year would probably have been too late. It rather adds to one's glory to be one of the thirteen women in all, I think, who have studied at Leipzig.

This letter is being written in the intervals between rushing into Mamie's study to see that the tomatoes do not burn. She has just discovered that Madame Lavigne's is within a square of the most celebrated ice cream store in Rome—six cents for a plate of ice. It will be double nice to have nothing but French spoken if, as it seems, an Italian Pension will be out of the question. Frl. Matilda recommended to us a doctor under whose charge her brother, who lived in Rome, was—she says he is most excellent and that if we mention her name he will take a personal interest in us. Now that we have decided to go I live in a sort of dream of anticipation. It consoles me a little about the expense when I think that if I ever do become a professor this is my one chance to see Rome as it will not be safe in the summer. We start next Fifth Day at 6 o'clock in the evening—the fourth of Third Month, but long before this letter reaches thee we will have taken our first plunge into the eternal city. I wish thee were going with us. It does seem too bad that so many never have this all surpassing pleasure. I hope it won't be so with you.

After dinner. Tomatoes excellent. Two slices of roast beef, three potatoes, one veal cutlet and the most delicious asparagus—you don't know what it is like. Imagine the tenderest milky white stalks with little blossoms, instead of green heads like ours, cooked in drawn butter. All this cost us 19 cents apiece. Mamie and I have been breakfasting at the rate of 1½ cents apiece since Mrs. Gwinn sent that hominy. However etcetera and books are very expensive. Tell Mother I spent $4. for a pair of shoes, $1. for a lace scarf, a long one to wear with my blue travelling dress, and $2. for gloves, and am grieved over the expense. Then my travelling dress facing and braid was so worn out it had to be rebound by Anna and my watch had to be

213

cleaned and my umbrella is at the menders so all my things like the one horse shay are giving out at once.

Minnie is afraid Mrs. Davis will report her to Mrs. Morris, who will tell Mrs. Gwinn that she had only her travelling dress so to our great sorrow we shall have to take a trunk to Italy. Mr. Gummere seems hard at work—he has gotten his thesis subject. I foresee we shall have to give up travelling entirely and just buckle to—fourteen hrs a day, right through vacations many of the men work. I do not see how Mamie can stand it. She has had no experience of the sort though she is very well and very nice. But this consciousness makes the enjoyment of Rome all the keener. With a great deal of love to thee and Mother and Daisy—

Rome
April 4, 1880

My dear Mr. Cadbury,

Perhaps I only wish to set off a Rome against your Paris, in any case you need not fear description. No, your last letter rather provoked me. It had the tone of virtuously settling down about it.[5] Severe respectability and money making. But Rome puts me in such a charming humor. For the first time I am in love with life—I quite understand why the poorest beggar puts his ragged cloak against his mouth at sunset. I cannot imagine the Romans with their suicide and legions here.

While you have so ungenerously been silent I have received two opposing accounts of you. Mr. Gummere told me what Miss Mott wrote—very favorable, but then I allowed for your shining with reflected light. Anna's [Shipley] was rather the reverse. Rome, Naples, Capri, Pompeii, Castellammare, Sorrento and Paestum—I have seen them all. At Paestum I felt for the first time the Doric column "the god whom ye ignorantly worship him declare I unto you." Lizards, blue Mediterranean, through the spaces, acanthus growing over the ruins—it was just as one would have had it. It is a sort of a blind faith that

5. **Richard** Cadbury was by now back in the U.S.

makes us care for Greece in America . . . Paestum and the statues have made me sure. I suppose the Louvre did the same for you. . . .

As your last letter contained a wish to be an actuary, you would enjoy the ruins—on the Palatine one can see exactly how the Emperors and private persons lived. The very roofs are over the houses—Pompeii was like a doll house, but here Miss Gwinn looks upon these strictly as bricks and dirt so I have no one to root with. Of course I made a pilgrimage to Shelley's grave and for once had the degradation of *feeling* all the sentimental trash one reads about it. You know I have Shelley to thank, and through him Godwin, for almost all the light I walk by. Do you remember our talk under the bridge? I wish I could tell you how much clearer everything is now. Does it pay now that you are back in America—trying to care for other things than the herd?

Leipzig
April 18, 1880

Dearest Mother,

The letter I began to thee in Florence is lost. I do hope it has not been a week since I wrote . . . . Here we are back in Leipzig and a most unwilling return it was but this is already four days after the University is advertised to begin.

Our journey was rather exhausting. We left Florence Sixth Day morning and the 16th at 7 a.m., reached Bologna at 11. Went straight to the Museum where Raphael's St. Cecilia is. There we met that charming Miss Hope again. She was prettier than ever and talked to us quite a long while. She knows Symonds the Renaissance man well and has been with him in Florence. She says she is one of twelve children and when she goes into the drawing room sits and draws or writes a letter, she "gets out as much as she can at the table and then considers she has done her duty." She must be thirty or thirty-five and is most ladylike—her dress is perfection . . . .

She introduced a delicate looking girl with her and said I must ask her about Girton. This young lady, it seems, had wished to go there. I said something about leaving Italy but she rejoined, "You are going back to an *ideal life.*" I asked her why she had not chosen it—to my surprise she flushed and her lips trembled and her eyes filled with tears—she said, "I am to be married in two months." Afterwards I found from her asking me repeatedly how I obtained permission and from her again half crying when I said my mother had helped me, that she had probably made a struggle and failed. Was it not a tragedy?

Miss Hope herself has a pokey old uncle and aunt whom she is travelling with. Miss Hope asked for our Leipzig address and insisted upon our letting her know when we came to England. Thee don't suppose she could intend asking us to visit her does thee?

Bologna is a sombre old place all made up of arched arcades covering all the sidewalks; the second story of the houses extends over them. There are two very high leaning towers there and one interesting church but we were quite ready to leave by 5 p.m. when we took a train and came straight through to Leipzig—thirty-six hours. We had no trouble and both of the two nights had a car to ourselves. The way of proceeding is this: "Is there a lady's car on this train?"

Conductor: "Not exactly, but it can be made one," we on both sides understanding, as he leaves we slip 10 or at the most 20 cents into his hand and he watches like a dragon. No one comes in and we sleep in comfort. A very funny German girl travelled with us last night who thinks too much learning brings grief and envies the peasants and adores "Childe Harold." We surprised Frl. Pochhammer as she had not received our letter.

I will confide a secret. It is now 12 o'clock noon and we have tasted nothing since 10 o'clock yesterday morning. We were sound asleep when the train stopped for supper. Mamie commenced immediately upon the crackers and gingercakes left from her box—but I don't feel hungry. I found thy letter written just before Bessie's wedding. . . .[6]

6. **Bessie** Nicholson married a Frank Taylor in 1880. I have not been able to determine whether he was any relation to the founder of Bryn Mawr.

I had the pleasure of reading my article in the *Nation*[7] today—thy additions are rather too romantic for the severe style I want to cultivate. Thee seems to be well content with thy children—Harry and Bonny and Daisy[8]— and all the rest too. If thee succeeds in making *them* as well contented as I am you will have fulfilled the whole duty of parents according to the modern view . . . .

Thee must excuse this letter as that of a starving person.

With dearest love to thee and father and especially to thee—if it had not been for thee I often think I might have been like that poor girl in Bologna.

Wintergartenstr 7, Leipzig
June 26, 1880

My dear Mr. Cadbury,

. . . Do you know civilization is gradually dispensing with man in his masculine prerogative of protector? The lady Miss Gwinn and I were to travel with received a telegram and we have travelled alone everywhere—not the slightest difficulty. There is an underground railway system of pensions extending from city to city. They are the paradise of old maids and thither we betake ourselves. One can study human nature in them—also numbers of solitary men drift into them, though why I can't imagine. . . .

Your letter put me into a bad humor—as perhaps you see. You know of course that the only thing I really care to do is what you are doing—try. But I dare not throw away the chance of knowledge—of images, and new furniture for my imagination which I can get here now and never

---

7. This reference is something of a mystery. No article in the well-known publication *The Nation* published at about that time could conceivably have been by Carey Thomas, even under a pseudonym. Her tone moreover indicates (as does her denial to Mr. Cadbury in a later letter that she wrote the article) that the magazine or newspaper in which her article appeared was not a well-known publication. I could not find it listed among Quaker journals of that time, or in newspapers in the Philadelphia or Baltimore area. It may have been a kind of newsletter limited to the Quaker community to which her parents belonged.

8. "Bonnie" is her brother Bond; "Daisy" is sister Margaret.

afterward. It is a delight to dip more and more into literature and see the *Weltgeist* rising before one—but—tragic perplexity—I have to push him back into his bottle and cork him up, nay throw him into the sea for the next three years. A degree and a German lecturer and the German student are—so much philology, so much grammar, so much dictionary and oh so little spirit—the latter is of course all I care for; but how can one individual change the preordained order? You don't belong to an enslaved race—I am hampered by a desire if I fail in the highest, to at least try and prevent other girls from having even the struggle I have had. If I were a man I suppose I would try for it and in case of failure smoke away the rest of my life in "domesticity." Though even from a man's standpoint that seems hard to imagine—one doesn't know how late in Venice or on the Roman hills the god might descend and touch one's lips. No I did not write that article in the *Nation*. I have no time even to try . . . I care more about Italy than anything else. This summer I expect to do very little except let the palaces and statues and Italian sun and color soak in . . . . I too liked your letter. I admire you for your bravery—it seems to me you have a fair chance . . . .

Leipzig
June 27, 1880

My dearest Mother,

I suppose thee has already rec'd my homesick letter written on Second Day. I feel better now. I went to see Prof. Wülcker yesterday. He has just married and his study is as swell as possible. At first he was very much embarrassed but I determined to extract the information we wanted and he ended by being as kind as could be. I told him we wished to take our degrees in Göttingen. He said he wished he knew Müller, the English prof. there so that he could introduce me but he did not. He showed me his photograph and said he was a cranky man with lots of notions and that we must by all means go down to Göttingen and consult him as to what course to pursue. He said it depended entirely upon the examiner whether one required philology or a wide literary knowledge.

He then talked about degree subjects and showed me three that had just been accepted: One "The Life of Massinger," only Wülcker said that if one took a modern English subject like that, unless you proved your Anglo Saxon knowledge in examination, "a misfortune might happen" (the German expression for "flunk," "fluck"). He told me that the next year he expected to take up Anglo Saxon Grammar from an historical standpoint and trace it into new English . . . . He strongly advised taking a degree at Göttingen instead of in Switzerland, and ended by expressing his opinion of the stupidity of not admitting women to degrees and classes at Leipzig. He was very satisfactory.

Of course we must now see the two Müllers—the English and German profs.—in Göttingen. I think we shall go there next week and the sooner the better. Unfortunately it will never cost any less—$6. there and back. Also we find that it is impossible to study Middle Hoch German without two immense dictionaries and we have bought one and hope to make that do. Then all the books we have to read must be bought—of course the students club together but we cannot do this. However, books are very cheap and will be invaluable in America. I hope the Minister will permit us to stay until we are ready to try for it.

Miss Channing came to see us last night just as we were undressing to go to bed, which never appeared to occur to her as a possibility. She says there is a swimming house here, much larger than the Phila. Natatorium, being in fact a house built over the river, where only ladies are admitted—*tickets 5 cents apiece.* She says the girls are hung on to long poles like fishes at the end of a fishing line and taught to swim. Mamie and I are going there this week to try—the bathing suits are delicious—low neck sleeveless, almost legless.

Tell Father I hope he will vote for Hancock. I rejoice that Grant failed. These little scraps of politics find their way into the German papers. Mrs. Channing and I had a warm discussion upon the Southern question and she lent me *A Fool's Errand*. You certainly must read it if you have not. It is a most fair and clever discussion of the condition of things down south, written by a northern man. Mamie and I were very much interested.

The fathers of the German girls who attend the high school by the University are in commotion, because a student has been seen to walk up and down before it. This impertinence continued a week, then he had the audacity to kiss his hand to the girls. Whereupon all the masters of the school expostulated with him. He still continues to walk. Two of the fathers lay in ambush, caught him and forced him to give them his visiting card. They expect to try him before the city courts, so we hear. Is it not a tempest in a teapot?

Wülcker said there was talk of a great national German university for girls which he considered very foolish as there were already so many where ladies could be admitted without extra expense. It sometimes seems hopeless to think of women's doing anything. When men have a choice of twenty or thirty to coop women up in one.

Tell Father . . . there is a most ubiquitous German—Karl Hildebrand. Mrs. Curtius said that when they were in Florence he was living there with his mother, sisters and a literary lady whom he treated as his wife and whom his family received as such but to whom he was not married. Since, he has married her—it was a legal quibble as in Geo. Eliot's case which prevented before . . . .

Did I tell thee that we discovered a most economical custom of the Germans? We were walking outside the city limits when we suddenly found ourselves in a park but divided into hundreds of little gardens, each surrounded by a hedge at least eight feet high and entered by a gate tightly locked. At the further end of each garden was a little summer house containing a table and chairs and in each of these houses was a family drinking beer while the children rolled on the grass. I suppose we walked for an half hour along the paths. Numbers of people were either leaving, locking their gates behind them, or coming and unlocking. Sometimes nurses with numbers of children. Is it not a cheap way of keeping up a country place?

Mamie is so happy when she is walking. Last week the afternoon of the day I was so unhappy I took half holiday and rowed Mamie up our dear little river under a half a hundred bridges into the woods. We pay 10 cents an hour for the boat. Then we walked through the meadow land from which as I saw by placard, our butter comes, and came to a milk garden filled with tables under the trees. We went in and got a deep flagon of milk—2 cents— further on we came to a park in the midst of the meadow where nurses and children were sitting and what was our disgust at finding that these little babies, one and two years old, relieved themselves with the same barefaced- ness which their papas and elder brothers show. Little girls as well as little boys sat or stood against trees with the utmost nonchalance—in public view. We walked on. The children are allowed to stand so early that they are so bowlegged as to be deformed. Also I told thee—did I not— that almost every older man and student has his left shoulder lower than his right?

Certainly Leipzig is a most delightful city in the sum- mer. We have not once been too warm and thee sees— swimming, boating etc. are so cheap. . . . Mrs. Gwinn sent Mamie eight cans of Whitmans chocolate the other day. Tell her when thee sees her, that thee asked me about a box and I said the duty we had to pay was too high. Curiously, the chocolate duty was only 50 cents. I want thee to send me some books by mail. . . also will thee send me my Romola. . . . I find I need summer shirts. . . . It is certainly impossible for Mamie to sew. She is so well—for the first time in her life has she been free from medicines for a year. . . .

I want to tell thee Mother dear—I had a baptism into sympathy with thee last week, resulting from my home- sickness and thy having been sick. . . . I love you both very much and certainly don't wish to say or think any- thing that displeases you. I am so glad Bessie [Nicholson] is happy—she certainly deserves to be—though I still, from my emancipated standpoint, consider it hard-hearted in her to desert her mother merely for a husband and *for fun.*

[To Margaret Hicks ("Clytie")][9]

Bellagio
August 30, 1880

[No salutation]

I opened your letter where of all places but in the Milan cathedral, with the sunset light streaming through the west window—the place of all places to dream in in Europe. At first I thought your letter a very nice one though I was so sorry that you should seriously think of giving up your intentions of being a practical architect. I could hardly believe it after all you had said. When I came to the end you must forgive me for saying that I found the explanation (I do not wish to be unjust but it seems to me you would at least have given it a trial—the work you had chosen and looked toward for so many years had it not been for this). I do not know why I am answering your letter so soon [Miss Hicks's letter was dated July 18]. I only rec'd it four days ago, it was sent from Leipzig to London thence to the Engadine and thence to Milan so it arrived two weeks late. Perhaps to have it over because I have nothing to say, as you know.

In one way your engagement was no shock. Since that first fall term at Cornell I have known that Mr. Volkmann was in love with you—it was such a patent fact to me that I was amazed that "the corridor" was so considerably silent on the subject. But of course I hoped all along that

9. **Scant** though it is, correspondence with Miss Hicks shows that Carey had at this time been neglecting her if not rejecting her despite Clytie's pleading letters: "My darling—Why do you not write to me? I have waited and waited and tried to be patient but—I do not understand. . . have I offended you? It was so very unconscious, beloved, if I did. . . . You are not ill? Where are you? I want you. . . ." etc. This letter from Carey is in reply to a long one in which Miss Hicks writes of how she longs to be with her friend, gossips about mutual Cornell acquaintances, poses philosophical questions (reason versus passion and emotion) for ten and a half closely handwritten pages, and ends by casually announcing her engagement to "Mr. Volkmann—I can't help being happy, though I am afraid it will **displease you.** . . ."

you would care more for other things so in one way I am bitterly disappointed. In Phila. the last time I saw you I thought you were in love with him and that was what made it harder than it otherwise would have been to write to you—what was the use?

Although all this was so, I must confess that the light on the fretted pillars looked a little less golden and fairy-like when I looked up from your letter. I had not realized before how much I had looked forward to being with you again at some future time, though of course I knew it was most improbable. *Tu a changée tout cela.* But this apart—I cannot help being grieved to see another woman with a fair chance for success and influence give it up. I know you do not think it is giving up but do you think I ever did you the injustice to suppose that your theories on this subject were purely abstract?

I think that every girl falls in love with one of the first two or three men who have ever fallen in love with her. This has been substantiated by the experience of every girl I have ever known. If she does not yield to it and devotes herself to other things she is as sure to get over it as men are.

Among men whom I know there are at least six who after having been desperately in love and desperately "cut up" over their refusal, in less than a year have been ecstatically happy over their engagement to some other girl. I am inclined to believe that no woman and of course no man is an exception. We talked over this I think and so what is the use of repeating it? It is not that I idealize work; you know that you always thought that I thought too little of it—but I think each one has his or her independent thought life to live and of course must be able to express this freely in some work. Every one whom I have told of my "architect friend" has said what a nice field it was for a woman and how many branches there were for her to work up. I suppose you can judge but it seems to me that on no subject are people more intolerant of amateur work than in architecture. I have heard a great deal of discussion of plans owing to the Baltimore University and Hospital Orphan Asylum, and now Taylor College, all of which Father is interested in. Of course you can judge and I hope you are right.

Do you not remember my saying you could never be a practical architect and marry—though I believe it, yet I *wish* you were going to try. If one marries at thirty or over when one's pursuit is definitely settled there seems to me much more chance. You know of course this is only a transition state; when things are a little further along the march of progression (*Gott sei Dank!*) I think it will not be so, but now I do not think there is a man who realizes that liberty and money independence and "life work" are as much to a woman as to himself. Every time I have expressed this to a man he says "is it possible for women to feel so. I always thought that a girl when she fell in love gave up all that and considered her husband's work hers."

Since I have come abroad you know what in America I blindly felt I now see face to face—the life in pictures and statues and in higher study. I may never be able to use it outside of my own life; but, the mere looking through its open portal has been enough to make me forever discontented with any other. After Oberammergau, which was marvelous, the moment the Christ came on the stage I felt that he was acting in a sick excitement, I don't know how else to express it, which affected one immediately. The impression deepened, my heart was in my mouth the whole time he was on the stage, every gesture noble and graceful, every word tender and Christlike. I would not have missed it for anything.

Well, after Oberammergau and four days of Munich we spent a week in Switzerland—Zürich, Schaffhausen, Lucerne, Rigi (we saw a perfect sunrise there) and then joined Miss Garrett in the Engadine where I had my first taste of glacier climbing. Have you tried it? The joy of springing over the clear ice that breaks into those marvellous chasms full of liquid bluish air. But delightful as that was I rejoiced when we reached Milan last week—the cathedral and the Brena and the old churches more than make up for scenery. Leonardo's head of Christ was lovelier even than I imagined, and his Last Supper more dramatic. Why is it, do you think, that one bows down before all great pictures and poems, without one's own will coming in, it is like magnetism and one's former life seems barren because without them, and one's future life full of homesickness because lived without.

Oh, that is the worst of pictures and statues and Rome! Since we have been on the Italian lakes—Lago Maggiore and those lovely islands, I little thought when I effused over Jean Paul that I should ever be on the scene of his *Titan*—yes the palace at Isola Bella is the only one I have yet seen that I should like to live in—we spent most of the day rocking in a little boat between blue sky and bluer water and bluest hills thrown into deeper contrast by the Simplon snows. Lake Lugano is beautiful also. Now we are waiting till the rain, our first rain, be over to see Como.

No, Julia is not with us. Her grandmother died and she comes abroad next January. Mamie is asleep in the next room while I am writing in our little parlor to the beating of the lake under my window. I must soon close. I hope you will excuse my writing as I have done—I used to know you well enough to permit me the liberty. I am very much disappointed in you and I think you have made a mistake but it is a very common one. Then too you have seen nothing of family life and I suppose idealize it—you have not had the struggle I have had to lead the life you wish and so of course giving it up means a great deal less to you than it does to me. You see I am trying to make allowance and not to judge you by my rule.

Is your engagement met with applause by the "us who lived in bliss"? *Why* was Pres. White asked to resign? It seems to me the height of ingratitude just as the administration is at a close. Where is Miss Clements now—and why do you not speak at Commencement according to your most fixed principles? . . .

I wish I had seen any women who erred on the side of consistency—you have been fortunate. In a few days we shall be in Venice—then only Athens of the cities one dreams of will remain. Mr. and Mrs. Garrett and Mary will also spend September there. I hope you received my letter written just before I left Leipzig—just as I decided to try and write more regularly comes your letter—perhaps I should not have succeeded anyhow.

Goodnight—you know I wish you every happiness even though it be of the last kind that I should ever have chosen for you. What right have I to choose? None—only the fancied right that having cared for you very much during two very pleasant years gives, and after all that is four years ago.

Yrs very truly,
[Not signed]

Casa Allrestro Bandeni
Siena
October 14, 1880

My dear Mr. Cadbury,

The fates or what not have done their best to thwart my laudable desire to answer your letter. First, Nero is lost. No eloquence could induce the *poste restante* to deliver him. What may this portend? Shall we read success or failure in the omen? . . .While at Venice impatience to receive another Nero overtook me and I wrote to Mr. Gummere for your address, which letter I suppose missed him. Here at Siena of all places your letter turns up in a corner of my travelling bag, so you will receive a much more peaceable letter than if I had written from Venice. In Leipzig I combatted your letter. In Siena—I have just re-read it—I agree. It is an open secret written in every curve of these unutterably blue Sienese hills to write something, to paint something or if not that to try, for it is worth a cycle of scholarship. A heart must be far harder than mine is to walk through gallery after gallery of the masters. . . marking where they worked or lived or died! And then you know, I have told you often, that Germany and a degree was a makeshift. Even so I consider three years of study a trifle to pay for even as little of Italy as I have seen. . . . In return for your advice, which I think I shall follow—do you come to Italy. It would have aided me far more had I made a beginning as you have; but even now, distrustful as I am, I *know* that I shall have a better chance because of Italy. If I could I would never leave it . . . . Here in Siena's "many fountained streets" I am a mystic . . . . But then one must confess Rossetti and Gautier and Baudelaire are bad omens for the future of Eng. and French poetry . . . . I do not think anything will stand that does not appeal to the purely everlasting which is always noble. It is too heavily weighted; what between, as you say, the public who *won't* from principle and the public who *will* from low curiosity, it falls into the hands of would-be artists who read to probe the technique—like ourselves. When one thinks that so much of Alfred de Musset and such really lovely ideal writing as *Mademoiselle de Maupin* contains, is hopelessly lost just because of this—to take extreme examples—it is a lesson. As for Flaubert and Zola, it may be the age needs such moralists if it would only regard them as such but in Art they are abortions. I always think of those terrible charnel houses filled with victims of the plague which Italian talent executes in wax. Also work to stand must not be anti-Christian, as yet . . . .

Leipzig
November 13, 1880

Dearest Mother,

Thy letter came nice and early this week and was also charmingly long, also one from Bessie King and Julia came by the same mail. You each presented a different side of life. Mamie and I were horrified by Cora Johnson's story.[1] I remember her well. I must confess I might easily have done all except drink the tea—that is one of my fixed principles. Thee knows that we *are* careful in the extreme, and it seems to me there is much less danger here than at home—so much more provision is made for dissipation

1. The gist of Cora's sad story is as follows: girl of high moral integrity, fine family, but headstrong, insists on going about alone, gets lost after dark in dead of winter just outside Philadelphia (or Baltimore). Blizzard. She is half frozen when "rescued" by kindly appearing "gentleman" in a carriage, who takes her to his home and gives her tea to revive her. Tea is drugged. She eventually regains consciousness and gets home somehow, and whether she is or is not pregnant is not clear, but upon realizing the worst, she kills herself—or tries to (it is not clear which).

and I cannot help thinking so much more unchastity among the upper classes; why else those repeated advertisements, new ones each day, of quiet families a few miles out of Leipzig or Dresden where best nursing, most nourishing food and *absolute* secrecy are guaranteed to ladies in *delicater verhältnisse.* I sometimes wonder about these conservatory girls. They are so young and most of them out of the class which is not bound by any particular tradition and so very poor that they live about in all sorts of places. Yet one never hears any scandal. (Leipzig is almost given up to providing homes for the 3,236 students and the conservatorists—men and women—It is as Howells says of Italy in winter—one half employed in frying fritters for the other half to eat.) They say Leipzig has a brilliant social life outside of this room renting and floating population but of course we cannot judge.

We have settled down into quiet comfort again and our rooms do look very cozy—we bought ourselves some very beautiful cretonne last week and now at last a little of thy talent developed in me for I made both our lambrequins, pieced them, hemmed them, and put them up—made Mamie a table cover out of cretonne to match, and replaced the green baize which covered the glass doors to Mamie's wardrobe, with blue satin cambric. . . . Also we, or rather Mamie, bought a bust—the young Augustus—he crowns regally my bookshelves. One can furnish rooms luxuriously abroad for so little—warm, eastern cretonnes and stuffs and rugs for a trifle—bronzes and busts of all sorts of porcelain. That hateful customs duty cuts us off—

Second Day evening—

Right here as I was writing Seventh Day a headache descended upon me . . . even today I had to miss my lectures except one from 5-6. Now, however, I feel convalescent. Mamie as usual was as sweet as possible and read me all Blake, a great deal of Keats and Browning. It certainly would be dreary to be alone when one feels sick.

Bessie King's theory, which Mr. Gummere retaled [*sic*] to me with such horror, of marriage at sixty to nurse and be nursed, has its advantages; though I of course believe in

228

sticking to one's principles at all costs. If it were only possible for women to elect women as well as men for a "life's love" as Miss Hicks writes, all reason for an intellectual woman's marriage would be gone. It *is* possible but if families would only regard it in that light! *A priori* women understand women better, are more sympathetic, more unselfish, etc. I believe that will be—indeed is already becoming—one of the effects of advanced education for women. I do not suppose *men* are as satisfactory to men but then I only see my side of shield and they may see well to metamorphose themselves into fit rivals.

According to thy theory, Mother, unless a woman marry, she can only associate with women or with her father, brothers and uncles—no one cares for association that is not friendship, and intimate literary friendship which is far more intimate than society friendship. Thee considers it a great wrong to permit it with an engaged man, almost as unwise to encourage it with an unmarried man and, I suppose, criminal to allow it with a married man. About the first and last perhaps thee is so far right that there is always more intensity in a man's friendships for a woman than for another man and I suppose it is just possible that it might result in his wife's instead of representing all womanhood for him, sinking into his mistress and his friend changing into his love (excellent were it not for the wife). It does seem so provoking that men can't be cool and nice about it as women are; there would then be so little trouble.

A propos of this, it is only abstract reasoning—thee is entirely wrong about any possible objection to my intimacy with Mr. G. He is in love with Amelia [Mott], our talk is the most abstract possible; however, it really makes so little difference to me that I shall follow thy advice if the opportunity ever occurs. I think myself the experience *looks* better to carping eyes, where it is not based upon previous acquaintance, before the engagement, though that makes no real difference. The trouble is it takes so much waste time to get so intimate with a man that he tells you the inner workings of his mind, and if I am ever to carry out my hopes I must know how men think and feel. Here it is already done—thee sees it is like asking an artist to throw away a model—a tool.

About my friendship with Mr. Cadbury I do not see any reason to break it off; besides it would be basest treachery. If thee will write me a promise not to tell Father, or show it to him, or of course anyone else, I will send thee his last letter which came yesterday just to show thee how nice he is—in my way, not thine exactly; but then thee knows we can appreciate our different kinds of niceness. At least I think I appreciate thy kind.

Thurs. morning: I found another blank side to the sheet. I feel completely well this morning . . . . I was shocked to see the small endowment of ["Taylor" crossed out] Bryn Mawr College, that is only about $40,000 a year is it not? . . .

November 21, 1880

Dearest Mother,

. . . I have read over thy letter which came Fourth Day according to a very happy habit thy letters have lately; thee tells me so many interesting things but still no diagnosis of thy catarrh for which I am anxiously awaiting. I agree with thee in thy belief in quack medicine. I do hope thee is already benefitted. It surprised me very much to hear that your Silver Wedding is past—twenty-five years does seem a lifetime to be married . . . .

Yes, Garfield is elected in great measure because the Democratic party dared to announce a principle which could be used by the Republicans as a whip to drive every manufacturing hand to their pole. I believe it will be 100 years before a party is brave enough to support free trade again. I do think mere justice should make you consider that all protection in favor of Northern manufacturers is so much money taken out of pockets of Southern and Western agriculturists. It is the most flagrant injustice. With all the money and invention in America it would not take twenty years before our own manufacturers could compete and all the rest of the country would be paying a *just* instead of an infamous price; most of the lobbying would disappear from Congress.

I consider there are four issues in our Government. First: Hard money (I am willing to give the Republicans one four years more to finish that, though they are so cowardly they delay resumption and will probably quash the whole thing by the silver issue). Second: Free Trade. Third: Civil Service reform introduced into every corner of the Union (this will entirely remove our disgraceful presidential crises), and Fourth: Universal Suffrage for Woman. I consider all talk of freedom and justice a huge joke until this is put through. Mamie and I were saying the other day that we read speeches and poems and novels which fairly bristle with apostrophes to ideal justice and far reaching freedom with a cynical smile. It keeps me from being enthusiastic, personally enthusiastic, for any one of these profs. here. Even Swinburne who has stormed every other institution of man is silent here. Only Shelley leads the poets in this as he has done and will do for the next few decenniums in everything.

We were reading the younger Dumas' last book *Les Femmes qui tuent et les femmes qui votent* the other evening. He takes up the cases which have come up lately in France of women's murdering their rivals, or of fathers shooting men who have ruined their daughters. He mentioned especially that lady who threw vitriol in her husband's mistress's face. She gave as an excuse that not only was she [the victim] his mistress but he swore he would marry her after her own death and she took the only means she had (the law gave her none) to prevent her children's falling into that woman's hands. The jury— *did nothing.*

In all such cases, Dumas says, the juries *do nothing.* Man's laws are so unjust that he himself cannot execute them. He, Dumas, says it passes his intelligence to see why women should not vote. The question is not if all women are equal to all men, but if they are intelligent enough to vote and defend their own rights which are now ground to the dust. He proposes that all men be made responsible for their illegitimate children, that all rape, etc. be punished to the extent of the law, that marriage be made as far as possible in favor of woman and [because] as yet it seems impossible to make a woman quite free in

231

marriage, that such women as are in a position which puts them outside the need of the protection of marriage and who are unwilling to place themselves in the power of a man, should not be *forced* to accept a civil contract so much to their disadvantage but should be allowed to make their own terms (this is the only thing thee would disapprove of). He would of course give women all university and professional privileges and first and last the *ballot*. I have much more hope of France's than of America's leading the way.

I wish I could convey to thee an idea of the way women are mentioned by the profs and in German books. I suppose American men regard them in that light—of course they do because they act thus, but at least they do not *say* so. It has turned Mamie into *such* a woman's righter that I have to laugh at her (thee must not tell Mrs. G. this; she would be in despair). I believe Mamie thinks women should inhabit one continent and men the other and her reasons *are plausible.* I think Plato's *Republic* is the ideal and that the Greeks were right there as in everything.

I have been betrayed into such an harangue but the kettle must boil over some times. Mrs. and Miss Channing have outdone themselves upon the election question— their cool Northern insolence in talking about the South to us is laughable. They are Mamie's first experience of that exquisite thing—Yankey politeness. They *mean* to be as kind as possible; but every time they call, as Mamie says, they emit a volley of insults not only about politics but everything. Mrs. Ch——has a slangy manner, and Miss Ch——a rollicking manner and they both dress badly. But all this would matter not if they only were in the least lofty and not overflowing with little bits of gossip and chock full of prejudices. And the worst of it is that these prejudices are what everyone else would call libertinism. I mean of behavior. They think it very wrong of us not to speak to the students, not to bow to them and allow them to call, etc. They saw no reason against a young conservatory girl and a young conservatorist rooming together alone with an old servant—no one else there and their rooms adjoining and they very intimate—he an

Englishmen, she an American. They thought no scandal could arise. They could not see that, then, if this were allowable, every man and his mistress could live and travel together in what the world regarded as innocent friendship. According to their views Boston is either a community of saints or sinners. Mamie and I incline to the latter view. I think they really like me—and I feel as if it were vaguely my fault . . . .

Gracie's picture came . . . . Tell me about Mary—give her my love.

Leipzig
November 23, 1880

My dear Mr. Cadbury,

"Nero" with the interrogation point came before your letter preferring Italy to him as the subject of my letter, therefore you must let me say a few words; all the more because one owes admiration when one is so lucky as to feel it. Yes, you have given me the first real thrill of admiration that I have ever felt for the works of any of my contemporaries. "Nero" is vastly better than when I saw it before—the scene with the furies is really grand; those lines "lordly indifferent," etc. are glorious. Nero is, to my mind, much more firmly drawn. . . . Yes, you have dramatic power, and just for that reason you will let me, will you not? criticize a little. I think it is a little too long, that is that some of the speeches have too much padding. . . . Also I think you are purposely obscure. . . a great pity. . . . You must take sides with your character. This and the fact that there is hardly one melodious line in it seems to me its chief faults. . . .

I agree with you that we must write ourselves into our work. Goethe was right in his "every poem is concrete in its core." Also love in some form or other is our tool—it arouses the sympathy of our audience, it is something they can each parallel and above all it symbolizes. . . that higher falling in love with the "beauty of holiness," with abstract thought, with yes even with fame in its best sense. . . . This I grant you—but I do on my side honestly think that family life is too dear a price to pay. Don't you

233

remember our talk under the bridge? You thought so too then; witness your remarks about buying coal for a family.

I think that most men and women are happier perhaps married though they do not seem to me "satisfied completely" but still to them it makes little difference; "death in their prison reaches them, unfreed, having seen nothing still unblest." For those of us, and Heaven knows we are few enough who do care to live, whose every would be trade requires us to throw outselves into manifold influences, to send our roots if need be into the ether, never into the earth—how can you think that it is best to root ourselves to one spot, to put travelling out of the question, to lose one's independence—not to be able to risk any money on a literary venture, etc. Instead of being able to give our off hours to ideal work, to spend them in daily gossip with some ordinary man or woman. I cannot see how this helps toward creative work. I believe it is squandering one's birth right for a mess of potage and also I believe the blessing is lost. Very few of my friends have been engaged or married but they fully justify me. Mr. Boyesen with his little gift of lyrics and novellettes has not done one thing since his marriage two years ago and a Cornell man who wrote very ably on political subjects and who had a noble ambition has, since his engagement, given up all his plans and entered business, *etc.*

I despair of you when you write in that way—for Heaven's sake don't marry until you have seen Italy, and Greece, and all the realms of fancy. . . . You cannot think that family life as it is now lived is the stuff that dreams are made of, will really adequately help one. I shall write, to begin on, a love poem of the purest water, a lyrical love drama, and prove you in the wrong, Sir Poet. . . .

For a woman there always remains stirring up women to revolt, waking up girls; it is delicious to plant theories of independence and —oh all sorts of things— it has the excitement of a revolution, the heroic thrill of martyrdom—no but seriously if you knew as much as I do of the unhappy vacant hours of girls in our class of life, married or unmarried, you would see that it is being a very gospel-bringer. . . .

My love drama is going to try to express a moment I have never seen treated—it is perilously near immortality and yet moral to its core. I would tell you the motive but brutal prose tramples its life out—it is too evanescent . . . . Of course you know without my telling you that you are to keep my secrets in return—you know I am supposed to be here lost in roots and old manuscripts . . . .

XMAS 1880
MERRY CHRISTMAS!!

Dearest Mother,

We have been in Vienna ever since Fifth Day and yet I have had no time to write, but I knew thee would not expect a letter before First Day. Where shall I begin? (All our lectures closed Third Day the 21st. We left that night at 9 and went direct through to Prague reaching there at 7 the next morning. It was a lovely sunny day and it is a dear quaint old city full of queer buildings and a beautiful river which divides it and is separated by islands and flanked on either side by high hills.) Prague is a wonderfully beautifully situated city all crisp and sunshiny and misty. Thee knows it is the capitol of Bohemia and the heart of Czech (this is the most outlandish speech that ever existed. There is a great anti-German movement now and so everyone is trying to return to Czech and all the signs on the shops are written both in German and Czech; it looks like this: "Z thn Sczyt"). There is a great palace on top of a great hill and a lovely view of the city and a wonderful clock. But the most interesting of all was the Ghetto, the Jews quarter where until lately they were all forced to live; it is hundreds of years old—it is said that the Jews came here after the destruction of Jerusalem, and we visited the old Jewish graveyard. The stones are great blocks of granite all carved with Hebrew letters and crowded against each other elbowing each other as roughly as their poor owners had to during life. Almost all the stones have the symbols of the different tribes they belonged to—i.e., a jug means the tribe of Levi and so on. I never saw as deserted a looking place. But the old Synagogue was even more curious. It is as large as the sitting room perhaps, and tiny little seats with stiff little reading desks and all sorts of chandeliers holding seven candlesticks, the candles of which are never blown out but after each allowed to burn out according to the old ritual, the guide said. Every Saturday worship is held there, in exactly the old way just as the Jews held it when they fled from Jerusalem. My inherited taste is strong enough to make Jews awfully interesting to me.

I wish I could describe thee the funny mystic gratings and Hebrew scrawls and all the dirty dark gloom of this synagogue. There are nine others there which of course we did not take the trouble to go and see. So altogether our day in Prague was a success. . . .

We left at 7:30 that evening, without thinking, in a way train. We had four shawls and a foot warmer but we needed them all and our train being a way train just sat down to rest by every little stone in the wilderness. . . however at 9 a.m.—two hours late—we arrived in Vienna—the coldest place we ever felt. We drove on a tiny cab that holds only two to the pension. . . .

Frau Pohl is a sweet, kind, coquettish woman. . . her husband is also nice and rather cultivated—a disappointed genius, an inventor who has squandered his money. The daughter is a large eyed sentimental girl who looks languishingly at a gruff handsome Chicago Dr. who is rude and silent and speaks with a nasal twang. There is also a Dr. who poor man has just received such bad news from home—no one knows what it is—that he will not come to the table. Dr. Darling and his sister complete the number—red haired and snub nosed and Irish, but immensely good natured. . . Dr. Darling is very funny and they and indeed the whole pension speaks the worst, the funniest German imaginable. . . .

Tell Father if you think of going to Italy and of course you will—that either he or thee or both must study a little Italian; it is hardly any trouble and as soon as you hear it spoken you understand by instinct; it adds ten times to the pleasure—to say nothing of expense. . . .

Dearest mother—I came to the conclusion the other day that it certainly couldn't pay to have a daughter like me. . . .

February 6, 1881

Dearest Mother,

. . . Zärncke has been having a Gothic quiz twice a week extra. I went in and it is splendid fun. He takes a verse of Gothic and calls upon a man to recite—this man is made Zärncke's text for the whole hour. Zärncke asks him every conceivable question and if he gives wrong answers makes fun of him and leads him on until in some wonderful way of Zärncke's own the whole thing is made as clear as daylight. It is amusing to see a bearded man sitting there nonplussed like a schoolboy. Thus far they have all been stupid; but Zärncke—he only shines more brilliantly the darker their answers. He has not called upon me yet but I should not care if he did as I am prepared. It is excellent practice; I would not have missed it for anything. Zärncke's lectures are inimitable. The men applauded Wülcker vehemently yesterday and from his embarrassment I suppose his wife has just had a baby. He was married last year . . . .

That there is a charm about one's own family I have never denied. I think it is different from anything else and about one's own mother and father I am sure of it. I think our family is a lovely one. Mamie says it is like a family in a Sunday school book in all its branches . . . .

Leipzig
February 10, 1881

My dear Mr. Cadbury,

. . .My drama must wait till I return. As I have told you I do not think my sex is against me. I do not have to support myself. And, by the way, why do you think I consider practical life a lowering—you are a man, you cannot help yourself. How else are your Neros to be pub-

237

lished! You are fortunate in having non-intellectual work. Then certainly Mrs. Browning has not sounded the depths, nor has Christina Rossetti with her broken woman's heart in her hand. . . . She is a poet of with but one string. . . . We must go back to universal feelings, I go with you that far—or forward to Nero. We need a Romantic revolution and a Victor Hugo for our words. . . . One thing you say that I cannot let go. You misunderstood me—I must have spoken carelessly. If a girl with freedom of choice considers marriage with a man whom she loves will increase her happiness and usefulness, I have nothing to oppose. What I do think—and so strongly that I can hardly express myself, is this: you know nothing about it and how could you? Many girls, most girls, all girls who are not even devoted Christians compress all their life into a few society years. Public and family opinion is such as to force them into marriage as a profession. If this be not openly expressed they themselves feel the complete subjection to their fathers. (I know of girls who are treated like children.). . . I assure you that what applies to a man applies to a girl—a life devoid of wider interest is a blank—be it married or unmarried. Heaven help girls and women if they lose the outlet of prayer and religious work before the new era is ushered in! A very religious life fills the void partly, as a free intellectual or active life would do completely but eight children do not anymore than they would yours. I do not think even you, philanthropist hater though you be, would be quite unmoved if you saw so much suffering as I do. No girl will tell you—you are a man. If I felt the void I should not. Let me correct your statement. It is no woman's *duty* to marry; whether she be in love or not, it is her duty to consider true marriage, if you choose, a completion to life but a completion which may come or may not but will surely not come if she marry without love or if the man whom she love be in any way a hindrance to her attaining the highest that she desires. . . exactly so I think it is with a man. I am no fanatic. That marriage would continue I do not doubt. . . . In a transition state I think it would be quite often a *duty* and a pleasure not to marry until the supply of parties of either sex equalled the raised demand. Then you must take into account that very many women never fall in love. . . .

You do not know very much about women or you would never write a girl such letters as you write me. I determined to give our correspondence a **fair trial**. I **allowed** you to write as familiarly as you chose. I've replied almost as freely as I write to my girl friends. If I have hitherto taken no notice of your "impertinences" as you justly term them, it has been because the only possible notice I could take was to close the correspondence. I hoped you would see from my silence how much I disliked them. As in your last letter you increase them and even comment upon my silence, I think it better to tell you frankly that in spite of, nay with my Greek as always I consider such letters, even though written in fun, an offense against good taste and that as you seem unwilling to hold to the letter, as well as the spirit, of our bond, I consider our experiment at an end.

[Undated]

My dear Mr. Cadbury,

I was hurried away by indignation at the close of my letter. I intended to put the closing of our correspondence conditionally, but as I mailed it on the instant, there was no help for it. Since, I have concluded that you are too really "nice" to be intentionally disagreeable, though appearances were so against you in your last letter that at first I thought the contrary. Also I think I should have said that of course I would be sorry to stop writing—there are so few of us who care for ideal work that one cannot afford to lose any sympathy of that sort. But you cannot help seeing that I cannot allow you to write me quasi-sentimental letters. You know you would not talk so. . . . I was so provoked with you that I mounted the rostrum and delivered you a tirade upon women. To be sure it is all true; but it is awfully degrading to mix oneself in reform. . . . I only wished to say that my anger put me in the wrong. I am willing to shake hands across the ocean, to stop the woman question and the "impertinence" . . . to begin again. If you don't care to—alright, only remember I did not stop the correspondence in a pet.

M. C. Thomas

Leipzig
February 27, 1881

Dearest Mother,

. . . If possible I wish to spend a month of next summer here to get started before the semester begins. Do not talk too much about my taking degree because I am awfully afraid I cannot find a German university which will let me try and if they will give me fair play even then, I do not know. Of course I shall have to go ignorant of their theories—I shall wait till I am ready and have my thesis written and then try Göttingen and if they refuse, the other non-Prussian and non-Saxon universities. If all fails I shall have to go to Zürich but that will require at least four months of study there first because of course the profs will be indignant if I do not care to hear them but only care for the degree . . . .

Zärncke is the most delicious man, he stamps his feet and groans with impatience and yet is so good natured and clever. I admire him more than any prof. I have ever seen; he is perfect; the stupidest themes become full of intense interest . . . .

Have you read Tennyson's latest volume of poems? . . . Swinburne admires it greatly. He says "Rispah" is glorious, that it shows that all great poets are bisexual, that in it Tennyson has the tenderness of woman. He thinks it forever places him above his rival Alfred de Musset. Swinburne himself has published a new volume. Is it not nice? Booth is now acting in England with the greatest success. . . . We leave next Sixth Day for Italy reaching Rome by the 13th as I told thee. It does seem very charming to have it so near. . . . I dreamed Harry died the other night and that I most impolitely reproached the other children for not having been the victims. . . .

Leipzig
July 6, 1881

My dearest Mother,

I hope thee will not be anxious at getting no letter, though to be sure this is only one day late. . . Thy letter came Third Day as it usually does now, and was very interesting. . . . I like to hear what the children do and everything. . . thy letters a few weeks ago sounded displeased. Thee misunderstood me. Letters are really so stupid a means of communication. Did I tell thee that Mamie and Julia and I and indeed Mary and Bessie have all had a misunderstanding which it cost a great deal to rectify and we have each lost our temper over it? Now Mamie and I are pacified but we haven't yet heard from them. Then as thee knows I had it bad—homesickness. I felt just as Aunt Hannah says she used to, when she came in town after her marriage and found Grandma out. She would sit down on the steps and sob. It is a sort of nightmare that wakes one up at night—its only manifestation being an overpowering desire to see thee and this being impossible to conceal it from Mamie, which I did not succeed in doing, and tried to live it down.

I went in swimming with Miss Channing. The bath is almost as large as the Phila. Natatorium but has its own German characteristics. In one end penned in by fence railings are the children who can't swim jumping up and down like water bugs. These wear nothing except little tunics like circus acrobats. They range from seven to thirteen or older and when one swims to the railings and looks through have a most emancipated appearance. The older girls and young ladies have short trousers down to their knees but mostly to their hips and their bathing waists are just two pieces of linen tied together over the shoulder—no arm holes and no sides. Even this failed to distract my mind and it was attended by a mortifying circumstance. When I reached home Mamie exclaimed at my changed appearance. I looked in the glass and my face shone like a star with a whiteness which was dazzling. I suppose Leipzig is so dirty that though I wash my face with care often twice a day, the soot gets ground in. Mamie was so impressed that she determined to go the next day.

Seventh Day at 4:10 a.m. (the only through train) we started for Göttingen. There were numbers of people in the street even at that hour and several pairs of students strolling home after a carouse I suppose. At 10 o'clock we reached Göttingen in the rain—a rambling, muddy, dirty little town of about 20,000 inhabitants. We took the one cab which was there and drove into the town to the largest book store where we bought a University directory and threw ourselves on the good nature of the community which directed us to the street where one of the two Müllers—on whom our fate hangs—lived. We did not know which was the German and which the English prof. but concluded to be non-committal until he made some leading admission.

The door of the tumble down house was opened by his wife, a thin, lively woman, not a lady. She took the most active interest in us as soon as we explained our errand. She regarded us in the light of a baby show or some other enormity, I suppose. Her husband had been ill for two weeks and saw no one, but as soon as she heard we had come from Leipzig only to see her "Mann" she rushed up stairs and I am sure *forced* her husband to see us for she soon led us upstairs into the presence of the crustiest, mustiest old prof. in the smokiest of wrappers and caps. We stated our business, told him that we had studied in Leipzig for the past year and expected to study there two more years, told him what we had read and asked him if we were on the right track. He said yes, but told us that in Göttingen the dissertation was the chief thing, that it was required to be something absolutely new and no literary subject or remarks were desired, that often he sent back theses that would have been accepted elsewhere. I said Wülcker had suggested tracing back the *gnellen,* the sources, of Beaumont and Fletcher's plays into Shakespeare and Ben Jonson. This he repudiated. I then mentioned a subject I had asked Wülcker about and which he had approved of: separating the two parts of Caedmon in regard to their word and rhyme-rise and following the subject matter—the creation—back into Greek, Latin, French, etc. and down into Milton. Both Ebert and Wülcker said this would be capital, and it was something I should have cared to do. But Müller would have none of it. On the entreaties of his wife he suggested two subjects (a thing he said he never did for his own students, but "as by being women we were to miss the incalculable privilege of hearing him"—he consented). You probably will not understand how dreadful they are—one was "the Ablaut reihe in Engl." You know *was* and *were* are the only instance of it in Modern Engl. and this involves a dreadful philological study of Anglo Saxon and Old Eng. The second subject was—a prize subject upon which no one has yet written: "the declension of nouns in Engl. from the 13th to the 16th century." If this were too extensive he advised a sub-division— "the *e* of the dative and when it passed into the impure *e* of the nominative and become lost."

He is as nice as he could be and told us dictionaries, grammars, etc. and let us in to his crusty, philological, cranky, dogmatic mind. If we attempt to take a degree there it would have been impossible without seeing him because Leipzig methods are much more liberal and philology is not the one thing—literary subjects such as several Wülcker showed me are accepted: "Who wrote the Phoenix," "Byron in Literature," etc. Thee knows the Grimms—Jacob and Wilhelm—"the great twin bretheren" were at Göttingen and I imagine their influence is still straditionary [sic] there. We left with the kind permission of writing to him when we needed advice and of calling upon him in the summer if needful. It will not be. We know the method of the horrid man now.

This dear old woman could hardly part from us—she made us come into the parlor and questioned us and encouraged us and promised that her "Mann" would always be at our service. She then sent her daughter with us to the other Müllers. He was much nicer but also said the speech was the thing—no literary knowledge counted. He expected a student to take any Middle High German he layed before him in examination and trace the words and forms back into Alt Hoch German and Gothic, also read from Gothic or Alt High German. He asked about our books, said we were safe if we were under Zärncke's direction, and added he should look forward with great pleasure to examining two ladies. He then sent us to the Dekan[2] in his name because the statutes had been changed in the past two years and because the woman statute had altered for, as the Dekan observed, these cases came so seldom he couldn't say. . . . He was very polite and said he would write as soon as he had time to examine the rules.

So at 1 o'clock we found ourselves through our business and with excursion tickets over three days (we saved ourselves $1.50 apiece on the regular fare by them). We went to an hotel and got a beefsteak and potato dinner for 30 cents apiece. Oh, it was delicious! and then I yielded to Mamie's overpowering desire and we took the 2 o'clock train for Cassel—one of the prettiest cities in northern Germany, famous for its gallery. At 3 o'clock we were there and in a few moments wandering through a most lovely park and palace called "On the——?" It was laid out by the architect who designed Versailles in the Watteau Palace style—long avenues of trees. In one of the Pavillions is the Marble Bath where Jerome Bonaparte used to bathe in red wine which was afterwards sold to innocent purchasers. . . . It was lovely. Artificial as it is I like the style—wide lawns and water views and white statues against dark backgrounds of evergreen. Later we went to the Museum where we were disappointed—Rembrandts and Vandykes . . . .

Table d'hote time came. We must take the 4 o'clock train and do without supper if we were to get home—our money was just enough to pay our bill and buy tickets back to where our excursion tickets were good. One expedient

2. Dean.

suggested itself—telegraphing to Miss Channing for a telegraphic order. We did so—for $10. (more than we needed) and then went and dined—the first good dinner since we left Italy—soup, roast beef, cauliflower, spring chicken, salad—potatoes in different ways, ice cream, strawberries and cheese. All this for 60 cents apiece. By three o'clock the postman was counting the 40 marks into my hands. Is it not convenient? We then took the horse cars run by steam to Wilhelmshohe and I never imagined such a lovely place—thousands of people were there because First Day is the only day the water plays. . . . 3 o'clock struck. From the great castle [on top of the mountain covered with firs and on a mass of artificial rock] the water started from a great reservoir in the center of the rock under the Hercules; burst out in twelve fountains in front, rushed through Triton's grotto, whereupon they blew their horns so mightily that we standing below heard them; leaped over the ruin to one side, foamed down the cascades into the lake in the center of which, as if by magic, a fountain sprang up ninety feet into the air with a force that reminded us of nothing else but Niagara . . . .

We reached our hotel at 9 o'clock, still bright light . . . . The next morning at 6 a.m. we left and the hotel keeper was in such a hurry that he charged us for only one night. We did not notice it till we were in the cars, and we cannot feel bound to send it back because it was a horrid little room and our sleeping there one night more cost him nothing extra . . . . Mamie has gotten so fat during our two days lark that her dress won't button. Our trip to Göttingen cost $5 and Cassel $2 extra. Mrs. Gwinn's five $20 notes have arrived.

I am finishing this before lectures but will write again this week if I have time. I was utterly disgusted with those Göttingen profs. I agree with thee—I want a literary training and yet I do think a degree most needful and it seems fully possible to take it. I am sure I can—it is only the waste of time in studying rather off my principal interest. It is a comfort to know definitely and I feel better. . . .

Isle of Wight
October 2, 1881

My dearest Mother,

We spent a part of a day at Matlock. . . then took a coach to Haddon Hall. . . . On to Chatsworth, the finest show place in England. It belongs to the Duke of Devonshire but it is altogether uninteresting—like any German palace. Its park is lovely though. We went to Lichfield for Dr. Johnson's memory and more for its most perfect cathedral. . . then to Kenilworth and. . . the "Regents Hotel" [where we] had the pleasure of seeing your names in the hotel book and splurged on a 5 shilling dinner which was delicious. We found that the Earl was at Warwick and that no one was admitted except on a personal application to him. Mamie wanted to give it up and refused to have anything to do with it but I decided a note even if we did not know how to address him could do no harm, so I wrote "Would the Hon. Earl of Warwick kindly grant the privilege of seeing his castle to two ladies—Miss Gwinn and Miss Thomas—who live in Germany and who will be passing through Warwick tomorrow," addressed it and sent it. The next day we got out of the train at Warwick and walked up to the lodge in spite of the assurances of the villagers that we could not see it. The porter asked us our names and thereupon handed me my letter with "yes" written on the back. I would not have missed the castle for anything; it is worth a thousand Chatsworths and we had the satisfaction of seeing the Earl himself, a little dried up man of sixty, walk into his ancestral hall and take a cane from the rack and sally forth under his primeval trees. Stratford-on-Avon came next. I wish you had seen it. Shakespeare's father's house. . . also the church which contains the bust of him in the chancel put there eight years after his death, but far the nicest thing in Stratford is Anne Hathaway's cottage, a mile across the fields. . . an old woman lives there who is the direct descendant of the Hathaways. . . . The old woman showed us Mark Twain's and General Grant's names where they had signed in the autograph book. We arrived everywhere just after Tennyson and his nephew Hallam Tennyson; their names were before us in all the books. . . .

London
October 15, 1881

[To Mary Garrett]
[no salutation]

There have been many reasons why I have not written to you—of one—that of retaliation I am sure you will not accuse me. So much has taken place, we have seen so much, although so little that I have a wish to cut the thread which I can't take up and just talk as if nothing had intervened [such as] castles, thatched cottages, abbeys, fountains, ruins, baronial halls, cathedral towns, the Scottish lakes, the English lakes, the Isle of Wight, Charlotte Brontë's moors, England's own soft mists that almost make up for Italian skies. It needs Turner to interpret England, and England Turner. . . . I feel less like a ghost now; I have set foot on our literary heritage, but in London the National Gallery and the Elgin Room are the places whither our feet most often turn. . . . In Liverpool whither we repaired for the purpose we saw Irving and Ellen Terry in *The Cup,* Irving in *The Bells,* and them both in *The Belles Stratagem* and in *The Merchant of Venice.* . . .

You say that unless I can write to you as a friend you would prefer that I should not write at all. I could not write to you in any other way if I tried, and if I could I should not care to write. I had wondered a great deal about your not writing, but I understand how it was. After all letters are very unimportant in the long account of a year. You need not suppose I would for a moment think of telling Mamie the contents of your letter. I have no wish to make her angry with you. I think you might have noticed that in my letter I carefully kept from expressing any opinion of Julia's conduct, only my sorrow for it. However, the expression makes no difference. I knew you thought so. You should remember, I think, that even granting what you say, Mamie is so much younger than any of us and our friendship counts by months where yours and Julia's counts by years.[3] Then I think I was very

3. As early as 1881 Carey appears to have been jealous of Mary Garrett's and Julia Rogers's friendship. At the same time, Mamie was not at all fond of Mary Garrett.

much to blame in Rome and I don't like to think that you are unjust to Mamie on that account. However we will leave it—if you explain Julia to yourself as you do, you can understand at least how very different Mamie's conduct looks to me. I have too much faith in your justice to believe that you will be anything but most fair to Mamie in the future. If I did not care about your liking her I should never have said even this much. You must excuse it.

It is 10 o'clock, Mamie is asleep and I am writing before the fire; it is cozy. I wish you would appear—we would draw the sofa before the fire and I would first see for myself if you really looked better. Then you would talk and I would tell you how great a difference realizing that Bessie is ill has made, and how statues and pictures and mad ambition have raised a sort of mist between myself and Mother. I love her even more across it—so much that being with her this summer has made being without her now very miserable, so that my eyes fill when I think of her, but I feel the mist is there. I do not know whether she does. I have felt afraid of the Elgin sculptures—they make me unspeakably wretched. I feel my eyes crushed shut before them—it is no use. I can never rise to them; they make the life of one who cares for them a fitful fever, and one can never be the same afterwards. Bessie's feeling is much more healthful—she does not care either for statues or pictures that way. I have been thinking this summer as I saw how these things affected Father and Mother and others that there could be no excuse for the passion I cannot help giving them—no excuse except its sanctification in reproduction (like sexual passion). It is otherwise, and perhaps then, the misery of "varying from the kindly race of men." Ah, false Tithonus, where is my goddess, my Aurora? Do you know I have absolutely had a sobbing fit over this letter? I am almost glad you were not on the lounge after all. Still if you had been I could have kissed you goodnight as I cannot now. There is "nothing between us" now, is there?

Leipzig
November 10, 1881

My dear Mr. Cadbury,

I am sorry to have left your last letter so long unan-
swered; it waited for me some time in Paris, and after that
came Father's and Mother's sailing and England. I am no
longer an American ghost. I have claimed my heritage—
my castles and ruins, abbeys and cathedral towns and
thatched cottages, my lakes, the homes of my poets, my
dramatic landscapes, my English mists, my purple
heather. Never did the laurel wreath seem so desirable as
walking across Charlotte Brontë's moors, or sitting in the
little garden of Anne Hathaway's cottage, or climbing
Helvellyn by the path Coleridge and Wordsworth and
Southey took . . . .

I carried away one overpowering, glorious impression
from Switzerland—that is Monte Rosa. I watched it one
whole day lying on an opposite mountain and saw the
moon lights fade and flush into Alpine glow after sunset.
I never expect to see anything more beautiful—but for the
rest—the mountains crush back my thought somehow.
Well, and Leipzig, the four walls of my study after all—
Europe. If it had not been for Zärncke I should have
thrown down my books in a pet long ago; he is most
admirable, none of your piteous, dwarfed pedants. He has
shown me the possibility of a perilous path—few there be
that find it. During his lectures I feel like saying, "You
and I know your lectures are masterpieces, it is our secret," but alas, like an actor they will die with him.

You will get to Italy too late, they are putting in a
steamboat on the Grand Canal. . . now I know it is simple
truth, if I lived in Italy I should never write a line. . . .
Before I go again I shall win the right to go. . . . Do you
ever feel put on your mettle to make good your right "vary
from the kindly race of men"? But I forgot—you are far
from the Lotus-land or even from stray bits of Phidian
marble. I see I am entering the confessional. I meant
rather to tell you that you must consider the grating

between us closed. Your former letter displeased me *extremely*. As you say, you have won the right to some indulgence and so you see I have answered your letter without rancor, but even the author of "Nero" cannot be excused for allowing his dramatic taste to lead him into such personal applications as in your former letter. It is too absurd to tell you in every other letter that this or that sentence is unsuitable and yet I cannot let them pass as if you had said nothing daring. I resign my censorship. You have an admirable knowledge of *what* to say but you do not know or do not care to regard, what *not* to say. Nevertheless I hope you will send me "Samson" and whatever else you write. Try and suspend your judgement of my method until six years hence. Till then keep a place on your library shelves. Do not backslide. I am more afraid of that than you can be lest I should never begin. "The rest is silence."

Yrs sincerely,
M. C. Thomas

Leipzig
December 10, 1881

Dearest Mother,
MERRY XMAS! MERRY XMAS!
. . . Our holidays begin next Fourth Day week, the only holidays we have spent in Leipzig. I feel a little afraid I shall not like Gertrude so very much as I do now—men and girls are apt to lose their charm for me after the first, but still Mamie and Bessie and Mary Garrett have not—so I will hope . . . .

Thee knows that to the German man a knife and a toothpick are like the chopsticks of a China man—forks and spoons are an aside. Yesterday at our hotel a man absolutely put his toothpick behind his ear (like a clerk's pen) whenever he had done using it. They are certainly the most horrid race in the world as far as personal habits are concerned. . . .

I asked Fräulein Pochhammer if she would be willing to talk to me two hours a week at 25 cents an hour. She agreed, but afterwards wrote that as it was no trouble to her she could take no money for it. I shall have to make her some sort of a present, I suppose. I think it will be a help, although she does not correct me quite severely enough. I find her really well read and cultivated and she tells me a great deal about German life. She says that most of the marriages she knows of are so unhappy in the first place, so many children and absolutely nothing to support them with, she says she thinks to herself, "Well, if you do not marry you can at least never be unhappy, though perhaps you may not be quite happy as if your marriage were one which only comes once in a thousand unhappy ones." I have been thinking of her German, and so I fear my English sentence is confused thereby.

It is very amusing to hear a sentimental German woman talk. Any cynicism is better than such sentiment. The sense of humor in an Englishman or an American saves him from those unutterably soft depths. Now mother, how can thee argue that a profession is discredited because a man or woman of genius who pursues it happens to be like nine-tenths of the rest of the world? Thee might say that poetry was lowering because Byron was brutally dissipated or that Turner's water colors are degrading because he lived with a woman who was not his wife, or Goethe or Alfred de Musset, or Heine, or George Sand. I believe the artist and his art, the poet and his poetry, the actor and his acting, are as far apart as the heavens from the earth and I am sure thee does if thee will only think about thy own argument of not judging a creed by the fallible men who profess it . . . .

I am very sorry thee told Aunty Hal and Bessie about Bryn Mawr and I do not want thee to tell Aunt Hannah. Can thee not tell Aunty Hal to ask Bessie again to say nothing of it? She might tell Frank and Frank might tell Frank Allenson and then everyone would know, also Aunt H would never think and would tell Mrs. Shipley. Thee sees there might be circumstances under which I would not want to go there; it might start like a primary school and make the professors work too many hours a day so that no time was left for independent work—there might be a thousand *"mights"*—I feel sure that I could make

251

French and German a success though—the field is glorious . . . .

Plattenstr 43 I, Zürich
June 1, 1882

Dear Uncle Allen,

The photograph arrived before thy nice letter and I was delighted with it, esp. with little Miriam . . . Edward looks very much the same, but older of course. Aunt Rebecca looks natural also but I do not think it is so good of thee. It was very kind of you to think of sending it . . . . I want to thank thee for the *Atlantic* thee so kindly sent. I read the article on Leipzig with interest. It seemed to me very accurate.

I suppose thee has heard of our sudden move to Zürich. I had just prepared myself for an examination at Göttingen and expected to take it in August. I relied upon the letters of a Frau prof. in Göttingen whose husband had brought my case up and had rec'd word that there could be no objection: my Cornell degree and my three years at Leipzig putting me in the position of a man. Unfortunately this Frau prof. was the intimate friend of the women with whom we lived and who for financial reasons was very anxious to have us stay. Fral. Pochhammer had deceived us before, but I never thought of distrusting her; however when I went to Göttingen myself I found she had kept back all the necessary information—*formally* there *was* no objection, but each of the forty-two profs had to be asked his opinion upon the woman question and if two or three disagreed my fate would be decided in the negative. The head of the Philology interested himself very much for me, wrote my petition himself, made me send him my degree, a sample of my thesis, all my Leipzig certificates and did his best to put it through. He failed, but wrote me the nicest letter saying that he hoped my successful scholarly work would meet with the deserved recognition at some other university, etc. You will understand what a disappointment this was because I should have preferred a Göttingen degree. I had prepared myself for the requirements and not only are the Zürich examinations much more difficult but they are different, requiring Old and Modern German and English literature in addition to other things and adding to the two and a half hour oral examination, which German universities demand, a clausura examination of six hours and a paper upon any subject the examiner may propose to be prepared in three days time with the aid of books of reference. A dissertation is also required, just as in Germany, and it cannot be less than 32 8mo [*sic*] pages of print. If my pride had not prevented my giving up I should have lost heart at first, but now I am almost glad of the change of univ. residence. Zürich has many profitable lectures, esp. most admirable ones upon Old French, which I was going to the Univ. of Paris for later. This quite reconciles me to the savage rules here which prevent my coming up for examination under three full University years in Germany—viz before next October.

Thee doubtless remembers Zürich and the lovely snow mountains which circle the horizon upon every clear day. It is interesting also to see coeducation in its stronghold. It seems to work admirably and I am especially pleased with the respectful way in which men treat the women. There about twenty studying here and of these thirteen are in the Medical department. There are so many things I have to talk to thee about. I feel as if a whole year more were a long time to wait before returning and yet I enjoy every moment of the time and wish life were a patriarchal length in order to enable one to read and see one's mind and eyes full, as Uncle Robert says.

I suppose Mother told thee that Engl. Philology had led me into German and now I find that the Old French will be a great advantage. The three are so connected. What they call "the new philologie" and the "young Grammarian" movement seems to be carrying all before it. It certainly simplifies everything; it is like evolution in science but Mamie begins to put her fingers in her ears when I start to ride this hobby of mine. Nevertheless it is worth riding. I have been very much struck by the very thing thee mentioned in thy letter—the great difference between knowing a subject and being able to impart one's knowledge. Among all the lecturers we heard at Leipzig only two had the latter gift. Indeed I have ceased to think that scholarship as such is one of the world's best things because almost every prof. we heard *knew* everything in his own special line, had edited texts, written original studies upon important and unimportant subjects, and yet so many lacked "literary sense" and unbiased thinking and real *ability*. Realizing this, as I did during the last year, was a shock. Yet there is one man, Zärncke, whom I admire more than I ever thought it possible to admire any one man. Of him personally, of course, I know nothing (I have no doubt his knife and his toothpick play as important a part in his dinner as in that of other Germans) but on the lecture cathedra he is beyond praise. The ablest of the "young grammarians" are his scholars and think the sun rises and sets in him, so we hear from people who know them—and he really is little short of a genius. I prize the privilege of having heard all his courses of lectures more than anthing else since I have been abroad, except perhaps Italy, and Italy is more a birthright than a privilege—"the day dream of the Germanic races" some German calls it. No, I feel as I should never live a life which would cut me off from revisiting Italy again and again and when I am old and have done my day's work in my own land and all my dearest friends are dead, I shall take some Roman flat for the winter, a corner of some Venetian palace for the Spring, and a room in a villa at Frascali for the summer, and be happy.

Mamie and I are going to spend this summer between Siena, Florence and Lago Maggiore. I shall have to read Old Engl. and German seven or eight hours a day or else the statues and pictures and Italian scenery will make me forget all such base lore, but the rest of the day I shall revel—living in Italy only cost us $12 a month more than in Zürich and the St. Gottherd tunnel has brought us within ten hours of Milan.

I have been very egotistical, but before I cease I will tell thee our plans for this next year. After I take my degree we shall go to Stüttgart for two months to stay with some warm friends of ours there and practice speaking German.

Thence to the Univ. of Paris. If I find I have $25 to spare we want to go to London in the season and taste the pleasures of mighty Babylon. Seriously, Rossetti's pictures are the chief attraction. There is to be a great exhibition of them and we may never have the chance again.

. . . I cannot believe either thee or Aunt Rebecca looks much older in only three years . . . I found Mother and Father did not seem older. If it had not been for their coming over I could not have plucked up heart enough to stay this next year . . . . I often think of thee and Aunt Rebecca and of your kindness to me. I feel as if I owe you both a great deal. Thy very affectionate niece . . . .

Thee knows I do not want my degree spoken of to anyone outside of the family.

Zürich
June 25, 1882

Dearest Mother,

It is Fifth Day between lectures. A student and I are occupying this lecture room waiting for the rest to collect—hot outside and in but all the lecture rooms have a view of the lake, which makes up for anything. The students spend all their spare time in looking out of the windows and I imitate them whenever I can find a spare window. . . . One student belongs to a duelling club and they spend most of their day in practicing fencing. He says eight duels have been fought this month, the students all travelling into Germany to fight them. They are absolutely prohibited in Switzerland. The last one was kept secret but the police found it out and each member of each duelling club had to pay a fine of $20 and the chief actors were shut up in the common prison for fourteen days with thieves. After that he says they have preferred to go to Germany to fight. Every evening from eight on they have a *kneipe*—all the members of the club and drink and smoke, etc. Last night they hired a great gallery hung round with lanterns and had their *kneipe* on the lake till morning—all night long. It is certainly a demoralizing kind of a life for men who have to settle down and work but I do not wonder they cling to the duelling and all the fun.

Every time the police authorities have tried to suppress duelling in Germany the professors and older men have come forward and prevented it—they say if students do not choose to study they shall not be made to do so and robbed of their amusements. It is extremely interesting to hear what this dueller has to say for himself. He is the most easy going man. He is now sound asleep at 1:30 p.m. . . .

We read [your letter and one from Mamie's mother] in a dear little ice cream parlor back of the general salon, over plates of apricot water ice (we allow ourselves a ten cent plate every Saturday).

There was a very decided chance of my being allowed to try at Göttingen. The head of the philosophical faculty thought it possible and was as much surprised as could be at the result. He apologized in his note for having been mistaken and spoke as nicely as he could about my work. I cannot say I regret it entirely because I wrote my dissertation with the aid of books which it would have been almost impossible for me to obtain anywhere except at Leipzig where the library sent for books which I wanted.

Of course my dissertation will do, dearest mother. I am only waiting for two books to come from England to copy it and lay it up in lavendar. What I mean about the extra delay is this: Breaking off at Leipzig in the middle of a term of course made me begin the term here so late that I could not be examined till next term. The rule is that you must have six Univ. terms, or three years, now I have had five terms, and this half term begun at Leipzig and finished here. As I came so late it will not count as a whole term unless I hear lectures to the very end instead of taking my examination a month before the end as I should have at Göttingen. Thee must not feel worried about it. I could go up for examination now and get through if they would let me. Their method and the things required are more difficult and so I want to study as much as possible through summer so as to pass as well as I can but that I shall pass I do not doubt.

The students here say the profs rarely give more than "cum laude" even for an excellent examination, and very often just "rite." The universities differ greatly in their customs about degrees. I want to be examined as soon after the Univ. opens next fall as they will allow. Probably the second week in November. I am quite sure I cannot take as good a degree here as at Göttingen because I had about prepared myself for that, and now have to prepare myself again for other requirements. It is a nuisance but still I do not regret the trouble . . . . Please do not tell anyone that I am going to try, nor the time, because something might happen.

A married woman took her degree here last year and died before the degree could be made out. She left a will saying it was her own fault, that she had worked fifteen hours a day although she knew she had a low fever all the time and that she did not wish her death laid to the charge of women's education, it was her own consummate folly. And so it was . . . .

I have told thee have I not of Mamie's sudden leap into a non-nervous condition? It came like a flash after the Easter vacation. I think her constitution has recovered its tone—of course she was completely broken down when we left home and last summer was very nervous, but now there is the greatest change. I tell her she has become thoroughly reasonable . . . I hope her staying is right. She genuinely wished to return but Mrs. G——will not allow it. She also wrote she had a very nice visit from thee. Be sure and tell me all thee knows about Bessie King. If thee thinks she will not get well I had much rather know it . . . I am so glad I saw her in London and all this year . . . .

[No date, 1882]

Dearest Mother,

Thy letter was very nice and a great comfort, although I have gotten through my slough of despond and feel very cheerful. I would not give up my Ph.D. for anything—the difficulties are like the retarding element in every proper love drama as Zärncke says: they make it ten times more desirable . . . .

As for Paris thee knows that is necessary for my French and thee needn't feel the least anxiety—I shall find some nice family and live with them. I already have the address of one. The attendance of women at the University is the regular thing there. Thy stories are very dreadful and it makes my blood boil to think that women have not the power to vote against such enormities, but for myself I know I shall be safe. Lots of girls go—and I feel a perfect capacity to take care of myself and not one atom afraid of anything. Nothing could make me "die of shame" except doing wrong myself. Thee will have to "trust" me when the time comes, I am afraid. . . .

I am heartily glad Bryn Mawr does not begin till 1885. I hope by that time to be able to make myself *very desirable* and I have no doubt I shall desire a career only unless I feel that I am thoroughly prepared—up to my own standard I mean, not up to the ordinary professional standard which is very low. I am afraid of Mr. Wood's getting in and interfering with the position that I want. I hope he is stationary at the J.H.U. . . .[4]

Mamie is going to Berlin next week for two weeks. . . I wish I could go too. . . but I do not want to spare the time and then statues and pictures upset me. Wouldn't it distract thee to have the clouds open and the heavenly Jerusalem peep through? Mamie has had an inspiration in regard to her going home. Mrs. Gw——has been writing that she does so hate to have her come without any chance of seeing anything more, that she would prefer her staying over six months more. . . . She—Mamie—proposed to her mother to return at once in Aug. or the middle of July. . . and then come over again in April and join me in Paris. . . . Don't speak as if I had written thee of it, only if she speaks to thee of it, *be favorable*. . . .

4. Probably Henry Wood, professor of German and English at the Johns Hopkins University, 1881-1925.

Florence
September 8, 1882

Dear Mary [Garrett],

I found the Swinburnes today at my bankers, and among them greatly to my delight Blake and the study of Shakespeare which I had not asked for. I arrived in Florence later than I had intended owing to [brother] Harry's desire to see me. As he was anxious to travel seventy-two hours for that purpose I decided to devote the ten days to showing him Milan, Verona, Venice and Florence. . . . In Venice we sat on the piazza and ate ices and listened to the music till ten every evening, took all our meals at the Quadri and were true Italian vagabonds. We were never out of a gondola except when we were admiring some Bellini and I believe Harry thinks he will never see anything again like Venice. Yet the Grand Canal is covered with steamers which run every few minutes, and Ruskin's blackened palaces will grow dingier than ever . . . .

Florence
October 10, 1882

My darling Mother,

. . . Our rain culminated in a tremendous thunderstorm at 1 o'clock night before last. For the first time the lightening frightened me; it seemed to quiver in all parts of the room and then came such a crash of thunder that we were sure the house had been struck. We got into bed together in order to be killed in a less lonely manner and at last went to sleep. The next morning we found that the lightening had indeed torn off the roof of the Carmine, a church two squares off, and had killed two people in a house near by.

Our two English ladies, the photographer and the artist, started for Venice in spite of the floods; they have to walk an hour where the tracks are gone and cross a bridge of boats, but still what is that to not seeing Venice?

Miss Newton is left and a table full of Germans who are amusing after the fashion of a menagerie, as they talk incessantly . . . .

259

It is worth everything to read an English book now and then and feel the beauty of our noble words; there is no such language as English among European tongues, and then our glorious verse—as Swinburne says, England alone has caught the torch of song which Greece let fall. So long as I cannot be an Englishwoman I am at least thankful for being an American. My next letter will be written from Zürich . . . We should love to go to Nice, Mentone, Cannes, etc. Looked at from one point of view it seems as if the delay in getting the degree were just arranged to fall in with that plan. It is the loveliest part of Europe and all winter long full of oranges and lemons and roses. Then the lower towns in Provence are charming with their Roman ruins and cathedrals and associations of troubadors, etc. Mamie declared it is the only thing for which she stayed over this other year . . . .

Thy long and interesting plea for the Old Testament was duly considered. Of course inspiration passes through a medium but the higher the inspiration the less human coloring. Take for example the New Testament—the Evangelists I have no doubt were quite as vindictive and bigoted as Moses, Joshua, Samuel, etc. The Jews are the same now and were the same then—a most terrible set of people to my way of thinking, and grand only as a very deep narrow rift between two giant cliffs is grand, from which its very narrowness enables one to stand at its bottom and see the stars at noonday, but the revelation was so full that the Evangelists wrote like men in a dream things they knew not. Paul was further removed and wrote quite a little of Paul into his epistles. But I will save the rest for some long talk some night when Father is off at some Y.M.C.U. meeting . . . I must confess to never having read such a mass of sermons, hymns, gospels, exhortations as what I must consider the one-sided nature of Old High German inflicts upon me.

Zürich
November 25, 1882
Evening After the Ex!!!

Darling Mother,

"Hail the conquering hero comes." I never dreamed that I would have anything so very delightful to tell thee and

Father of—that is enough for the first; now read composedly on and I will begin at the beginning and tell you everything in order. No. 1. *My dissertation.* I handed it in last August in order that the professors could read it at leisure with the aid of books which were not in the library here and which they had to send for. When I came back after the vacation the Dekan told me that he had rarely, if ever, heard the chief professors speak in such high terms of any thesis, of the learning or rather wide reading and clear critical arrangement shown in the treatment of subject matter; in short they were delighted with it. This I did not write thee because I wished to tell thee everything at once. No. 2. *My three days Examination at home.* This took place three weeks ago and here again I can't tell thee all the nice things they said about it—was in Engl. literature as thee knows. After it I was quite ill for three days with a terribly severe headache and fever. I sent at once for Dr. Heims, the most prominent woman doctor here. She did everything possible for me when she heard I was on the point of passing my examination. Mrs. Putnam and the two Misses Putnam took possession of my room and me, gave me medicine, read to me etc. . . . in a week I was well enough to go up for my written examination of six hours on *German Philology.* That also was accomplished most satisfactorily. This was a week ago and then I began to get very much excited. I knew from the manner of the professors that they thought I ran the chance of taking a good degree—they begged me to be calm in the oral examination and told me that so many students became unnecessarily confused from mere terror. As thee may think, this made me more frightened than ever. . . . The oral examination consists of a three hours examination before the philosophical faculty of the University and after the candidate has left the room a vote is taken which must be unanimous and the result is communicated by the Dekan. This semester two men have failed and another man in my subjects took a "rite." There are thee knows four degrees—"rite," "cum laude," "magna cum laude," "summa cum laude"—"Rite" is the usual degree, "cum laude" is considered very good, "magna cum laude" is rarely given and "summa cum laude" almost *never.* So the students and professors here told me. I had set my heart on a "magna" but it seemed to me almost impossible to hope for it because I had the added embarrassment of speaking German and the decided drawback of being examined by professors under whom I had not studied (I was only here two months last semester, thee knows). Also I knew most of the profs not at all, which cannot help making a difference. I thought of all these things, I became more and more nervous, I could not sleep or eat during all this past week. If it had not been for Dr. Culbertson's medical assistance I do not know how I could have gotten through it. She said she had three reasons for defeating my nervousness! I was an American, a woman, and a girl whom she liked. I took everything she gave me, strychnine, valerian, etc. Today before the examination she made me drink two cups of strong tea without milk and herself walked with me to the door of the University. I wore my brown brocade and velvet, the one I had on at my Cornell Commencement, and a pair of seal brown gloves to match.

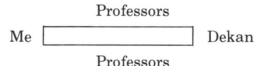

I was shown into a large room with a long center table covered with green baize. They told me to sit at one end and each prof as he examined me took his seat at my right or left, and all the others listened. These were the chief divisions—Anglo Saxon Philology one-half hour, Engl. and Anglo Saxon historical Grammar one-quarter hour, German Philology, Gothic, Althochdeutsch, etc., three-quarters hour. German literature one-half hour, Mittelhochdeutsch one-quarter hour, and a quiz upon the development of Engl. literature one-half hour. As the time for each came the Dekan would strike on the table and the examiner would give place to another. As soon as I got into the room I felt perfectly calm and was able to answer with perfect distinctness. I made almost no mistake and knew everything they asked. All the laws of the development of Gothic out of Indo Germanic were never clearer to me than at the moment of the examination. The clock struck 6 (I had entered at 3) and the Dekan asked me to retire. I did so and found the *pedell* [proctor] and his wife waiting outside to console me during the time of the deliberation of the faculty. They said they were sure I would get a "cum laude." I felt as if I might possibly get a "magna cum laude." You can imagine what those five minutes of waiting were. I never never felt such a sensation of choking anxiety. The message came to enter. I did so and stood at the foot of the table—the Dekan rose and said he had the pleasure of welcoming me as a Dr. of Philosophy of the University and of informing me that the faculty had bestowed upon me the highest honor in its power to give—"SUMMA cum laude." He then handed me my documents and shook hands.

Mother, is it not too splendid to be true? I never dreamed of taking the highest possible degree—a degree which no woman has ever taken in Philol. before and which is hardly ever given. Often twenty-five or forty years will go by without its being given because they are so very strict here at Zürich. I can hardly believe it now. The *pedell* and his wife could not comprehend it—they said it was unheard of. But still it is true . . . .

Dr. Culbertson was almost as pleased as I was—if that were possible. You know that taking a degree here is very different from a degree at our colleges where whole classes go up. Here no one takes a degree except the few picked men who intend to be professors either in the Univ. or in the higher gymnasia. A number of women have taken medical degrees but I believe only one has ever taken a "Dr. of Phil." Now think what it is to get the highest degree among these few. There, I have crowed out all my delight and will try to write like a reasonable being. One more conceited remark I must make—that is, it is very unusual for a student to take a degree under five years or at the least four, and thee sees I have only studied three, beginning from the very beginning too, as my Classical studies were of no assistance in the New Philology.

Thee knows I am only so pleased because I hope it shows that after awhile I can succeed in the line of work I have chosen. If with my present knowledge I can write a dissertation that is good, I ought to be able to investigate other more important subjects equally well with the knowledge I hope to gain. . . .

I leave here on Second Day night and reach Spezia Third Day where Mamie will join me from Florence. Spezia, thee knows, is where Shelley spent the last two years of his life and the house is still standing where he and Mrs. Shelley and Leigh Hunt and Byron, etc. used to talk till morning. I believe I care more to see it than any other place, so we are going to start there and make our way up the coast, which is said to be the most beautiful in the world, to Nice. It is so lovely to be able to take a rest in the loveliest part of Europe and I hope we shall be able to make it cost very little. . . .

I feel as if the taking of my "summa cum laude" were robbed of half its pleasure because I cannot tell you about it and receive *instant* congratulations. . . . It's the very nicest thing that has ever happened to me yet—except having such a nice home and such enlightened parents. . . .

Give my love to all the children. Tell Nell she had better come to Germany as it is just splendid. Ask my dear boy Harry if he is not glad?

With the dearest love to Father and thyself,

Thy loving daughter,
DR. M. C. Thomas!

Be sure and tell Uncle James—

Spezia
November 30, 1882

Dearest Mother,

[After an inspirational description of Shelley's house and the scenery.]

. . . My pleasure over my degree is still as great as ever. I must tell thee all the nice things or rather some of them, that the profs said. No woman has ever taken a "summa cum laude" before since Zürich has admitted women— either in medicine or science or philosophy and the friends of coeducation are delighted. All the papers of Zürich are going to contain an account of it[5]. . . . I am trying to remember some of these things so as to show you how very much pleased everyone was. For the first time in my life I rather enjoyed being stared at. Dr. Culbertson said that at First Day (the day after the examination) dinner the fifteen students who dine at the pension could not eat their dinners for looking at me and when we left the table they dropped their knives and forks and preserved a profound silence until the door closed after us. It was so on the streets. . . . Altogether the whole thing was as nice as possible . . . .

I care as much for the "cause" as for myself. I only wish I could have a chance of working for it as well as I feel that I could work. Of course I suppose it is impossible and that they would never give it to me but I should love to have the presidentship of Bryn Mawr. I believe I could make it the very best woman's college there is, so that **English and German women would come and study there—that is. I believe it could be so managed and I do not believe any other person whom they could get would have the interests of other women so at heart and, at the same** time, would have the requisite training to enable her or him to see what was needed. I have an American Univ. education to begin with, two and a half years at Leipzig, one of the first Universities of Germany, six months at Zürich and the highest honor the University could award my scholarship, all the higher because I came to them from another University and could expect no favor, eight months at the University of Paris, and if necessary I could reside at Cambridge to see the working of the Engl. system. If it were not that Father and Uncle James were on the board and the other trustees were more or less friends of yours; I mean if it were any other college about to open I should write and propose myself as a candidate—In this case it is out of the question of course. I feel

5. There follows a detailed description of what each of her professors said and of their hopes for her future: they expect great scholarship and original discoveries and books from her.

that as a professor I. . . could. . . be as admirable as I know how, but after all under a president who did not understand the necessity for harmonious working it would be a waste of energy compared to the forward impetus of a college in unity with itself. Even in Leipzig I saw so much inefficient teaching because the profs are in great part appointed by political influence, etc.

I wonder what a college would accomplish whose every prof. was the right man or woman, in the right place! What ever the Bryn Mawr trustees decide upon I hope they will select a *young* man or woman for president who knows what is demanded for the needs of today and I hope they will send such an one abroad if he has never been. The reason I care so much is that neither at Smith nor Vassar nor Cambridge have women the opportunity for the highest education and here in this new college it could be combined with more elementary work to the disadvantage of neither—if any other woman (and of course I think a woman would be better fitted for the position than a man) can carry this out I shall be happy— for after all what I have at heart is that this new opportunity for women may not be wasted—and a little orthodox Quaker pride that we shall be the people to provide the highest woman's college.

In any case I want Father and Uncle James not to allow them to appoint a prof. of English or of German or French literature without telling me so that I may apply if I wish—I do rejoice in my "summa" for this reason also—it ought to secure me a profship in any woman's college in the country. . . .

Mamie had a nice time in Florence and arrived with a bouquet as large as a bushel basket given by the prof. and a most breakable rose vase a gift of the countess.

Mentone
December 20, 1882

Dearest Mother,

. . . Thee cannot imagine anything more desolate and more lovely than a group of palms beside the sea. Olives too are melancholy; they are silver in the sunshine and

266

black as ink under a cloudy sky and twist themselves into all sorts of human forms. It is so long since I have had the time to idle that I revel in it. . . . It is so lovely to sit by the beach and see the blue waves break into such snowy foam, always in the same place, never rising nor falling, always in the same spot. . . . Yesterday we took our Christmas drive to Nice—four hours on the cliffs overlooking the sea, "the most beautiful drive in the world. . . ." The road is steep and one looks down hundreds of feet to the sea and up at the sheer crags with romantic little villages, or robber castles. It costs $2.50 the drive. . . .

A long very nice letter from Anna Shipley saying she is to be married in June and that at Christmas they begin building on their lot in West Phila. I suppose having opened Miss Hicks' letter thee read it—such a flippant letter. I wonder that I ever liked her. She is to be married the 28th of Dec. The nicest thing my mail brought me was two letters from thee, short though they were . . . . Mother how *could* thee say "different to" in thy letter—an English vulgarism probably caught from Mr. Harris. All English grammarians lament over it and all correct writers— Matthew Arnold, Swinburne, etc. do not dream of using it. It is almost our one point of difference where we Americans are correct. I have had to spend at least one whole day correcting my first package of proof. My dissertation looked at dispassionately at this space of time seems to me too too stupid, too unimaginably dull!—it deserves *more* than the highest degree—to have an intelligent being for four months of her life eat dust and grovel in the mole holes of the earth to collect *such* data. Thee and Father *must* read it—I insist upon it. Harry shall administer it in doses of a page a day. It is the least you can do, when I had to write it, and all the time think that they thought it splendid at Zürich. You will then have all the conditions for a Greek chorus on the vanity of the overvaulting ambition of man.

Monaco
Here I had to pause to pack and then twenty minutes on the train brought us here to this garden of the gods. It is

lovely, lovely, lovely . . . . and I can never give thee any idea of it—the "charm of the serpent" perhaps gives it its unearthly bloom for there twenty minutes off where the lights blaze is the great gambling house of Europe where hundreds of people are now losing and winning millions. There are four towns in this little principality—Monte Carlo where the great Casino is with its gambling hall, its reading rooms and grounds which are most lovely—every kind of tropical and brilliant flower. Clustered about this are the four great hotels where the wicked people stay all of which belong to the owner of the Casino. Second, Monaco on its beautiful peninsula where the natives live and all about which lie the most wonderful gardens . . . . Third, a little cluster of hotels and villas down on the beach where the good, ill people stay who come here for baths and climate. Fourth, another *good* settlement I do not know where it is. . . . It is so marvelously beautiful because the cliffs go sheer down to the sea and the gardens hang over the edge and the tiny breed of sea gulls circle around the waves all day long. We are entranced. . . . They say a law has had to be passed requiring visitors to pay every day at the hotels; they (the visitors) are so often left without a cent. They say the women are as furious gamblers as the men and we saw hundreds of them driving up to Monte Carlo today. If they had only placed Monte Carlo somewhere else and not in this loveliest of places. Thee must not be afraid that we shall go into the Casino. The hour before we leave we shall walk through once to see it; everyone does—the Garretts and Julia, etc.—but that is all. Nice lies an hour away and we shall go there in a day or so. We live here on the Riviera for a little less than $2 a day so that makes $30 a month more than we spend in Zürich. . . .

London
January 23, 1883

Darling Mother,

. . . I am struck dumb at the thought that Aunt Hannah is entertaining Walt Whitman. He is a great poet undoubtedly; he and Poe are our only *great* poets—many of his things are glorious, and *I* of course should be charmed to entertain him but to think that one of you should receive in your house the man who has written more grossly indecent things than perhaps any other man whose books are printed in an open manner, this consoles me for many things. He takes the view that everything that is, is lovely and of good report and upon principle he glorifies the sexual functions. He rejoices that he has vigour enough to be the husband of all women alive. He longs to call out to every unmarried girl, etc. I am using of course the most euphemistic language; he calls things by their names without scruple—I remember yet how he phrases Rossetti's line which was so objected to that he omitted it in late editions, "monstrous maidenhood intolerable." Because I disagree with him on this point would none the less make me anxious to meet him. He is our greatest living genius and I believe he honestly thinks outraging so-called decency the right thing to do and he does it in a whole souled way which wins him my admiration, distasteful as it is. Where he is not either prosaic (another theory of his) or as above, he is glorious. Tell me if they like him as a man. Do approve of Aunt H's having him.

Does thee know I have today seen Christina Rossetti, the greatest woman poet in England in my opinion? She and her mother Mrs. Rossetti were in the gallery looking at Dante Gabriel Rossetti's pictures and I saw her very closely. She looks like Sarah Smiley only much ennobled . . . I felt vaguely disillusioned—for the first time brought face to face with the author of beautiful things. . . . Dear Mother how I do hope that the time may come when you will not have to worry over money. John for one is nearly afloat. . . [speaking of Harry] Dr. Culbertson thinks Phila. Med. Sch. almost as good as the Harvard and what perhaps it may lack is more than made up by the more studious spirit. . . . Since talking to Dr. Culbertson I do hate to have the boys live away from home. I believe she thinks nothing in the line of extra knowledge can balance for the risk of sending a young man to Paris or Vienna to study . . . .

269

Thee knows they have the Vice Regulation Act in force in Zürich and Dr. C. said the women are brought up to the Univ. hospital every other day and all shut into one small ward till the prof. and fifty students, sometimes one hundred, come (and five other med. women students among them). Then the women are one by one placed on high stools in the middle of the room, while all the students crowd around. The women have nothing on but a chemise which is turned up around their necks and then they are examined and treated, with brutal jokes. They themselves show no shame but glance about, probably recognizing acquaintances. She says it makes her so faint and heartsick that it keeps her awake at night. Much of this exposure might be spared and the women's legs might at least be covered and the students and profs behave properly. She says one needs no better argument against the use of such measures than to see the condition in which the women are sent back to their trade again. She says that this prof. with these same unwashed instruments will examine poor respectable women who come to him and again make the same brutal remarks. She says she would rather die than go to a hospital to men physicians to be treated before men students. Two nice women in Zürich are suffering from this same incurable disease caught from his instruments. She says it is not conceivable that increasing civilization will not make it a horrible sin against decency that any woman should be treated by any men and vice versa . . . .

Bruges, Belgium
January 30, 1883

Darling Mother,

Oh, Mother, those pictures [of Rossetti's, in London] were so glorious seeing them was like taking some stimulant which affected the imagination rather than the body. . . .

The people at our boarding house were so degraded, not dangerously so, of course, but their talk at the table is so abhorrently low, they have no reverence for anything beautiful. . . I suppose they are all by birth "ladies and

270

gentlemen." The books and pictures abroad are dearer to me than ever but I do long to be among people who are not actuated by ignoble motives. One elderly man who sat at the table and looked so respectable, so dignifiedly serious, so profoundly gentlemanly, was carried off by the police, having drawn a false check to pay a large bill at Swan and Edgar's. He went owing Mrs. Christie $150. Also a Dane and his son, who seemed so childlike and innocent, left owing them $50; they kept their luggage but that was all they could do. The law should certainly offer some redress. These men probably make the rounds of all the boarding houses in London doing the same thing.

Uncle James wrote me a long and most kind letter advising me to write to Doctor Rhoads. . . . He sent me a copy of Doctor Taylor's will (that is the extracts printed for the use of the trustees which he also said was confidential). . . . I will answer his letter when I have thought more about it. His not thinking it unsuitable makes me think about it much more seriously. Whatever thee has said has been discouragement. This may either be because thee thinks I am really unsuitable or because thee does not wish me to be disappointed. Thee and Father need not be afraid of that . . . .

I should like for your sake and my own to be able to be pecuniarily independent but if I cannot do it honestly and in work that I believe I could do well and joyfully, you will have to wait and so shall I until it comes. I know you are so immeasurably kind that I shall not let that weigh any more than it should in thinking about this. An ordinary teacher, or a wretchedly paid, overworked shadow of a professor at Wellesley or Smith like Miss Whitney I shall never be. I cannot tell thee my horror of their ignorance and habit of thought. . . .

Now having cleared away all other considerations I want thee and Father to tell me what you think. If you are not in unity, of course I shall do nothing. I believe there are two courses for Bryn Mawr—either to go on as Haverford or to be at once a power which shall extend to every place where women are interested in educating or being educated. I know thee objects to my using Haverford as

271

an example, and I would not do it to anyone but thee, but to have Bryn Mawr like Haverford would be to have it a failure as far as any influence on anyone but Friends or any influence on learning in general is concerned. And certainly no Friend's children who are devoted students will go there because girls are not like boys. Boys are often sent to Haverford because it is more difficult to drink or be grossly immoral there, whereas at Smith or Vassar, there is no risk of the same kind to which girls are exposed. If it is to be the former, I do not feel as if I had any call there even as professor . . . .

I do feel as if, if I were given liberty to select professors (within certain limits of course) and to endeavor to organize on a thoroughly sound, consistently new school basis, there would be no doubt of the scholastic success of the undertaking. I believe the best students would come to it from all over the country, because there is nothing of the kind to meet the need. A few fellowships, however few, would give the tone and the professors could work up the raw materials. I read Doctor Taylor's will very carefully; he seems to me distinctly to desire the scholarship to be as high as possible. He, of course, also wishes that the teachers would "inculcate the doctrines of the New Testament as taught by Friends" and this resolution has been adopted by the trustees. As thee knows, my views have been much modified since coming abroad . . . .

My interests and education have, I think, fitted me for work in the direction of the higher education of women and I should wish to confine myself to the educational part. I should feel right to say this in my letter. I do not think they can find anyone who would be able to combine the two with success. I thoroughly understand what Doctor Taylor wished and I cannot see why the fact of Bryn Mawr being a sectarian college need interfere with its scholastic influence . . . .

Thee knows that whatever I have anything to do with, I hope thee and Father will always have a great interest in and if, as Uncle James says, he should wish to see an enlightened Christian influence like thine, then I can see no surer way of obtaining it than by appointing your daughter president. . . .

I am so unhappy about the smallpox in Baltimore. Mr. Gwinn's letter told Mamie of it. Do be careful. . . .

Stuttgart
February 23, 1883

Darling Mother,

It is Fourth Day evening and I hope to get this letter off in good time. . . . Mrs. Gwinn sent Mamie the [Johns Hopkins] trustees' statement which seems to me very dignified. I am absolutely speechless before Mr. Garrett's behavior in the face of the fact that Johns Hopkins' will says no word in regard to the University's being placed at Clifton. I always thought the will ordered it but that of course the trustees had the right to set it aside in view of the great disadvantage it would be. I do wonder what Mary thinks of it?

Wagner is dead. Thee knows Liszt never married but lived with a Countess for fifteen years by whom he had two children, one of whom (a daughter) married Liszt's celebrated pupil, Hans von Bülow. Wagner by this time was married but living separated from his wife. He had the reputation of never looking at a woman without her falling in love with him. He and Professor Lübke of the Art books were at one time rivals when Wagner was called to Munich, where Hans von Bülow and his wife, Liszt's daughter, were living. She entreated her husband never to let her come near Wagner whom she had never seen. For six months she avoided him, then her husband, who was intimate with Wagner, insisted upon her meeting his best friend. She said if she did he must bear the whole blame. She fell desperately in love with Wagner—eloped with him, and after the death of his wife [he] married her.

It is quite like a third class novel is it not? I am sorry Wagner is dead—there is no one to take their places; no one great man under forty years of age whom I know of. I had my article on Rossetti nearly ready but the atmosphere here is such that I have not been able to finish it and I fear it will soon be too late. . . .

273

Our plan is this: to leave here the first of April, and go to Paris to a little hotel there till we find a family. The Grüneisens are so kind and are asking for families already among their friends . . . .

Stuttgart
March 8, 1883

Darling Mother,
. . . Mother do take Grace to a woman doctor in Philadelphia. I am sure she ought not to be so delicate and it may be some little thing which will make all the difference in her happiness. Another of the Grüneisen's girls was found to be in a very critical state just from some slight displacement which had been disregarded for years and which could have been easily remedied at first. The woman's doctor here treated her for the year she was here, during which time she improved so wonderfully that she sobbed and implored her mother to leave her another year so that she might be a well woman. Yet her mother not only took her home but insists upon her going out when she is feeling most ill, will not let her consult a doctor, says it is the greatest disgrace to have any trouble of that kind, refused to believe the doctor here when he told her that if her daughter married, within four years she would not only never have any children but would lead a life of misery and suffering. The girl's father who was devoted to her did not speak to her for three days after she returned home after an absence of two years, so furious was he that his daughter should in that way be delicate. . . .
Poor women, how we do suffer, and apart from fathers, how few mothers are sensible! Aunt H's letter was very edifying. Her indignation does me good. Please remember to ask her *not* to mention the American doctor's name and not to write or speak in any public way about Zürich by name because it is no worse there than elsewhere and it might have the effect of closing the doors to women if they should hear of criticisms being directed against the medical school. I should be very *very* unwilling to be the instrument—the University is so generous . . . .

Stuttgart
March 27, 1883

My dearest Mother,

We are on the eve of beginning our packing . . . I tell Mamie I am sure you are taking my passage and expect to order the spendthrift to come home. I hope you understand—it has worried me dreadfully, but my degree, and the Grüneisens' not being able to take us at once, my clothes giving out—everything was unfortunate. Unless it is *absolutely* necessary I do not wish to come home because I think these six months will be a great help to my future plans . . . .

I am sorry thee feels as thee seems to about Bonny's [her brother Bond] enthusiasm for Walt Whitman. It was the only properly enthusiastic letter of his I have ever read. If a boy or a girl can ever "go off" over anything except each other I think it is the best thing that can happen to him or her. I do not care what it is that excites the feeling.

I feel guilty because I should never have written so freely about Walt Whitman had I thought it would prejudice thee against the man. A life of him, which I read, said that personally he was morally irreproachable, and even if it were not so, a really great man is by no means too frequent a guest in our American homes. Also, dear Mother, his standpoint is logically the standpoint of all men, and because he preaches what all the world practices I cannot think he is to be blamed. And even if his writings were objectionable, he himself cannot be or Aunt Hannah would feel him to be so. I hope Bonny was not quenched. I even think the Grüneisens worship for that stupid man, the Kaiser, makes them a shade less commonplace. . . .

Paris
April 1883

Dearest Mother,

. . . How fortunate it is that thee took Grace at last and what a pity it was not several years ago. I cannot understand how a girl not having inherited anything of the kind from her parents comes to be delicate. Grace has never exposed herself or done anything except sit up late. It is a proof, is it not, that even strong healthy people ought not to have more than four children because our strength goes in a descending scale down to Nellie and Frank. Do be firm and prevent Daisy from studying too many hours . . . .

Paris
June 12, 1883

Dearest Mother,

. . . My woman doctor is so nice; she has just been in to see me and finds me quite well and considers that I do her much credit to recover so rapidly. My inflammation has disappeared. I was particularly tired as I had my letter to Dr. Rhoads at last in satisfactory shape and wished to copy it at once. I am going to tell Bessie about it in strict confidence, so that if any thing comes of it she may be on my side with her father. I shall also write my long delayed letter to Uncle James at the same time. . . .

We have found a thoroughly satisfactory family through our French teacher. . . just outside of Paris five minutes walk from the barrier and the barrier is five minutes walk from beyond the Arc de Triomphe, so thee can imagine where it is. It is at "Neuilly". . . . we each have a pleasant room on the ground floor, the use of the parlor and the lady of the house to talk to whenever we wish. She is very nice, and the "bonne" as the Parisians call their cook is almost as nice as the old lady; she has been with her for seventeen years. We are to pay $50 apiece a month. We cannot, however, go there till the first of August and that is trying, is it not? . . . I *understand* French now perfectly—the University lectures close in a week or two, so we have thought we might spend three or four weeks in going slowly through the towns of Normandy and Brittany. Thee knows they are full of interest. . . .

Caen
June 29, 1883

Dearest Mother,

. . . Of course dearest Mother it is not that I am ashamed of teaching or of any profession in the world. I believe every man and woman who hasn't a large independent fortune should have one—But I feel a little differently about teaching on account of the disgraceful sort of people who engage in it, disgraceful in regard to culture and attainment. I do not wish to enter their ranks openly until I am far above all of their wretched incompetency by my studies. Besides, I am not a born teacher who likes to teach even babies for the mere sake of the teaching—I could not endure it unless in my own way . . . .

c/o M M Hottinguer & Co
38 Rue de Provence
Paris
August 14th 1883

Confidential
Dr. J. B. Rhoads[6]
Germantown
Philadelphia
My dear Friend,

My old desire to see an excellent woman's college in America has made the management of Bryn Mawr from the time of its first endowment a matter of great interest to me. This interest must be my excuse for writing to thee, as the newly appointed Vice-President of the Board of the Bryn Mawr Trustees and Chairman of the Executive and Building Committees, in regard to Bryn Mawr and in part in regard to myself.

It is now three years and a half since I came abroad, meaning only to pursue study for its own sake. My conviction of the value of a liberal education could not be made deeper, and my conception of what a college might become, clearer, by gradual training under German scholars

6. Dr. Rhoads was a medical doctor.

277

who in a certain sense aid in making the science which they teach; and I began to doubt whether it would not be a more justifiable way of life, to aid in procuring this liberal education for other women, than merely to pursue my studies quietly at home. When last Ninth Month I was more successful in my examinations than I had before thought possible and received the rarely awarded degree of Doctor of Philosophy, *summa cum laude,* I felt that I might without presumptuousness, in case no one better fit should yet have been found, offer myself as a candidate for the presidency of Bryn Mawr.

I can do this with the less hesitation because I am personally convinced that it is best for the president of a woman's college to be a woman; and among women I know that, thanks to my father and mother, my opportunities, not only for study but for observation and for comparison of methods, have been unusually good.

After graduating at Howland School, I went through the Classical Course of Cornell University, taking there the degree of B.A. I have studied for three and a half years in Germany and Switzerland, am now attending the lectures of the College de France and the Sorbonne, and am anxious to spend some little time at each of the two women's colleges at Cambridge.

A man placed at the head of a woman's college feels all the circumstances by which it differs from a man's college as limitations only; a woman sees definitely the especial needs, aims, interests, opportunities and possibilities. In view of this immediate sympathy and cooperation, as well as for the sake of the power given by recent and continuous study to understand the needs of a new college, I have not been able to regret my comparative youth which to thee perhaps may seem a disadvantage.

However this may be, and without further reference to any possible president-ship of mine, I should be glad if thou wouldst permit me, simply as a woman much interested in Bryn Mawr, to speak to thee of what I should desire for it, and to make a few suggestions, of which none perhaps may be at all new to thee. Only thou mightest be interested in seeing how far my own experience as a student may have led me to the same conclusions with thyself.

Since there attends upon the opening of each new college a certain amount of public interest which, when once disappointed, is not easily aroused again, but turns on the contrary to an enduring prejudice against the college, I am anxious that Bryn Mawr should open with a full number of competent professors and with as high a standard as it may intend to reach or maintain—that it should not, for instance, imitate Vassar, which began with a preparatory course that was to have been dropped afterwards, but has most unfortunately been retained. On the other hand, since the absence of the regularly organized preparatory schools that exist for boys greatly embarrasses a girl who means to enter college, I consider it very important that a year, or if possible two years before the opening of Bryn Mawr, there should be sent to all Friends' schools, and published in the *Nation* and in all the leading journals, a full list, made out by the president and such professors as shall be already appointed, of the entrance requirements and of the fellowships to be competed for—that is, if it should be decided to create fellowships, as I hope it will be.

I am anxious that Bryn Mawr should not duplicate other existing colleges. Coeducation is gaining ground. Vassar, Wellesley and Smith have the start of us: in the West there are Friends' schools and colleges of a lower grade open to both sexes. Bryn Mawr, if it be not exceptional in character, can expect at most but fifty or sixty students, and these, for all post-graduate studies, will be drawn away. Moreover, the best undergraduate training can never be given by a college which is not also able to guide advanced students. I should wish Bryn Mawr not to be a competitor amid the ranks of ordinary colleges, compelled to contend with them for its share and as it were to go a-begging for students; but itself to give America what is lacking there—a place where elementary college work is better done than elsewhere, and at the same time a place where women may at last be able to pursue advanced studies among women.

I should thus wish Bryn Mawr, taking girls at the beginning of their college course, to give them a systematic training under professors qualified to prepare both their own graduates and those from other colleges, so that these girls may either take their place afterwards as original scholars, or carry back with them into their own homes a love and understanding of study and culture: and this end could not, I think, be better served than by establishing in imitation of the Johns Hopkins University, at least ten fellowships each of two or three hundred dollars apart from board and residence. Let these be competed for by the post-graduates from other colleges, and by the future graduates of Bryn Mawr, and the successful fellows will not be the only persons benefitted. Their presence will assist in giving to the new college the requisite scholarly atmosphere: it will raise the standard of undergraduate work, aid in college discipline, incite the professors under whom they study to original research and, as at the Johns Hopkins, draw other post-graduates to the college. . . .

I am not afraid that the character of Bryn Mawr as a Quaker institution will interfere with its excellence even as regards the choice of instructors, for I know that if we teach better than is taught elsewhere, we shall have students who in their turn will be better teachers than the students of other colleges can become. . . . [But] we must not deceive ourselves; an excellent college within the limits of any one sect or society is an exceptional thing, and must be obtained by exceptional measures. . . .[7]

At the first opening of the college no professors would be chosen whose influence would be opposed to that of the Society of Friends and those excellent professors who were not Friends in point of fact would be accepted until

7. Dr. Joseph Taylor's will specified that the Trustees of the College must be members of the Orthodox Society of Friends. In 1905, with the approval of the College's legal adviser and the Trustees, Carey Thomas designated a Board of Directors sufficient in number to tip the scales against Quakers any longer controlling college policy. She herself officially resigned her membership in the Society of Friends after her retirement from the College.

they could be worthily replaced by such of their own pupils as had obtained this highest of scholarships, accomplished their years of study abroad, and plainly proved their ability in the eyes of the Faculty. The term thus set to these provisional professorships would neither be too long for the interests of the college, nor too short for the acceptance of a scholar who respects himself. . . .

I am quite content that these provisional professorships (and they will doubtless be considerable in number) should be held in great part by men, although thou hast already seen from my plan as to the way in which the professorships should be refilled that I should desire a number of them ultimately to be held by the graduates of Bryn Mawr. The Society of Friends has no deeper claim upon the gratitude and loyalty of its members than its steady equity and liberality toward women. In this new woman's college, which may be better even than its colleges for its men, because it is more recent of foundation: which should be better, because it must provide for women the ulterior training which the men of the Society of Friends can so easily obtain in any of the universities of the world—it may be proud if it gives to such of its women as are scholars not only a training but a career. . . .

I fully recognize that the majority of the girls at Bryn Mawr will not become professional scholars, and that it is not even desirable that they should become so. Nevertheless I do not wish the above solely, or even chiefly, in the interest of post-graduates. The ordinary student never digests and appropriates more than a certain proportion of the instruction given; but I am convinced it is only from such solid and scientific instruction as is meant to pave the way for prolonged studies that there can possibly be acquired the mental discipline and the intelligent comprehensions of things, which are the best results of a briefer and more general education . . . .

Believe me with sincere esteem,

Very truly thine
Martha Carey Thomas

[No postmark]
September 1883

Dear Father,

Please if any one speaks to thee about [Bryn Mawr] do not treat it as a whim of mine, as an impossibility, but speak as if thee wished me to have it and as if thee believed that it was a seriously to be thought of thing. Thee sees if *thee* does not discuss it seriously no one else will.

I am a woman now, nearly twenty-seven years old and I believe I could make the college more of a success than anyone else they are likely to appoint and I want thee at least to give me the benefit of the doubt. If the Board does not care to make a good first class college of Bryn Mawr then of course I would not even wish to try for the position but if they do then I think it is their duty to consider my proposition duly and I want thee to help me as much as thee can to have at least as fair a chance as any other candidate would have.

Thee and Mother must not think that I shall be disappointed. I know that there are ever so many probabilities against me, but it was at least worth trying and now I am satisfied to let the matter rest—only do thee give me the advantage of thy approval should the matter ever be discussed.

I have been wanting to write to thee for so long, but my indisposition made me feel very unlike writing. I am now entirely well. . . . We shall not return to Paris until September when the warm weather is almost over. I will write tomorrow a letter to Mother.

Paris
October 2, 1883

Dearest Mother,

Just a note to say that thy letter enclosing Aunt Mary's very sweet card arrived. It is so nice that they all approve of it [her plans for the presidency of Bryn Mawr] even if as thee says they have no say in the matter. I believe, as it is the right thing, it will come to pass. If they should decide "yes" I wish Father at once to get for me a

M. Carey Thomas upon her return from Europe

letter of introduction [to contacts at Cambridge and Oxford]. Without letters and without a positive position I cannot go to either college and ask the questions I desire. Otherwise I will spend a week or two in London reading up college literature . . . .

We have positively decided to sail the Allan line and shall engage passage [sailing November 6th]. . . . I believe that it was much better for me to have this interval of rest before returning home. When I reached Paris I still looked so badly that Miss Slocum and Doctor Howard did not know me, but each day I look better and for a long time I have *felt* perfectly well again . . . .

Dear dear Mother thee does not realize how I desire that you may be proud of me and find me a comfort. Thee must **not think that because I am not a missionary in your** sense that I have no missionary spirit, and if thee only will try and believe that I am coming home with the hope and trust of being good and useful and happy. I love you so much that I want you to be satisfied with me as I am satisfied with you. . . .

This is the last very long letter I shall write because I shall see you soon. . . . From this time on "whatsoever things are of good report" I hope to live among—

[From Hannah Whitall Smith]

Philadelphia
January 15, 1884

My dear Carey,

I have been sticking my "oar" into the Bryn Mawr pie. I interviewed Doctor Rhoads, and as much as told him he was not fit to be the president, and that *thee* ought to be put there. Then I wrote to F. T. King and also to Philip Garrett. Thee knows what I would say about the college. I told them we *women* were watching them and that they **must get a person of culture and one whose life was devoted** to literary pursuits, or they would have nothing but a good *school,* and much more to the same purpose. Then I urged thy claims, not as thy aunt but simply and only as a *woman* interested for the sake of her *sex.* I told them none of my family knew I was writing, and would not approve of it I was sure. But that my deep concern about the College would not let me keep silence, etc. etc. etc.

Now, Carey, I have stirred the dear old fogies up, and they are going to make some sort of a proposition to thee, just what, I do not know. But I am now going to stick an oar in *thy* pie too, and tell thee how it looks to me.

If they should still insist upon keeping Doctor Rhoads in a position of great authority and should ask thee to *share* it as it were, not putting thee at once in as president, but giving thee a sort of tentative position at first, I cannot help thinking it would be wise for thee to agree to it. Thee could then *prove* thy capabilities, and could make thyself so absolutely necessary to them that they would have no alternative finally but to make thee president. I feel morally certain that Doctor Rhoads would very soon realize his own insufficiency for the position, and would be only too glad to resign all his share to thee.

I cannot help wishing very much that thee would at least make the experiment, for the sake of woman. There is no one else but *thee* to save this college to our sex, and I beg of thee to throw thyself into the breach. If thee should consent to a sort of compromise now, it would not bind thee; if thee found thyself hampered, thee could say so, and give them the alternative of arranging matters differently, or of losing thy services. I feel sure that no matter what position thee might take, thee could soon work thy way into the very highest, and could have things go pretty much as thee might please.

And for the sake of womankind, it would be worthwhile to yield a little to the prejudices of these dear good brethren. Woman's usual weapons would perhaps have to be thy stronghold for a little while, I mean management and influence, etc. but they would win at last. Doctor Rhoads told me himself that he should not take the position for long, only until the present emergency was tided over, and I do not believe in fact that his health can stand it.

Now, dear Carey, do not reject any proposition the dear brethren may make without first carefully considering it. I do not know what they are going to say, they would not consult a *woman* I suppose to save their lives; but I do know that they are *exceedingly* anxious to secure thee and thy help. And if they have to throw in Doctor Rhoads as a "sop to Cerberus," why, let them do it, and thee just get in an entering wedge, you see. I will venture to prophesy that before a year thee will have them all at thy feet.

I feel as if this was a vital matter for women. And *no one* but *thee* can stand in the breach. For all our sakes do thy best.

With warmest love
thy Aunt H.W.S.

[From the Minutes of the Bryn Mawr College Board of Trustees, 14 March, 1884]

. . . On motion of President Rhoads, Martha Carey Thomas, Ph.D. [has been] appointed Professor of English and Dean of the Faculty. Until the opening of the College as well as after it shall be in active operation, she shall assist the President in arranging the details of the courses of study, and in the adoption of the best methods and means for imparting the instruction to be given in the College. During the first named period she shall receive a salary of $1,000 a year, her salary after that time to be agreed upon hereafter . . . .

[From the Minutes of the Bryn Mawr College Board of Trustees, 11 April, 1884]

Martha Carey Thomas, having accepted her appointment as Dean of the Faculty, has been authorized to visit the colleges for women in New York and New England in order to learn the details of their management and report for the benefit of Bryn Mawr.

[In her notebook is the following entry, after a lapse of six years, in the journal titled "Mr. Gummere," which Carey Thomas began in January 1878.]

February 2, 1885

I entreat that no one will read this part of my journal as it is *entirely private.* And I beg that Mamie if she loves me will not read it as it is something I have kept from her—I write it down as an experience and a madness, a temptation and a delusion. Just as the pages about Mr. Gummere seem to me impossible, so this will doubtless in as many years as have passed since my last entry.

I came back from Germany with my *summa cum laude* with my memory stored with beautiful pictures and memories ready to work. I accepted in March the deanship of Bryn Mawr and since then I have been busy with the organization of the college and with my work. I trust it may prove worth the sacrifice of time and the constant worry; after all, it has saved a million dollars for women's education even if it be not what Mamie and I have planned. Now, as this journal seems to be a mortifying record of avocations, not vocations, especially of emotional disturbances, I will proceed to take my bearings and then describe my last trial of that kind. Mamie and I are still intimate. We have seen each other almost every day since we returned in November 1883. I still think that our friendship and love will outlast our lives. She is in person and intellect, taste and belief perfectly satisfactory to me. I owe her everything except the isolation of mental life which thing no one can have who loves another person very dearly.

APPENDIX

I was born in Baltimore on January 2, 1857, the eldest of ten children. Three brothers in succession and two sisters in succession came after me at intervals of two years and a few months. (Another brother and sister who came later died before they were two years old.) Then the youngest living brother and sister were born, only a year apart, and were so nearly of the same age and so inseparable that they were thought of as twins by the rest of the family.

The families of my father's parents had been living in Maryland for eight generations, and I grew up in a bewildering group of cousins: Thomases, Leipers, Careys, Ellicotts,[1] Poultneys, Coales, Hopkins, Kings, and Tysons. It was the age of large families. I have counted up 252 direct descendants of the original Philip Thomas who

1. A short typewritten history of the Ellicotts, by a descendant, Malcolm van V. Tyson, dated 1925, is in her papers. It tells of the great influence of the Ellicotts on the early history of Maryland: in agriculture (they initiated the cultivation of wheat, favoring it over tobacco because it did not deplete the soil) and in manufacture of various sorts (they invented, among other things, the grain "elevator" and "hopper" but refused patents, preferring to share freely with others). They were successful merchants and city planners. One branch was prominent in the planning and growth of Buffalo; another ancestor, Major Andrew Ellicott, is claimed to have been responsible for carrying out the plans for the city of Washington, D.C., "when L'Enfant had to be dismissed on account of his peculiar disposition."

landed in Maryland, at West River, in 1651 and there must be many more I have overlooked. Large families were the rule, and the Thomas families run to fifteen, eleven, twelve, ten, nine, eight, seven and six children. My great-grandfather John Chew Thomas led all his ancestors with fifteen children by one wife. My grandfather Thomas had eight by two wives and my father led his generation with ten children by one wife.[2]

Although my mother's father and mother had moved to Philadelphia before she was born, her family on both sides had been settled for generations in New Jersey. The Thomases and Whitalls were Quakers from the time they set foot on American shores if not before, and many were ministers and elder members of the hierarch of Quakerdom.

In those early days Quakers were compelled to intermarry or be expelled from the Quaker Meeting although the Quaker sect was then as now few in numbers. From generation to generation Quakers married Quakers to the physical and mental detriment of their descendants. In an article whose name I have forgotten, I read with a shock of surprise a reference to the well-known inherited craziness of the old Quaker families caused by this compulsion to intermarriage retained by the Quaker church. My grandmother Martha Carey Thomas was certainly unbalanced—almost a religious monomaniac. In many Quaker circles everyone is closely or distantly related to everyone else. Until I went to boarding school and college I knew no one who was not a Quaker.

The Thomases came from Wales to Maryland in 1651, but with the exception of two marriages with first cousins who were also of Welsh descent, their Maryland marriages seem to have been with Quaker women of English stock. . . . My father's maternal family records have been lost; we think the first immigrant Carey must have come originally from England and not from Ireland because in

2. In her copious autobiographical notes and lists is the following: "In our family—not reproducing itself—only eighteen grandchildren. In **twelve [*sic*] marriages eighty-nine boys, fifty-seven girls. Thirty-two more boys."**

the eighteenth century the later rapid rise of the Irish immigrants to political power and consequent wealth had not yet begun. We also think he was English because of what we have heard of the great reserve and quiet dignified character of our ancestor James Carey the banker.[3]

My father used to point out a little wooden four-roomed house standing on the banks of the Jones Falls stream which then ran through the center of the city and tell me that it was the first house built and lived in by his great-grandfather Carey, the immigrant. He said that he knew nothing about him except that his son's son was his own mother's father, who was the head of a large shipping and importing business and president of the chief bank of Maryland. I was ashamed and never showed it to anyone.

I now think that to belong through one of my two great-grandfathers to a family that took only two generations to bridge the gap between this little riverside shack and Lowdon, the delightful country estate (at present Lowdon cemetery) where my great-grandfather James Carey kept open house for all Baltimore, is an heredity to be proud of. My mother's family was English on both sides. I therefore count my heredity as one-eighth Welsh and six-eights English, assuming the probability but not the certainty that the other one-eighth, my Carey great-grandfather, was also English.

My father was eighth in descent from Evan Thomas of Swansea, Glamorganshire, Wales. . . . His son Philip Thomas. . . in the year 1651 sailed to America in his own ship, according to family tradition as told me by my great-aunts Henrietta and Julia, and landed in the province of Maryland only seventeen years after Lord Baltimore's first Colonists. He brought with him his wife, Sarah Har-

3. The implication that the Irish are *not* reserved, quiet or dignified, reflects a conventional prejudice of her day and one that may have also been inculcated in her childhood: most Irishmen being Roman Catholics, and "Papism" anathema to Quakers. Moreover, Carey Thomas's mother was a leader in the W.C.T.U. and the Irish were not known for abstinence. On the other hand, at least some of her prejudices were cultivated in adulthood to accord with those of the ruling economic and social Establishment—a fact that reinforces the reputation she had, among those who knew her well, for conventionality.

rison, their son Philip and two daughters, and what is of great interest to his American descendants, a gold-headed walking stick and silver service, each piece engraved with a coat of arms. . . with the motto *Secret et Hardi* confirmed by the Heralds College as being the arms of Sir Rhys ap Thomas of Carew Castle. . . [one of whose sons] born 1449 commanded half of the army at Bosworth, was one of the largest landed proprietors in Wales, fought beside the Earl of Richmond (later Henry VII) on the field of Bosworth, and in a hand-to-hand fight is said to have slain King Richard III. . . .

In 1672 George Fox landed near West River Maryland and remained in America for thirteen months attending two Yearly Meetings in West River. He was amazingly successful in converting to Quakerism or at least into sympathy most of the leading people of Maryland, many of whom, both men and women, became preachers and elders in the Quaker Church as was the Quaker custom. It was a time of relaxation and dissipation such as is usually found in pioneer counties and never more so than in the Maryland of the sixteen-seventies. The Quaker discipline required temperance and sexual morality. Quaker children were thus ensured an unusually sound physical heredity. This may perhaps explain in part the almost controlling influence of the great Quaker families down the next two centuries on the industrial development of Baltimore and Maryland—but in 1850 the original impetus seems to have spent itself. I remember well enough the drinking that went on in Baltimore during my girlhood among the people we knew, to realize what must have been the conditions on the Maryland plantations. On New Year's day when they [made] rounds of calls, at parties we expected the young men we knew to be half drunk.[4]

---

4. Since Carey Thomas's family and circle of acquaintances were active in the cause of temperance, this statement does not square with her contention that before going to Cornell she "never knew anyone who was not a Quaker." On the other hand, it is conceivable that among Friends were some who tippled and all too readily showed the effects.

Samuel, the only surviving son of Philip [Thomas] the Bristol emigrant, was born in Maryland, married Mary Hutchins by whom he had ten children, and lived until he was eighty-eight years old. He was a minister of the Quaker church and is reported to have served as a committee of one on drowsiness in meeting. He seems to have been remarkable for nothing else except for the acquisition of more land. Philip, his eldest surviving son, who seems to have inherited some of the ability and public spirit of his grandfather Philip the emigrant, was a member of the Governor's Council, Judge of Register and of the Land Office, and member of various state committees until his health broke down and he became a complete invalid. He married twice . . . .

My great-great-great-grandfather Samuel, born in 1725, [was the offspring of Philip and] his second wife, Ann Chew. Samuel married his first cousin Mary Snowden Thomas . . . . The intermarriages of Thomases and Snowdens had begun a generation before when a sister of Samuel's father had married a Richard Snowden. Samuel's son, my great-grandfather John Chew Thomas, married his second cousin Mary Snowden, related to him on both his father's and mother's side, his maternal grandfather and her maternal great-grandfather being brother and sister, and his grandfather on his mother's side, Richard Snowden, being his wife's grandfather. And Elizabeth, my great-aunt and one of the daughters of John Chew Thomas and Mary Snowden, married Samuel Thomas, her father's first cousin—then the Thomas families moved away from West River where the Snowdens and Thomases had lived for generations side by side on neighboring plantations, and fortunately the intermarriages ceased, but not before they had introduced into our branch of the Thomas strain a slight mental instability that seems to show itself only when united by marriage with someone of somewhat similar unbalanced strain.

There was a streak of craziness in some of the members in the family of my great-grandfather and grandmother. My mother used to tell us of her fright during one terrible night soon after her marriage when she was left alone—

when my father had been called out to attend an ill patient and she was alone in the house. One of my father's first cousins was visiting them, became suddenly insane and spent the night pounding on her locked door and shouting, "Awake, awake, the light is in the East!" And she and my father had another somewhat similar experience with another first cousin belonging to the same family. In the second generation of our own immediate family two of the children of two of my father's half brothers (and one of his own nieces and two of his own grandchildren) have been at times mentally unbalanced, in the latter both cases as a consequence of marriages into families with unbalanced heredity.

The Thomas family had been living on their many acres of land for two generations without distinguishing themselves in any unusual way. When they died their land was subdivided among their many children, sons and daughters. (With a decided British preference for leaving land with a property to the sons and other property to the daughters.) It did not seem to occur to any of their sons to engage in any profession or business. In the third generation, however, my great-great-grandfather Philip Thomas married Ann Chew and her splendid Chew heredity brought forth ability, a new sense of responsibility for public service and a hitherto unknown scientific interest into a branch of the Thomas family.

From John Chew, who came to Virginia in 1622 . . . descended the many eminent physicians in the Thomas and Chew families who taught and practiced medicine in Maryland. His eldest son, Dr. Samuel Chew, moved to Pennsylvania from his plantation near Annapolis, became Chief Justice of three Philadelphia counties, and was very influential in public affairs. His son was the great Chief Justice of Pennsylvania, Benjamin Chew. Most of the Chew men studied law and devoted themselves to public service. Many of them were physicians, and some of them fought in the Revolutionary armies. The men of the Chew family must have had rather unusual vitality as almost all of them outlived one wife and were married twice which complicates their family tree as it seems to have doubled their descendants.

According to my great-aunts [Julia and Henrietta] their father, my great-grandfather John Chew Thomas, was a high-minded, highly respected gentleman, and my grandmother Anne Chew Thomas, an heiress, a very fine, great lady indeed. They kept open house as they had on the Eastern shore [of Virginia, whence they moved after the resentment of neighboring plantation owners became intolerable; the Thomases having freed their slaves, according to their principles] and many were the statesmen travelling between Virginia and to Philadelphia who broke their journey. Our great Aunt Julia, who as family tradition had it was a madcap in her youth and remained sufficiently one in her old age to delight us with stories, was a little girl of twelve as she told it, when she decided that she could not abide the ceremonious manners of the great George Washington who was then President for the second time. So the next time that he bent over to kiss her mother's hand, his powdered hair tied with long black ribbons hanging behind, she crept up and was just about to seize and pull his stately pigtail when she caught his eyes gravely looking at her in the mirror over her mother's head. She crept away, nearly fainting from sheer terror such as she had never felt since, and she dared not see him again. She took care to be safely hidden in bed from sudden illness when a visit from him was expected. . . .

My great aunt Julia is the only one of my great-grandfather's children that I really remember. She lived to a great age and died after I returned from studying in Germany. She might I think be called an unusual woman, although like the rest of my father's family her strength and vitality was put into religious work. She had about her a certain dash and spirit. Her criticisms were wily— she talked about things rather than people. She lost her temper royally when things went wrong; nothing was ever very dull where she was. She married late in life a stalwart Quaker over six feet in height and I remember hearing with awe because I had thought them so good, that they had to give up playing chess together because their quarrels over the game endangered an otherwise happy marriage. . . .

My grandfather had, I believe, one of the largest medical practices in Baltimore and took a prominent part in the organization of the medical teaching of the University of Maryland [where he became] a professor in the Medical School. My father also was a physician with a large practice and devoted much time and thought to the organization of the Johns Hopkins University and medical school. His son, my brother Henry M. Thomas, was a specialist on nervous diseases and organized the first nervous clinic in the Johns Hopkins Medical School and his son, Henry M. Thomas, is also a consultant physician in internal medicine, and director of the medical clinic there.[5]

At one time I wanted to study medicine and had I not been able to persuade my father to send me to Cornell, I had planned to go to Philadelphia and live with my maternal grandparents while I studied medicine in the only eastern medical school then open to women, the Women's Medical School of Pennsylvania.

After the death of my grandfather Thomas we moved from the smaller house next door in which I was born into the large house in which my grandfather had lived ever since he had married my father's mother, to whom it had belonged. It was built by her father, James Carey, the successful merchant, and had been given to his daughter Martha Carey when she married my grandfather the doctor. Her older sister Margaret Carey had married Galloway Cheston, also a very successful shipper and importer who built himself a large house adjoining the one

---

5. Fragments about her ancestry, heredity, and family end rather abruptly. While she does not appear to have searched for Carey ancestry beyond the owner of the poor shack whose immediate descendants grew wealthy, I cannot believe that she would have deliberately overlooked her Grandfather Whitall's exploits at sea, or even the legend of Ann Cooper Whitall. Indications are that she simply did not complete the section on her family background.

built for my grandmother. The two houses opened on the same garden and sunken stable yard. The two sisters planned to live here side by side but my father's mother died of consumption at twenty-five and his Aunt Margaret became a second mother to him. She was a very brilliant woman, spirited and witty with great social gifts and seemed to me as a child a very great lady indeed. My mother loved her.

My earliest memory I can date exactly. I distinctly remember the bars of my crib and that this terrifying experience happened when the brother who came next to me had just been born; there was exactly two years and four months between us. My mother, who was only twenty, and without any knowledge of managing babies, had allowed me to get into the bad habit of stroking her eyebrows as I was going to sleep. She used to sit by me and if I waked in the night she leaned out of bed and let me stroke them. Now that a new baby had come this awful tyranny had to stop, and as my mother had tried again and again and had failed, she sent for her eldest sister Hannah to come from Philadelphia to deal with me.

I remember I was shrieking at the top of my lungs as I always did when my mother refused to have her eyebrows stroked. The door opened and a menacing figure stood beside my crib and a stern voice such as I had never yet heard said, "Minnie, stop crying. Your mother will not come if you cry all tonight and all tomorrow. Here is a mint drop." And a whole large mint drop was passed through the bars of the crib into my mouth. I was so terrified that I stopped shrieking at once. To the amazement of the family I never again dared to ask my mother to let me stroke her eyebrows. Although I became devoted to my Aunt Hannah afterwards and owed her some of the greatest pleasures of my childhood, I was a little afraid of her for a long time. It was many years before I could touch a mint drop and every now and then, as I eat one, I still see the bars of my crib.

My next memory is teaching myself to read. My father used to tell me that I read to him long passages with difficult words before I was three years old. He said that he would stretch out his legs to me to climb up them from the floor into his lap. It must have been much earlier than this that I persuaded my mother to teach me the different letters. She would pin a piece of newspaper on a big pin cushion and show me a letter and tell me to prick it with a pin whenever it occurred. I can remember running after her with a big pin cushion in my arms begging her to show me little letters to prick, after I had learned all the big capital letters. Apart from the pin cushion I cannot remember a time when I did not read, and at every available moment ever since, sick or well, at home or abroad, I have been reading. It has been the greatest resource and happiness of my life; reading voraciously, incessantly, omniverously, and never more so than now. At seventy-five years of age I find it difficult to make myself write my memoir because reading is so great a temptation. During the thirty-seven years at Bryn Mawr College when I was occupied every moment of the day and evening, I read for my own pleasure from ten to twelve every free evening.

Another early memory, this one connected with my grandfather Thomas, is dated by his death. I remember him lying on a sofa in what seemed to me a darkened room. He was dying in great suffering from internal cancer. My mother used to take me next door every day to see him. As she said that she loved him dearly I remember trying to like going to see him and kissing him good morning but I knew I disliked it very much. I do not remember asking about him. If I was told that he had died it made no impression on me. Children often seem heartless because they are so absorbed in their own affairs. Indeed, I am afraid that I have always seemed so throughout my life.[6]

It must have been at this time that I went walking with my mother and lost her. Only once in my life, years later,

6. This sentence was heavily crossed out in her handwritten original. The confession is certainly not characteristic, and she may well have had second thoughts about recording it.

when my intimate friend and house companion[7] died, on April 15, 1915—— [here the fragment breaks off].

My mother and I were crossing a street; in those days Baltimore had surface drainage; when it rained, torrents of water rushed down the hilly streets. So, high stones were set at street crossings for foot passengers to step from one to another without wetting their feet. It was at one of these crossings that my mother forgot about me, or so I thought, and ran across the street to speak to a friend. I tried to follow her and got lost among the stepping stones which came almost to my shoulders. I could not see her anywhere. I thought she had forgotten me, and felt forsaken and alone. For a long time afterward I used to dream that I was standing among the stepping stones and wake up with the same terror.

My other memories are scattered. We used to play Swiss Family Robinson in our Uncle Galloway Cheston's cellar opening onto his yard which was next to our garden. Many diamond-back terrapins were kept there. Our house at the corner of Sharp and Lombard streets was everything that the heart of a child could desire. The garden was very large with trees and flowers and red-bricked paths. One side was a barn with a smoke room for curing hams and on a different level, down a long flight of stone steps with a cobblestoned court, there was a huge trough for the horses to drink from. When we were little we were afraid of falling in and of being drowned when we sailed our boats. The two Negro coachmen and their friends spent their spare time there, and were always ready to play with us.

Many were the accidents that happened there. Our mother used to say she always rang her front doorbell with a sinking heart lest something should have happened to us while she was away. And something usually had happened. One day she found Johnnie crumpled up on the bottom step with a broken shoulder. He was pretending to be Daniel trying to escape from the lion's den by walking up the straight wall of the area clinging to a rope tied to

7. Mary Garrett.

the railings, when the rope broke. And another day Bonny lay in the barn with the prongs of a garden rake sticking through his foot when he fell while trying to fly as a cock from a rafter in the barn. Harry she once found impaled on a sharp point of the six-foot-high railings between our house and the next, slowly revolving while his blood bespattered the dense crowd gathered beneath. I lost my two front teeth trying to storm the walls of Jericho.

As far back as I can remember we were always acting out stories we had read. One day we got hold of a great basket of potatoes and invited our friends to take part with us in a storming and defending Troy in the front hall. As soon as my little brother Harry could walk and almost before he could talk he was cast for all the more undesirable roles in our plays. Almost as soon as I could read I had found a copy of Pope's translation of Homer's *Iliad* with Flaxman's illustrations which furnished an inexhaustible supply of heroic battles to be enacted.

Baltimore was an old-fashioned Southern city as I remember it in my childhood before the founding of the Johns Hopkins University in 1876 brought scholars and scholarship and a breath of intellectual life. It was very provincial. Great Britain and Europe did not exist for me except in books. I had never seen an English man or English woman until visiting Quaker preachers began to journey across the sea. French and Germans were only teachers in girls' schools, and then mostly barbers or dressmakers who had failed to make a living at home.

The city was fortunate in having the Peabody Library and the Peabody Institute of Music founded and endowed by the philanthropist George W. Peabody. The music did not affect me because in those days music was considered wicked among Quakers. It was only years afterward that we had a family organ which was a halfway wrong because only religious [music] could be played on it, and a piano came many years after that.

My childhood before I was seven years old was full of joy. As the psychologists would say "my self expression was perfect." My mother and her two sisters had had a very happy youth because their father believed in making it so. They determined to give it to their children. In the background of all my childish memories is my beautiful mother, a radiant figure always helping us when we got into trouble.

I sewed beautifully for so young a child. There was a tradition in the family of a little hemstitched apron I made for myself. Later I never really sewed again. As part of my revolt I pretended I could not use a thimble.

I was deeply religious. I took down sermons for my grandmother. I was my mother's little acolyte. I accepted all her changing religious phases of belief. I loved to hear my mother read *The Duchess of May*, and Macaulay's *Lays of Ancient Rome,* and my grandmother Whitall repeat Cowper's *John Gilpen* and other narrative poems, all of which she knew by heart. I believed without reservation. Every day for nearly two years we had prayed that the dressing of my burn might not hurt, and every day it hurt terribly without shaking her [mother's] faith or mine. Ever since I could remember she had been looking for the second coming of Jesus in the clouds—so had I. In every thunderstorm my mother had to sit by my basket[8] holding my hand so that we might go up to heaven together. While she believed in hell I used to worry about it a little for other people, never for myself, for she had told me that I was a little child of Jesus and I believed that, with everything else she told me. But when my mother and her sisters came to believe in universal salvation I never gave Hell another thought. My childish sense of justice spewed it out as a hateful thing.

After eighteen months of enforced quiet, listening to reading and to the talk of my mother and her sisters and friends that went on around me, I got up a very different child: a Romantic Victorian. I think the change would have come in any case, but probably more slowly. When I began to read for myself my education began and changed my childish world.

My uncle, Galloway Cheston, who lived next door had a good old-fashioned library with all the English prose clas-

8. Her father had fashioned a basket so that she could be carried in relative comfort during her extended convalescence after her burn.

sics. I do not remember any poetry on the shelves. He allowed me to take any book I wanted to read, but only one book at a time. I read in this way all of Scott and Thackeray. Goldsmith's *Vicar of Wakefield* and Richardson's *Clarissa Harlowe* both puzzled me so much that I asked my mother what the Vicar's daughter could have done, but she (very unwisely I think now) would not tell me. My Uncle Galloway must have taken Fielding out of his library before he made me free with it, so I did not read *Tom Jones* until later when I knew a little more about sex.

My Uncle Robert Pearsall Smith, my Aunt Hannah's husband, had been a publisher at the time of my mother's marriage, and his wedding present to her was a complete set of "British Poets" bound in unattractive shiny black cloth. I used to lie at full length on our dining table resting on my elbows with my book under the hanging oil lamp and read and weep and weep and read, in true Victorian fashion. My mother could not understand why her mahogany dining table had to be repolished so often. I also remember taking off still more polish with my tears over the ending of Kingsley's *Hypatia,* but that was later, after I became a passionate feminist.

There was a shaky grapevine arbor in our yard on which the dining room windows opened. On moonlight nights I used to climb up to the trellised top, lie on my back among the leaves, and repeat to myself Wordsworth and Coleridge with feelings of ineffable joy. In those days I used to learn by heart the poetry I cared for most. Shelley and Keats I did not yet know. I came to Byron too late to care about him. They were too modern to be between the shiny black covers of our British poets. Byron I discovered later in a fat brown sheepskin volume. It contained all his poetry, each page printed in double columns. My father found me reading it, the volume far too heavy for me. I happened to have it open at "Don Juan," and as it was too heavy to hold open I had propped it up lying on a cushion. I had just begun to read it. I had **never heard of** Byron and had no associations of impropriety with Don Juan. My father snatched it from me and threw it in the fire and stayed to see it burn. It took a long time. I was so angry that for a long time I never spoke to him about my reading. I missed a good deal as he could have helped me. A flash of bad temper means nothing to older people, especially with children they love, but it has an effect on children out of all proportion to its seriousness.

My grandfather, whom my mother and his three other children adored, was kindness itself to all of his grandchildren. But one day he lost his temper with my little brother Harry. Harry was about to eat a peach from a dish of fruit on the dining table when Grandpa came into the room and spoke to him in a tone he must have used when he was captain of his East Indian ship. It was so severe and Harry was so frightened that he swallowed the peach, stone and all. After this, all of the grandchildren who were in the room were afraid of our grandfather, unreasonable as it seems. He was everything a grandfather ought to be, overflowing with affection and generous to a fault, full of life and the knowledge of life, humorous and witty, abounding in good stories. No one could be dull where he was. And yet I was afraid of him. My Aunt Hannah wrote his life and made him a perfect father and companion. And yet whenever I was with him after this I was afraid that he would speak to me in the tone that he had used to Harry. This incident and my father's loss of temper so impressed me as a child that in all my contacts with several thousand Bryn Mawr students I cannot remember once losing my temper.

One of the first things that happened when my burn got well was a summer in the Catskill mountains [with] my mother and her second sister, Sarah, and cousins Frank, Whitall, and Bessie. These were my first mountains, golden streams, splendid trees and waterfalls. I became active again and gradually the burn was forgotten by everyone, as well as by me. It was not until I was forty-seven years old in 1904 that the completely healed surface of my old burn began to give me trouble.

I had spent the summer in Spain where we had walked a great deal with a friend. There were few cabs. And on my return my father told me that I was limping a little. I had not noticed, but whatever the trouble was, it soon passed away. That winter I was skating when suddenly the burned leg gave way and I fell on the ice. I stopped skating and the two-mile walk home was very difficult. This weakness in my leg was only temporary, but I did not dare skate again that winter. The next summer I was in London with my friend Mary Elizabeth Garrett. We had heard Wagner's *Twilight of the Gods* the night before and the next morning I found that I could not walk. The scar tissue of the burned surface had contracted during the night, giving me the feeling that this leg was much shorter than the other. I was in great pain. We sent for King Edward's surgeon—the only surgeon in London whose name we knew. He said he had never seen such a contraction and advised a cure at Aix-les-Bains.

I feel sure that Dr. Weir Mitchell was triumphant. He was the leading Philadelphia physician, especializing in women's problems, and his opposition on the grounds of health kept many Philadelphia girls from coming to Bryn Mawr College. He had seated me next to him at a dinner at his own table, in 1888, and had told me that no woman could study and be well. He admitted I looked well, but said that he was convinced I had some secret disease that must show itself sooner or later.

I was too young, in 1865, to be admitted to Miss Kumer's School where Bessie King and Mary Garrett and all the older girls went. So I was sent to a small school opened by the Misses Norris, two well-bred energetic Baltimore women, who were without any special training but were teaching school in order to support themselves as was the fashion in those days. I do not remember anything about my lessons or the school itself except that the girl I knew best in the school, Mary Carey, a second cousin (one of whose brothers afterward became my brother-in-law) had a picture of President Lincoln on her desk and when the other girls saw it they slapped her face and tore the picture up and tramped on it.

The next day both she and I came up with pictures of Lincoln and set them on our desks and defended them as well as we could against all the other girls, who finally knocked us down and pulled our hair and tore up our Lincoln photos. The teachers were secessionists too—it seems we were the only girls in school who were "unionists." Feeling in Baltimore ran high, and as I remember this went on day after day. Each morning we came with a new photo and every day it was torn to pieces. It was at this time that I remember hearing a beautiful young Baltimore woman, a cousin of my father's, saying to him and my mother that she wished she could "wade up to her neck in Yankee blood."

Many years afterward, after I became Dean of Bryn Mawr, I heard with surprise that Miss Becky Norris (the cleverer of the two sisters) used to say that I studied so hard and knew so much more than she did that she had to sit up at night to try to keep ahead of me. I think this story must have been circulated later as I cannot remember studying at all.

It was during the time I was at Miss Marble's school that I determined to study Greek, which Miss Marble did not know. At this time in Baltimore Greek was a word to conjure with. No girls studied Greek and only college boys studied it in college. It was considered to be a purely masculine study and to have a grievous effect on girls. Mary Garrett's father thought Greek so improper for women that he absolutely forbade his daughter to study Greek and refused to pay for the lessons. Mary said nothing but went on attending lessons and of course in the end her father had to pay. This seemed to me splendid bravery, this act of defiance.

When I was twelve years old I used to play chess hours at a time with a girl friend until I realized that it kept me from reading and gave up chess. Cards we never saw. They were thought to be wicked like many other things. At Cornell two girls in the study next to mine used to play until midnight night after night. This seemed to me a great waste of time. Neither of them was good at her college work. I thought this such a waste of opportunity that I decided I would never learn to play—and it has been a good safeguard.

My reading during these years from the time that I got

well from my burn at nine years and went to boarding school at thirteen and nine months,[9] amazes me. I am sure that it was done then, as there was no other time in my life when I could have read so continuously and read just these books. They are the books of my generation.[1] I have found them mentioned in the lives and memoirs of my contemporaries. How I heard about them I do not know. I did not know Mary Garrett at that time; I knew no one who read. By the time I was nine years old, my mother and father, my mother's sisters, had all become so absorbed in religious and theological questions that they had given up all general reading. My father during the four years that he was a student at Haverford College (which was then little more than a strict Quaker boarding school) had the friendship and the run of the library of a very literary, well-read Quaker, Charles Yarnall. He benefited from it. He was up to the time of leaving college very well read, and his whole point of view was that of a cultured young man of a literary turn of mind. But two years afterwards he married at twenty-one. The practice of a busy general medical practitioner and his religious interest put a stop to any general reading. He was already beginning to preach in Quaker Meeting, and soon became a recognized minister. He opened his Sunday School for boys in one of the poorest parts of the city. Later he became president of the YMCA.

My mother became an active worker among the poor girls of Baltimore, attending magistrate's courts to try to protect the girls from the prostitutes. She was the first president of the Women's Christian Temperance Union,

9. The records of the Howland School, and Carey Thomas's correspondence from the school, agree that she began her studies there (near Canandaigua, N.Y.) in 1872, which would have her *fifteen* years and nine months.

1. Lists of "Favorite Books" and "My Guides in Literature" all include Shelley (whose name is invariably spelled "Shelly") and Swinburne. Under "Guides in Conduct and Theology" she has listed "M. Arnold, G. Eliot, G. Meredith, Mrs. Browning, Robert Browning, Darwin and Huxley." At one point she has noted: "I never read Dewey—too dull. William James never did amount to anything." Yet on another list of inspiring books, "W. James" appears.

and a little later carried on a large weekly Bible class for the society. Throughout all this time with her sisters she was absorbed in the study of the "new heresy"— ultimate universal salvation for all created beings—which did away with the frightful belief in hell fire. Of course I believed as my mother did . . . .

My step-grandmother Thomas, the third wife of my Grandfather Thomas with whom Aunt Henrietta, Aunt Julia, and my father's half-brother and sister lived, was a preacher and head of the women's side of the Baltimore Meeting in her time. She was a very good-looking and beautifully dressed woman; she dressed in the Quaker costume of that period. She had a musical voice and her long eloquent prayers in Quaker Meeting were much admired. As a child I used to wonder how anyone whose daily conversation consisted of insistent repetition of unimportant personal details could pray so as to influence a congregation, to say nothing of an intelligent deity. (No general conversation was possible with her.) When I made myself listen to her prayers, I found that they seemed to me nothing but disconnected, empty words spoken in a moving voice. But they certainly deceived the congregation—and perhaps God also.

The theory of Quaker preaching was one of those impromptu religious occasions which I thought very unfair. [We had to] listen to exhortations to our parents, which we resented as we thought them quite good enough, and prophecies in regard to our own futures to which we listened with terror. There was one woman Quaker preacher of great reputation from Ohio, I think, who came repeatedly to our house and lay down on the library sofa and went into trances in which she would moan and mutter and see visions and, in a ghastly tone talking all the time, saw and prophesied what was to happen to the people in the house. She was of course an ill, hysterical woman and what she said had no importance, but I could not know this. I used to listen to her through the crack, moaning and muttering in her trance, and the more she muttered the harder I prayed. I prayed as hard as I could that she might not prophesy that I was to become a

307

Quaker preacher. I did not then know what I wished to be. The only thing I was sure of was that I could not endure to be a Quaker preacher. I told God in my prayers that I had rather die, and begged Him not to let her say it. I used every device I could to avoid her notice lest this awful idea should occur to her. The world we lived in seems to me now, in looking backward, a nightmare. Every question that arose was settled by the literal words of the English translation of the Bible. After my mother's death I found that even her Bible had "ands" and "buts" marked as a help to the literal interpretation of disputed texts. It moved me indescribably to realize that my mother's splendid intellect was fettered by such—— [incomplete]

Among Quakers, Fox's doctrine of the "inner light" and inspired "concerns" gave an awful sanction to their words, however illiterate and provincial they might be. An uncouth carrot-headed ignorant boy from the wilds of North Carolina used to pay frequent visits to our house and my Grandmother Whitall's. One day my little sister Helen and my little brother Frank came skipping into the room in the stiff short little white dresses then worn by children, tied around the waist with beautiful broad blue sashes. He said sternly to my mother, "Mary, the Lord give me a concern to tell thee He forbids thee to rig up them innocent little things in them gay sashes." We never saw the sashes again. But much to my delight there came a time when we never saw the carrot-headed preacher. Later I persuaded my grandmother to tell me why. He had been found misappropriating funds for his own uses— funds given him for his various charities.

The worst of it was that this was exceptional. According to their lights our visiting preachers were as good as they were ignorant which, to me, who hated their illiteracy and their country manners, meant very good indeed. They suffered gladly the mischievous jokes we played on them which our mother never knew of. These jokes were all of my inventing because in looking back I realize that I disliked them with the intolerance of my own ignorance; the other children took part only for the fun involved, and feared them. Now I should be amused and touched by their simplicity, but then my whole future life seemed to me to be menaced by their "concerns," and their prophecies, and their prayers, which terrified me lest it arouse God to interfere with my reading and my getting the kind of education I was determined to have. Their ignorance and illiteracy and their biblical conversation seemed ridiculous after the dream companions of the books I was reading. And I revenged myself by inventing ways of ridiculing them which were enthusiastically carried out by the other children.

We children used to lay open nooses in dark corners of the visiting men's Quaker entrance hall, or on the stair in places where we could hide and pull the noose when they stepped in it. After a sharp jerk we fled and they had to disentangle themselves. Once my cousin Bessie Nicholson and I were caught—our victim proved a sport in spite of his plain coat. He gave each of us a five-dollar bill (a small fortune!) and told us he thought we had better play with that and not with visiting friends. He left the next day without telling our parents of our pranks.

Another time, in order to see what he would do, we took away the basin[2] of a visiting hayseed, as we called country Friends. To our delight he poured the contents of his wash basin out of the third story window on the head of a passing policeman who was so enraged that he wanted to arrest him. Our parents with difficulty averted this. But we felt that our joke fell flat when he told the policeman that he always did pour water out the window in his home town. He did not know what a slop jar was for. He had never even missed it! But he never came back again.

The worst result of the narrow Quaker horizons enforced on us was the almost complete intellectual lack of public spirit.[3] In the strict Quaker environment in which my grandparents lived in which I spent every summer

2. She evidently means "slop jar," and is using the term interchangeably with "basin."

3. She is obviously here referring to her own childhood era. In discussing her earlier ancestry, she has more than once pointed with some pride to the involvement in public affairs of some of her Quaker ancestors, as earlier pages attest.

until I went abroad in 1879, I never heard anything discussed except the different schisms of Quakerism, Quaker business, and food. Music of any kind, the theater and novels were all considered wrong.[4] No Quaker house at that time had a copy of Shakespeare and in 1888, a few years after the opening of Bryn Mawr College, one of the original trustees appointed in the will of the founder resigned from the Board because I insisted on Shakespeare in the college library. One of my uncles who was an Elder in the Quaker meeting and sat in the gallery[5] was asked to sit on the floor of the [Meeting] house because he had bought an organ for his invalid daughter. One of my mother's sisters became an invalid and she used to say it was almost worthwhile to be ill because she felt that she could read Mrs. Oliphant's novels.

The great division between the Orthodox and the Hicksites had just taken place . . . . I never saw a Hicksite until I went to Cornell University and I suppose because Bryn Mawr was founded by an Orthodox Quaker I do not remember any Hicksite girl ever coming. In Philadelphia in those days the Orthodox Quakers were the most well-to-do. They dressed in heavier silks, and at the time of the Hicksite Yearly Meeting we used to stand and watch the Hicks women go by clad in flimsy silks, the wind blowing their hooped skirts and showing what we called "Hicksite ankles."

The schism in the Orthodox church in my day was between the very conservative followers of Wilber called the Wilberites, and the followers of Joseph Gurney, an English Quaker evangelist, called the Gurneyites, to which my grandparents belonged. I was a passionate Gurneyite because Joseph Gurney had married, as his second wife, an intimate friend of my grandmother who returned to her New Jersey home as a widow and became a well-known preacher. She brought back to the United States from her long residence in England a clear English

4. Since her uncle's library contained novels, some taboos were evidently relaxed in her parents' generation.

5. Where Elders were privileged to sit.

310

intonation and pronunciation that seemed to be beautiful. I used to take down her extemporaneous sermons when I was a little girl of not more than seven, as it was before I was burned, and read them to my grandmother after Meeting, and sometimes she asked me to read them to Eliza Gurney herself. The two old Quaker ladies made an entrancing picture in my eyes—tall and stately, dressed in their stiff gray silks with the elaborate fluted cambric caps and kerchiefs so elaborately pleated that it took their maids almost half an hour to pin them in place. It was surely the most extravagant dress that was ever invented. Quaker men wore cutaway coats of the fashion worn by all men when George Fox first began to make converts to Quakerism, and broad-brimmed high hats, usually gray beaver, which it was "gay" to take off in greeting, or when one entered the Meeting house. A delightful Phila-delphia Quaker a little older than I, who was in love with my father's half-sister so that I saw him very often, wealthy and fond of travel, was never able to go inside a cathedral abroad because his conscience did not permit him to take off his hat, and he was too considerate.

Everything was carefully scrutinized to see if it was "gay" and one never knew in advance when a nervous conscience would feel that a perfectly innocent thing was "gay," or wrong. The unmarried brother of my father's mother Uncle Sammy Carey, who was a strict Philadel-phia Quaker, left my father his house and furniture. His carpets were for sure in good condition because he had put them down wrong side up, as the patterns of the right side seemed to him "too gay" . . . . We children used to shiver with excitement when our grandfather, who sat in the gallery, stood up to "offer prayer" as it was called (it was thought *gay* to kneel in prayer) and the Wilberite Elders stood up also and one after another put on their broad-brimmed high hats to show their disapproval of prayers by a Gurneyite.

My Aunt Hannah Whitall Smith, my mother's eldest sister, [in a book—untitled] describes her mother suddenly feeling that the pantaloons bought for her and two sisters had too many gay ruffles and tells how she felt it her duty to

311

cut them off while her little daughters were dancing around the table and weeping and entreating her, as inch after inch the ruffles disappeared. . . . My mother began by trying to dress me plainly and when overskirts became all the fashion she felt that it was wrong to let me wear them. As a child I never thought or cared about dress[6] until, when I was about fifteen, I was invited by a group of older Baltimore girls whom I did not know, to join their literary society—it met at the big house of one of the members, and when I stood on the doorstep about to ring the bell and I suddenly realized that they would all have overskirts and I was without one, I turned away and went home. My mother was so distressed by this incident that she immediately bought me dresses with overskirts and from this time dressed me and my younger sisters like other children. She was the most logical of persons and really reasonable. She was convinced that she had done wrong and the battle was fought once and for all.

My mother idealized the whole Jewish race[7] on account of the Old Testament; as a child I accepted everything she told me, and so I idealized them too. Nevertheless I do not remember ever meeting a Jew until Bryn Mawr College opened and then my troubles with them began: Exams on holidays, Kosher Meat——[8]

6. Later she cared very much. Both her personal maid and her secretary (they had lived with her, although at different times, and were in a position to know) testified that her wardrobe was extensive and her taste expensive. She had dozens of dresses for every conceivable occasion, all made to order to her very exacting specifications.

7. Evidence of this attitude is in a letter from her mother's sister, Sarah Nicholson, to her husband, written from "Newport" dated "8 mo. 20th, 1869: . . . Mary, Mother and I were sitting together and [Madge Kimber came] and told us there was to be a service in the Jewish synagogue at 10½. . . so we hurried and scurried. Oh! I can't describe to thee how I felt as I sat there with them, I could not keep back the tears. . . I would have loved to have gone up to the Rabbi and taken Him by the hand and told Him how I reverenced His people, because they had been so peculiarly God's care from time immemorial and still continue to be so . . . ."

8. The fragment breaks off here and there follows a list titled "Reason for Dislike." Some items are cryptic, as for example: "Ed Bettle on Helen's marriage." Others include, "I never asked a Jewish prof. to recommend a

Shakespeare and the dramatists were a sealed book to me as plays and theater were anathema to Quakers. After my twenty-first birthday I graduated from Cornell. Then, when I was allowed to choose for myself whether to continue the Quaker tabu, Mary [Garrett] gave me a dinner and a theater party to celebrate my twenty-first birthday, and my first play was *Camille,* played by Modjeska, who was then at the acme of her powers. I was so innocent and so excited and so carried away by my first play that as Mary found out later that night as we sat talking the play over, to her great amusement I had not a suspicion that Camille was the mistress of Armand or why his father had separated them. I was grateful she never told anyone.

Those two years 1878-79 were great Shakespearean years in the U.S. Edwin Booth was playing all his Shakespeare roles. Henry Irving and Ellen Terry and Salvini were also playing Shakespeare. I saw Booth and Salvini and Irving play together in *Othello.* Booth was the greatest Shakespearean actor of my generation. Side by side with Booth, as I saw him, Irving's shocking enunciation and uncouth mannerisms seemed to me a travesty. It was only in melodrama like *The Bells* that he was a great actor. Shakespeare was, I think, more wonderful coming as he did all glorious to me at twenty-one, interpreted by great actors. I had never really read him before. I knew most of his sonnets by heart, and many of the great passages in his plays.

[Reading and the theatre], pictures, sculptures, temples and cathedrals, travel, travel everywhere, have been the great joys of my life. Like Stevenson I was born wanting to pack and unpack my suitcase (only they were unknown at that time—my half of a tiny cabin trunk it was then) in every attic of the world; like Paul Moran [who] was such a traveller that he wished to have his skin, when he died, made into a suitcase.

---

candidate that he did not recommend a Jew," and "College—if one Jew the dept. and the college gets full," and "Like Quakers they stick together." Her youngest and favorite sister Helen ("Nell") had in 1903 married Dr. Simon Flexner, the first Director of the Rockefeller Institute, and a Jew. To the end of her days Carey Thomas showed the deepest familial affection for her Flexner brother-in-law and nephews.

Now [1934] Edith Lowber's death leaves me very lonely. No one of my other friends and no member of my family is able to live and travel abroad on account of other ties. But I try to remind myself that for an enthusiast dedicated to the cause of women's education, I have been very fortunate in my lifelong friendship with Mary Garrett from my twentieth to my fifty-eighth year; [Mary], who was really a great person as well as an intimate and devoted friend, and with Mamie Gwinn during our four years in Germany and at Bryn Mawr until that degenerate Hodder came into the picture, which was after all only for six years of the twenty-nine years of our friendship, and then for the past eight years, Edith, and in between, from 1915 to 1926, Lucy, Alys, Logan, Ray Strachey and my brother Harry and Zoe[9] every other summer from 1915 until his death in 1925, all of them delightful travelling companions, have been with me whenever I could leave Bryn Mawr. Grace,[1] Alys and Mary Berenson all offered to come and stay with me after Edith's death—her death leaves me very lonely.

From the time when my mother told me God was love and could not torture people in hell I never gave the future after death another thought. Life was enough. Shelley satisfied me about after death. Darwin and then Lucretius convinced me that immortality was impossible and if possible undesirable. And now at seventy-five and eight months when I know I must soon die I regard it with perfect composure. After my memoirs are finished I have had enough joy of living. I shall be ready to die.

I have always wanted to do what I have done. I do not remember any struggles. It is Victorian to care about immortality, unworthy to care for it. In a healthy world with quite possible, fair conditions, life is enough.

---

9. Lucy Donnelly, professor of English at Bryn Mawr 1896-1938; Alys Russell, Carey Thomas's first cousin; Logan Pearsall Smith, Alys's brother; Zoe Thomas, brother Harry's wife.

1. Grace Worthington, Carey Thomas's sister.